"Steve Sonderman is the heavyweight champion of the world when it comes to building a men's ministry. If you're looking for the blueprint on how to do it, you've just found it."

STEVE FARRAR
Author of *Point Man*

"Steve Sonderman is the voice I trust to talk about men's ministry in the church more than any other. While there are many good voices speaking about men's issues and ministry, there are few who have themselves grown a strong men's community in the local church context from the ground up. The architecture described in *How to Build a Life-Changing Men's Ministry*, if followed closely, will produce bushels of leaders for your church. I have used these principles myself at Saddleback with great results."

KENNY LUCK
Pastor of Men, Saddleback Church;
Author of *Risk, Dream, Fight*, and
Every Man Bible Studies;
Founder of Every Man Ministries

"Steve is a man's man who presents his readers with an incredible game plan for coaching the men in your church to victory. He will inspire you to be the coach your men need, and he will give you the tools to help them grow in Christ, serve Him in the church, and be leaders in their homes, workplaces, community, and the world. This is a must-read for any pastor or men's ministry leader!"

DR. TOM MULLINS
Co-Pastor, Christ Fellowship

"Whether you are in a big or small church, Steve's book gives invaluable insight into the opportunities available for strengthening men. *How to Build a Life-Changing Men's Ministry* is a book in tune with the times and the heart of God."

DR. JOSEPH M. STOWELL
President, Cornerstone University

"Steve Sonderman is a man of God who knows God and understands men. Having known him for almost forty years, I can tell you he says what he means, he lives what he says, and knows what he's talking about. Just what men need!"

STUART BRISCOE
Minister at Large, Elmbrook Church

"I have been looking for this book for years. No church can ignore this book. No seminary student should graduate without reading it. Full of realistic insights and practical suggestions, it's a much-needed message and a refreshing read."

HOWARD HENDRICKS
Distinguished Professor
Dallas Theological Seminary

"Just getting started? Need to rebuild your men's ministry? Steve Sonderman can get you there. Filled with actionable ideas and practical checklists, this field-proven book receives an A+ for teaching effective ministry to men. Steve is an extremely well-read, highly capable, seasoned professional who can save you years of missteps and disappointment. It's my pleasure to recommend this classic."

PATRICK MORLEY, PhD
Men's author and CEO of
Man in the Mirror

HOW TO
BUILD A
LIFE-CHANGING
MEN'S
MINISTRY

STEVE SONDERMAN

BETHANYHOUSE
MINNEAPOLIS, MINNESOTA

Published by Bethany House Publishers
11400 Hampshire Avenue South
Minneapolis, Minnesota 55438

Bethany House Publishers is a division of
Baker Publishing Group, Grand Rapids, Michigan.

Printed in the United States of America

In keeping with biblical principles of creation stewardship, Baker Publishing Group advocates the responsible use of our natural resources. As a member of the Green Press Initiative, our company uses recycled paper when possible. The text paper of this book is comprised of 30% post-consumer waste.

 green press INITIATIVE

Library of Congress Cataloging-in-Publication Data

Sonderman, Steve.
    How to build a life-changing men's ministry : practical ideas and insights for your church
/ Steve Sonderman. — Rev. and expanded.
       p.   cm.
    Summary: "Presents ideas and guidance for pastors and layleaders who want to start or
improve a men's ministry program at their church"—Provided by publisher.
    Includes bibliographical references.
    ISBN 978-0-7642-0748-8 (pbk. : alk. paper) 1. Church work with men. I. Title.
    BV4440.S66   2010
    259.081—dc22

                                             2009040933

To Colleen

You are a gift from God.
I love you.

STEVE SONDERMAN is associate pastor for Men's Ministry at Elmbrook Church in Brookfield, Wisconsin. He consults widely with churches from a range of denominations in developing local men's ministries. Sonderman is a graduate of the University of Wisconsin—Milwaukee (B.S.) and Bethel Seminary (M.Div.). He makes his home in Wisconsin with his wife, Colleen, and their four children.

Steve Sonderman is available to speak at retreats, conferences, and other special events or consult with your church or denomination about men's ministry. You can contact him at:

Steve Sonderman
Elmbrook Church
777 South Barker Road
Brookfield, WI 53045
(414) 786-7051
ssonderman@elmbrook.org

CONTENTS

RIDING THE CREST OF THE WAVE

I can still smell the summer of 1976.

As far as I was concerned, summer began in the middle of May and ended the first week of August—spanning the twelve weeks when our high school baseball team roared into the Wisconsin State Baseball Championship. A lot of the guys on the team had known each other since fourth grade, when we started playing with or against one another in an assortment of city and county baseball leagues. With a potent mix of seniors, juniors, and two sophomores, we started fast.

Then we had a midseason slump. With ten games to go we were barely above the .500 mark. I blew out my right arm. Not that I had a strong arm in the first place—but an outfielder has to be able to throw. I was moved to DH. After a 12–0 shell-shocking at the hands of Homestead High School, we had a team meeting on the way home. It was an intense moment on the bus when we vowed to do whatever it took to turn the team around.

What a ride! We won our last ten games, including the state championship game against our archrival, Nicolet High School. Every game of the streak was better than the one before. We rode the crest of the wave. Great fielding. Deadly pitching. Incredible hitting. In the three-state tournament games we outscored our opponents 35–1. (The lone run was unearned.) I can still remember running onto the field and jumping into the air as the final out was made, hugging my teammates and crying like a baby, hoisting the championship trophy toward the sky. For years we had practiced and played in backyards and rocky fields through all types of weather to prepare for this day. We had come from many backgrounds, but what was important was that we had done it together. We were a team.

I won't forget the exhilaration and excitement of winning and being a part of something that felt enormously bigger than anything I had ever experienced.

I won't forget. But I've more than matched it.

In '76 we rode the crest of the wave to a state baseball championship. For seventeen years I have been riding the crest of the wave with another team. Not a sports team. A ministry team—a *men's* ministry team. As I work shoulder to shoulder with other men on my leadership team, the exhilaration and excitement mimics the summer of '76. Tears flow when a man crosses over from trusting in his own goodness to make him acceptable to God to trusting Jesus as his Savior and Lord. My heart jumps up and down when I see men striving to be godly men in their homes, at work, and in their communities. I get ecstatic when men start to use their spiritual gifts to ignite the local church. When men start to really "get it." When they get excited about the things that excite Jesus.

I have had the privilege of ministering to pastors, men's ministry leaders, and other men around the world—from here in the United States to Asia, Europe, the Middle East, and Africa. In each place I see virtually the same thing: men riding the crest of the wave, men hungry to grow, men hungry to learn how to effectively minister to other men, and men hungry to have an impact in their country for Christ. The highlights include:

- Working alongside Max in the Philippines, going from barrio to barrio, ministering to men in thatch-covered churches, teaching them what it means to love their wives and follow hard after Jesus.

- Speaking at the first-ever men's conference in Krasnodar, Russia, with hundreds of men singing their hearts out, and then having them listen for the next four hours as I unpacked what the Scriptures say about being a man of God.

- Teaching nearly one hundred army chaplains from all over the European theater for three days on how they can more effectively minister to the soldiers in the Middle East and Europe.

- Speaking on the theme of *Braveheart* at the Mandate Conference in Belfast, with thousands of men in attendance.

- Ministering to a small group of men on the Indonesian island of Sumatra.

- Working with the Promise Keepers Canada staff to further their work across that great country.

From villages to mega-cities, there is clear evidence of God's work in the hearts and minds of men. I cannot imagine a greater ride. For me, there is no greater joy than to be connected to the local church at Elmbrook, and then have the freedom and privilege to minister the gospel of Jesus Christ to men all across the globe. But it wasn't always this way.

It was nearly two decades ago when I approached our then senior pastor, Stuart Briscoe, about leaving the college-age ministry. Colleen and I had four children of our own, and I had grown weary leading four hundred to five hundred college kids as well. Eight years of late-night pizza parties, bus trips, retreats, weekly large-group meetings, and the daily grind of youth ministry had taken its toll. I told Stuart I would be interested in working in the area of evangelism, missions, assimilation, or prayer. After hearing me out, he said, "Let me get back to you in a month or so."

When we met again, I was in for a surprise: "Steve, I'd like you to take over the men's ministry."

"What? That wasn't on my list. I've never worked with men before. What would I do with them?"

Stuart's response was quick and to the point. "The same thing you've been doing with the college-age students; just try to act a little more mature!" And that is exactly what I have been doing ever since. In my mind, there is no greater job in the world. We haven't always hit on all cylinders, but two stories illustrate what a fully functioning ministry to men can do in the context of a local church.

A couple of years ago, during a Sunday service, Stuart leaned over to me and asked, "Steve, look out there. What do you see?"

"A few thousand people; just like every other Sunday morning."

"No, really. Don't you see it?"

I shook my head and he explained, "I see a congregation full of men, and for that I want to thank you. Your work has changed the complexion of this church." God has made Elmbrook a church where as many men worship on a weekend as women.

Fast-forward to a few months ago. I was walking down the hall and our new children's pastor stopped me. "Steve, thanks a ton," she said.

"Well, you're welcome. But what for?" I had to ask.

"In all the churches I have worked or spoken at in the past twenty years, I have never seen so many men involved in teaching the young kids. You must really have an effective ministry to men here."

Those two conversations were extremely encouraging. Sometimes in ministry you can't fully evaluate how things are going, but we have seen many wonderful things happen in our church over the years. And just as important, these same sorts of things can happen in big and small ways at your church.

Men Coming to Christ—Through each man's personal evangelistic efforts—and through several events each year geared specifically to supplement the men's personal efforts—hundreds of men have surrendered their lives to Christ.

It is a sight forever etched in my mind. Once a year at a nearby hotel our men's ministry hosts an evangelistic outreach called the Breakfast of Champions. Over the years the men have really caught the vision for inviting men whom they have been sharing with and praying for. Our men understand the only reason to attend is if they bring someone to hear the message of Christ. And every year the same thing happens. Men pray and boldly ask their fathers, sons, co-workers, bosses, neighbors, or friends from high school to be their guests. The Elmbrook guys usually arrive around seven thirty and stand by a long window overlooking the parking lot. They watch and wait for their guest to arrive. Every car that pulls up fills the men with anticipation, waiting to see if it's the guest they invited. The men stand there with their tickets in hand, hoping and praying that this is the year their guest joins them. As the starting time draws near, the number of men waiting at the window dwindles, but they still have hope that their guest will arrive. When the program starts at eight, a few more trickle in, but there is always a group of men still waiting by the window. Sometimes they join the breakfast alone; sometimes they go home. Either way, they have stepped out in faith trying to reach another man for Christ. During the breakfast a man shares his testimony about how he came to Christ. Then there is a powerful message on how each man in attendance can have a personal relationship with Jesus, and every year we see many men commit their lives to Him.

Men Growing in Christ—More than eight hundred men have gone through our two-year discipleship course called Basic and Discipleship Training. These men are well-grounded in what it means to be a fully devoted follower of Jesus. Relationships have been healed, marriages reconciled, addictions broken, and lives have been transformed and set free to follow hard after Jesus.

I still remember Jim (not his real name) interrupting our first Top-Gun group and telling us that his wife was thinking of leaving him. We set aside the workbook for the morning and concentrated on listening to Jim pour his heart out and then gathering around him to lay hands on him and pray for him and his marriage. Jim's marriage was eventually healed; he grew in his faith and is now serving with his wife in a restricted country. Where would Jim, or his marriage, be today without a group of men committed to being transformed by the love and grace of Jesus?

Men Mobilized to Serve—Countless men have moved from the pews into action. We're working alongside the urban poor, tutoring students in Milwaukee, preaching in nursing homes, ministering to the unemployed, discipling college-age students, starting a ministry to executives, leading Bible studies in prisons around the state, leaving the comfort of home to minister in the Philippines, Romania, Guatemala, Kenya, Congo, and numerous other countries. We have a church full of men with ears to hear God's call on their life and a willingness to be obedient to His call.

Men who have come to realize that there is no greater joy and nothing more fulfilling than to give their lives for the sake of others.

Men Connected to Other Men—We have gone from five small groups to more than one hundred groups. These are scattered all over the Milwaukee area, studying the Word, sharing life, and being missional in nature. Everything we do in the ministry has been geared to moving men into small groups because we know it is the optimal place for spiritual transformation. So whether it is a specialized group for those with a sexual addiction; a Soul Purpose Discipleship group; a book study group; a video small group (such as *The Quest for Authentic Manhood*); or a group meeting for Bible study and fellowship, they all have one thing in common: They are groups of men committed to Christ and His people.

Men Empowered to Be Leaders—Through training aimed at nurturing followerers of Jesus, men have learned leadership. They are practicing leadership in their homes, communities, workplaces, and the world.

My good friend Rob recommitted his life to Christ in one of our first Top-Gun groups. He was so struck by the Servant Leadership Module that as a national sales manager for a good-sized company, he decided to rework all the training for their national sales force. Their training now starts by looking at the example of Jesus and how He leads through serving others. It continues by discussing how each of the salespeople are to be servants in the marketplace. Rob's life has been revolutionized by Jesus, and so has Rob's sales force.

As I look back, God has truly done an incredible work in our midst. And because I am confident that He is not finished yet, I look to the future with hope and excitement. I also look forward to sharing with you the lessons we have learned over the years on how to more effectively minister to men.

This is what this book is all about. It is about men ministering to other men. It is about building a team of men equipped to do the ministry. It is a tool to help layleaders within a local church start and run an effective men's ministry.

This book will help whether you are an individual thinking about beginning a men's ministry or you are already a part of a small group of men, whether you are starting from scratch or adding to what is already established. What I write here applies to churches of one hundred, one thousand, or even ten thousand people. The principles are the same, though the applications may be different. I have given points to ponder and exercises throughout that will help you to walk through the practical steps that make growing a men's ministry achievable.

If ever there was a time in history when local churches needed to build men individually and corporately it is now. That's one big reason for this revised and expanded edition. We have learned so much since this book was first published in 1996. In addition to adding two new chapters (chapters 3 and 12), sections throughout have been updated to reflect the paradigm shifts we're seeing in ministry to men.

As we survey our country's spiritual, financial, and societal landscapes, it becomes apparent that men not only need ministries geared especially for them but men are looking for them as well. Jesus once talked to His disciples about finishing the work the Father had given Him to do. He then challenged the disciples to look at the fields—to notice that they were ripe, ready to be harvested (John 4:34–38).

Christ's challenge to us is to turn our eyes to the fields and see the opportunities before us. We can be tempted to be angry that our world seems to be going from bad to worse. Yet what we see as problems in our society, we must grasp as opportunities for ministry.

Wherever I look, I see men who desperately need a ministry uniquely designed to reach them *as men*, working on the issues they face. For a moment let's look at the fields. Yes, there are challenges, but vast opportunities lie before us. Let's see why men are ripe for harvest.

The American Male Is Friendless

Competition, comparison, isolation, individualism, and self-sufficiency— these words describe today's American male. That isn't good news for men trying to make friends! They are wedge-driving words. Splintering words. Labels most of us have worn since the day we were born. And as a result, the average male over thirty can't name one close friend he could call at any time of the day or night to share his hurt and pain. Wherever I go I tell men that isolation is not masculinity, it is stupidity.

A recent survey asked men who their best friends were. More than 75 percent said it was a guy from high school, a guy from an old sports team, and so on. Interestingly, most of the men hadn't spoken to that friend or seen him for several years. Some friendship!

The Lone Ranger of the '60s and '70s is looking for companionship in the twenty-first century. He is looking for one or two good buddies to hang out with. Friends he can share heart to heart with. Friends who will walk with him at the birth of his first child, who will be there when he loses his job, who will provide wise counsel when his teenager rebels, and mourn with him when his parents or spouse dies.

Men, look at the fields, they are ripe for harvest! What an opportunity for you to develop a ministry that helps men to belong and to develop friendships—a place where they can get together and get to know each other better.

The American Male Is Emotionally Isolated

Herb Stanelle, a counselor for men, says, "Emotional isolation can be viewed as the systematic separation of a person from his feelings. It is the process whereby a man changes from an eight-pound 'cherub' who coos, laughs, screams, cries and drools into a 200-pound 'humanoid' for whom all of life is work and all problems have intellectual, rational solutions."[1] The emotionally isolated male doesn't see himself as a creation wonderfully made by God but rather the sum of what he does at home, work, and church.

That's the male self in a nutshell.

When men are asked what they are feeling, most give only a blank stare in return. Or they say they're "doing good" or "doing bad" (neither of which is a feeling). The price men are paying for ignoring their emotions is huge. It affects us physically. We suffer migraines, heart problems, and ulcers—to mention just a few common problems. It affects us relationally. We are unable to nurture our wives and to relate to them on an emotional basis, perhaps their most vital need. Gary Oliver notes in *Real Men Have Feelings Too*: "When emotional pain strikes, we often lack the ability to understand and deal with it. When the pain becomes too uncomfortable, the only other option is to attempt to anesthetize it. For instance, you can replace feelings with busyness. The busyness becomes workaholism. [Men] become insensitive and blind to their spouse's messages of discouragement, dissatisfaction and resentment."[2] From childhood the message we have heard is *Men do not show their emotions*. Big boys don't cry. To be a man is to conceal your emotions.

The men I run with are saying those messages are wrong. The American male, while generally emotionally isolated, is looking to fully understand how God wired him. He is seeking to uncover the emotions stashed away inside and to find ways to express those gut-level feelings in a positive and healthy manner.

Leaders of men, look at the fields. They are ripe. What an incredible challenge to develop a ministry where men can be real and transparent—to develop small-group ministries where men can share the three *Fs*—feelings, failures, and fears!

The American Male Is Confused Over Masculinity

What does it mean to be a man? It isn't hard to understand why we're confused. Every ten years our role model changes. In the '60s it was James Bond, the womanizer. In the '70s it was Alan Alda and Phil Donahue, the sensitive and caring types. In the '80s it was Michael Douglas, the work-obsessed marketplace man. In the '90s it was Kevin Costner, aggressive yet ethical, traditional yet adventurous, intimate but independent, a family man developing a rich inner life. These days, role models are all over the map. Worse yet, we haven't only watched these defective role models on TV and the big screen—we've lived with them at home. Many of us grew up with fathers who were emotionally cold, uncommunicative, or absent.

Chuck Swindoll, in *Growing Wise in Family Life*, says, "I'm concerned about a vanishing masculinity that once was in abundance. I mean honest-to-goodness men who are distinctly that—discerning, decisive, strong-hearted men who know where they are going and are confident enough in themselves and their God to get there. Over the last three decades there has been an assault on masculinity."[3]

It's no wonder that men have an identity crisis. But men are searching for answers. They want to know what it means to be a man. They are buying books like *Fire in the Belly* by Sam Keen, *Iron John* by Robert Bly, and *Wild at Heart* by John Eldredge. They are attending Warrior Weekends by the hundreds. More men are seeking out therapists than ever before.

Men, lift up your eyes to see the fields ready for harvest. What an opportunity to present the biblical base of man! We can present Jesus as the ultimate man, the man who knew who He was, where He came from, and where He was going. What an opportunity to help searching men discover their identity in Christ Jesus!

The American Male Is Success Driven

Climbing the corporate ladder. The big promotion. The bigger home. The nicer car. That prime corner office with floor-to-ceiling windows. Winning the big one.

The competitive nature within us always wants more. We have become convinced that *what we do* is *who we are*. How much we have and how fast we get it determine our status in society. Wherever we look we see men moving faster and faster, seeking to do more and more in order to leap higher and higher. We are obsessed with success. Success means status and position—and that's what it's all about.

Once again, the price men are paying for this obsession to succeed is enormous. With the pressure to succeed, our commitment to choose right over wrong is diminished if not vanished. The success obsession also exacts a price from families. When a man pours all of his attention and energy into work, he has little or nothing left for home and family. After ten to twelve hours at work, he comes home physically—but not always mentally or emotionally. His relationship with his wife and children suffers or withers. Most marriages end in divorce not because of a mistress *at* work but a mistress *called* work.

The fields are ripe! Men everywhere are realizing there has to be a better way. Stephen Covey says, "You can climb the ladder of success and then realize it's leaning against the wrong wall." When I surveyed five hundred men about the biggest issue they were facing in life, this was the most frequent question: *How do I balance home and work?* What an opportunity to build a ministry where men can study biblical principles of work, home, and recreation—and to grow a group of men who will hold one another accountable for how they spend their time, energy, and money!

The American Male Today Is Spiritually Searching

Over the years ministries like Promise Keepers, Men at the Cross, Iron Sharpens Iron, and many others have provided men the opportunity to respond to an evangelistic message to follow Christ, and thousands have taken that step. The obvious question men ask themselves after a great day or weekend of teaching, worship, and fellowship is *What's next? How do I continue this and grow in it? What happens the other fifty-one weeks of the year?* The only way to bring the fire home is to grow a strong, healthy men's ministry in every local church. Our isolated retreats, conferences, and mission projects pose an obvious danger. Men can have a great experience and then come home and slide into old routines—or worse, get inoculated with just enough Christianity to give them a false sense of security.

The number of books, magazines, and audio materials on spiritual growth and men's issues being bought today is another sign of male spiritual hunger. In the past it has been women who have kept most Christian bookstores in business. Today more men are buying Christian materials than ever before.

Let me say it one more time: Leaders of men: Lift up your eyes, for the fields are ripe for harvest! Men are ready to be built up together in a ministry designed to connect Christ with their real needs. Men today are ready for groups where they can help each other grow into

Christlikeness. Where they can talk about raising godly children in a godless society. Where they can meet on a regular basis to worship with other men through song, prayer, and study. Men today are searching. We have an incredible opportunity before us.

Building a Life-Changing Men's Ministry

In seventeen years, the men's ministry at Elmbrook has grown from fifty to hundreds of men involved weekly in small groups. The leadership team has grown from eight to one hundred forty.

If our experience is any indication, men's ministries are finally coming home to the church. For me, nothing in life is greater than working with men in this environment. God uses other means of ministering to men. But His primary means of reconciling the world to himself—men included—is the church. It is my prayer and dream that as you move through this book you will catch the vision and passion of what can happen when men come together to serve Jesus together.

I would suggest you work through the material in this book together with other like-minded men, slowly enough to complete the exercises that apply to you and your situation. I have no intention of laying out a model and advising you to copy it! Rather I will give you straightforward principles, ideas, and guidelines you can use to develop a ministry for your own setting. Every church in the world is different—different denominations, different leadership structures, different mission statements, and different philosophies of ministry. As a result, every men's ministry will look different as well.

Having done a stint as a high school football coach, I still find myself thinking and talking like a coach as I lead more than three thousand men at Elmbrook. Besides that fact, there are almost endless similarities between building a team and building a ministry. For these reasons I have decided to approach the development of this book like I would a football season. In the first chapters we will prep for the season, then move into developing a coaching staff, scout out the players, set a game plan, kick off, and then play the game—everything you need to know to get from here to the end zone.

No matter where you are right now in developing your ministry, you need to know where you're going. In the next chapter we will look at the end game, what God looks for in a godly man, and what an effective ministry to men looks like. So let's get started.

NOTES

1. Herb Stanelle, "The Emotionally Isolated Christian Male," *Social Work and Christianity*, Vol. 18, No. 2 (Fall 1991): 1.

2. Gary Oliver, *Real Men Have Feelings Too: Regaining a Male Passion for Life* (Chicago: Moody Press, 1993), 63.

3. Chuck Swindoll, *Growing Wise in Family Life* (Portland, OR: Multnomah, 1988).

WHAT ARE WE AIMING AT?

02

Youth soccer. Everywhere I look in our community on Saturday mornings there are kids running around playing soccer—and adults screaming on the sidelines as if they were at the Super Bowl. In our community alone there are some 1,800 kids playing this fall.

Having grown up on football, basketball, and baseball—and then coaching high school football for five years—I swore I would have nothing to do with soccer: playing it, watching it, letting my kids play it, and certainly not coaching it!

Of course, a few years ago I found myself coaching soccer!

It went like this. My two daughters came home from school with a registration form for the local youth soccer league. I told them that their mother and I had signed a prenuptial agreement that none of our kids would ever play soccer. They didn't believe me and went to their mother, who made me sign the forms. That was bad enough. Then came the tactic all kids are taught in school: "Dad, they said they're short on coaches, and if you don't coach, the team may not be able to play." *Great. Solved that problem. I guess my kids won't be playing soccer.*

But then my soft side took over. I heard myself say, "Sure, I would love to help."

I went to the library and took out all the books and videos I could find on soccer. Of course, I had a twofold agenda. First, to learn all about this game I knew nothing about. Second, if I had all the books, none of the other rookie coaches could study up. (Yes, I am very competitive.)

At the first practice I sat down with the twelve kids and said, "Okay, kids. You need to know that I have never played, watched, or coached this game, but there are three things I know. First, this is a ball. The second thing I know is that over there is a net." I pointed to the goal behind me. "The third thing I know is that the point of the game is to get this ball in that net. That's the goal."

One girl raised her hand. "Mr. Sonderman, what about plays?"

"Plays are way overrated," I responded. "There will be no plays."

"What about positions?" another girl asked.

"Positions are way overrated. We will only have a goalie, and that's it. I don't care where you run. I don't care how you kick it, or where you kick it—just get it into that goal. I don't know how we're going to do it. But girls, that's what we're going to try to do."

That year we set a record for the most goals scored against us. But we also set a record for scoring the most goals and we ended up winning the city championship in the spring!

It's not a whole lot different in ministry. We have lots of people kicking the ball all over the field but never getting the ball in the net. We need to know where we're going. What's our goal? What kind of men do we want to grow? Ministry needs to be principle-centered and purpose-driven. We can run a lot of programs, we can stage a lot of events, we can burn through as many Bible studies as we want—but unless we know where we're going, we will never get there.

Jesus in His final moments on earth told His disciples: "Therefore, go and make disciples of all nations, baptizing them in the name of the Father and of the Son and of the Holy Spirit, and teaching them to obey everything I have commanded you. And surely I am with you always, to the very end of the age" (Matthew 28:19–20).

The key verb in this passage is not *go*, but rather *make disciples*. A disciple in the time of Jesus was a follower, learner, and imitator, and this is what we are to be developing in our ministries. We are to make disciples, who make disciples, who make disciples. Notice Jesus does not say to make men into better dads, or better husbands, or better employees. Our mandate is go and make them into disciples of Jesus. So instead of kicking the ball all over the field, let's make sure we keep in mind the goal—to make disciples.

As we saw in the first chapter, we have incredible opportunities right now to develop men's ministries in the local church. Yet the men we want to grow strong in God have been warped and misshapen by their world. They have been influenced by society. Many have made countless poor decisions. And they are greatly confused about what it means to be a man—much less a spiritual man. One of the first projects for your leadership team is to talk and pray through how God sees men and how that affects your goals in ministry.

So what does a disciple of Jesus look like? What should the end product of our ministry be? If you and I could take a piece of paper and sketch the ideal man, what would he look like?

The guy we are aiming at has four characteristics: integrity, intimacy, identity, and influence. As we understand these four marks of a mature godly man, we begin to see what type of ministry it takes to build that man.

Men of Integrity

When Len Climber became president of Holiday Inn International, he wanted one thing: for people who heard or saw the name "Holiday Inn" to instantly think "Good, wholesome, family fun." Climber did everything in his power not only to sell a company image but to shape a company culture worthy of that image. And in just four years Holiday Inn became the fastest growing, largest hotel chain in the country.

Then Climber resigned. Why? His board decided to connect a Holiday Inn to an Atlantic City casino. They violated his code for the company. They overran his conscience.

Climber's resignation cost him millions. An interviewer asked him why he left Holiday Inn. "It was very, very easy," he replied. "It had to do with my integrity."[1]

Biblical men are men of integrity. *Integrity* comes from the Hebrew word for "whole," "sound," "unimpaired." It means to possess a genuine heart. It evidences itself in ethical soundness, moral excellence, absence of hypocrisy, and a willingness to keep promises. No hidden messages. No hidden agendas. Men of integrity are true to their word. Like Len Climber, they say, "This is what I stand for. This is what I believe. This is right. If you want to do something else, fine. But I will have nothing to do with it."

Little in society is under more fire than the character quality of integrity. Its absence is felt in government, the military, sports, business, and, yes, even the church. The integrity crisis is a national emergency. Ken Blanchard, author of *The One-Minute Manager* and *The Power of Ethical Management*, observes: "All across our country, there is evidence of a deterioration of ethics. Nowhere is this decline greater than in the world of business. . . . Individuals seemingly have come to check their values at the door when they enter the office. The attitude in many businesses appears to be profit at any cost, especially if a company's gains come at the expense of a competitor—and sometimes, even if it is at the expense of its customers."[2]

Integrity will show itself in the men of our ministry in three ways.

Integrity shows in convictions. Through study, encouragement, and accountability we want to help men to become men of conviction—men who know what they believe in and act on it. We just passed the twentieth anniversary of China's Tiananmen Square protests. What went through your mind when you saw on television or in news magazines the nineteen-year-old student who held up his hands to stop a tank? Conviction. That young guy was ready to pay the ultimate price because he knew the rightness of what he believed in. Months later, high school- and college-age students with pickaxes knocked down the Berlin Wall—in some places with armed soldiers pointing guns at their heads. That's conviction. That's what I want. I want to be a man of conviction. And that's what we want to develop.

Integrity shows in congruence. We want to develop men whose walk matches their talk. It's been reported that 81 percent of what we communicate to our kids and to our wives is conveyed by what we do. We cannot settle for men who look good in church but who everywhere else lie, cheat, and sleep around. We need to help men develop consistency between what they profess on Sunday and how they act at work, home, and in their neighborhoods Monday through Saturday.

Integrity shows in character. Many men masquerade on Sundays.

They disguise their sins, failings, and weaknesses and look good from the outside. Some men can manage that deception in front of their families and co-workers. But who are our men when no one is looking? Do they cheat on their taxes? Do they lead double lives? Do they stumble with pornography—or lust or greed or covetousness or other sins of the hidden heart? Our ministry needs to build men who are strong because they have come to grips with their brokenness and been healed.

POINTS TO PONDER

1. Where is a lack of integrity most clearly seen in our community?

2. What integrity issues do the men of our church deal with?

3. How is integrity developed? What must we include in our ministry to help our guys become men of integrity?

4. How is my integrity as a leader? What steps can I take to grow in that area?

Men of Intimacy

The second mark of the biblical man is intimacy. *Intimacy* comes from the Latin word *intus,* "within." It's a sharing of life with another. It's allowing others into our heart—the inner chamber. It's journeying into their heart. And it means we become one.

We want to help men develop intimacy in three areas of life.

The biblical man experiences intimacy with God. I'll be blunt. We all have a lot of guys in our churches that come on Sunday mornings because their wives drag them there. Their whole idea of Christianity is playing church. So what's the problem? They're settling for secondhand religion. They're just going through the motions—stand up, sit down, throw a buck in the plate. They're missing out on an authentic, growing, vital, living relationship with Jesus Christ.

Men move beyond the motions when they realize God made them to know Him—even deeper than that, to commune with Him. To enjoy Him. To experience Him. We are made *by* God *for* God. They can know what it means to wake up in the morning, jump out of bed and onto their knees and say, "God, thank you so much for the life you've given me." They can enjoy God's presence moment by moment, day by day by day. We want to work toward that end. Not just punch the clock for an hour on Sunday morning.

The biblical man experiences intimacy with his wife. Men need help to see their marriage as more than "the marriage thing," something to scratch off the to-do list of life. Men spend a lot of time, energy, and money dating or courting. We write letters and e-mails. We send text messages. We phone. We buy flowers. We do anything to catch the woman we want. Then we get married, have the reception, the honeymoon . . . and it's over. What's next? What's the next project, the next deal, the next hill to climb? We drop our marriages and leave our wives behind. Most of us stay married, but as far as our time, energy, and money are concerned, the marriage thing is done. And our wives feel it.

A biblical man realizes intimacy with his wife is both deep and wide. It's a deep sharing of hearts. A journey into the deepest cavern of who a man and a woman are—an exploration of what it means to become soul mates. But his intimacy with his wife is also wide. It encompasses their entire relationship. It's emotional—laughing and crying together. It's social—dating, going out together, having people over. It's intellectual— reading, sharing ideas, discussing politics, talking about life and life issues. It's physical—holding hands, kissing, touching. It's spiritual—praying together, worshiping together. Intimacy between a husband and wife involves all that they are—sharing dreams, hopes, fears, failures. And slowly—through small groups, through one-on-one counsel—we want to rock a man's view of marriage, to help him move beyond "the marriage thing" to experience real intimacy. Total-*person* contact with his wife.

For the first five years of my marriage we had a rule in our house: "Don't rock the boat." I was busy. I had been called to our church to start a college-age ministry. Everything I did revolved around the start-up, working day and night to guarantee a good ministry. So when I went home my rule was "Colleen, don't talk to me about your problems or the kids' problems or home problems." And my wife's rule was "Steve, don't talk about work. I don't want to hear more of your ideas, more of your plans, more of your strategies. You always have a new vision and I don't want to hear another one."

That was how things went for five years. One day I came home and Colleen met me at the door—that was new. She said, "I have great news."

"So, it was a great trade, huh? Who was it—the Packers, the Brewers, or the Bucks?" It had to be sports-related. That was the only good news I was waiting for.

"No, it's none of those."

Well, we already had two children, so I guessed. "Okay. Number three's on the way."

"No, it's not number three."

"No trades, no pregnancy, what's left?"

She said, "I'm going to rock the boat."

"You're gonna do what?"

"Sit down, honey." I sat down. "Steve, I don't like your lifestyle. I don't like the way you work. I don't like your habits. And we're going to change all this."

"Oh, welcome home," I said. "It's really been a great five minutes."

That night we had a very long conversation. And for the first time I shared with her my greatest fear—the fear I had kept stuffed inside me my whole life. I was afraid of failure. I had never told anyone that. And through a lot of crying and kicking and hugging that long evening, we moved past the "Hi, how are ya? Everything's fine, honey" kind of relationship. We sank the don't-rock-the-boat rule. We shared our hearts. We shared life. We broke through to intimacy.

Real ministry takes place when you move men toward intimacy. When you can explain to them what's going on in their hearts so they can open up with their wives to share feelings, failures, and what's really going on inside.

The biblical man experiences intimacy with other men. It's one thing to have intimacy with God. It's another thing to have intimacy with your wife. The biblical man needs one more thing. He needs to learn how to open up to other men, to have male friendships.

If you look at the Bible you'll see that the guys God used surrounded themselves with other men. *Moses.* Who did Moses have? Aaron. *Joshua?* Caleb. *David?* Jonathan. The story in 1 Samuel 18 describes a wonderful friendship in the making. God actually knit the souls of David and Jonathan. They became one in spirit. What about *Jesus?* He had the three—Peter, James, John—and the rest of the twelve. What about *Paul?* Barnabas, Timothy, Luke. Everywhere you look you see men surrounding themselves with other men.

We have built our ministry around Proverbs 27:17: "As iron sharpens iron, so one man sharpens another." What we're about is helping men to connect with other men. As noted in the first chapter, most men don't have friends. We can put them in situations where they can at least begin to break down walls and get to know one another, draw on each other, and depend on one another. Christianity isn't a solo sport. In the same way it would be suicide to climb Mount Everest by yourself, so it is spiritual suicide to try to make it on your own spiritually.

Twenty-four years ago I was asked by a college friend to join a men's small group. This was new territory for me, and I was very unsure what they would do. Would it be a bunch of guys meeting in a sweat lodge giving group hugs for the entire time, or what? We met a couple of hours a week to talk about what was going on in our lives and to ask ourselves the tough questions. It was encouraging. When things got tough with our marriages or our kids or our ministries, we could call day or night. It was challenging. They would see my blind spots, sins I was pushing off. They could look me in the face and say, "Shape up!" When I was lying, they knew it. And they weren't afraid to call me on it. When I took a step of faith or said no to sin, they cheered me on. We committed from the beginning to never allow one of us to walk through the valley of the shadow of death by ourselves. Years later, we still meet. Men have lost their wives, their jobs, and everything else that comes a man's way, but we have gone through it together. If there is one thing

I have learned through the years, it is that sharing life together is better than struggling alone.

We need to develop situations where men can get into those types of relationships. It's the "so what?" factor. We can take twenty or thirty guys to a large men's conference, and they get stoked. Then they come home and say, "So what? What's next? What do we do the fifty-one other weekends?" By placing men in small groups we can move them into intimate relationships that challenge them, help them grow, and give them a sense of belonging.

We have a long way to go to build men of intimacy. As males we seem bred for independence. We isolate ourselves behind thick walls. I've tried to jackhammer through some of those walls with guys, and it's hard. Walls don't break down quickly. But there's nothing more exciting than seeing those walls slowly come down.

POINTS TO PONDER

1. Describe obstacles for the men you work with in these areas:

   intimacy with God

   intimacy with their wives

   intimacy with other men

2. What will you need to incorporate into your ministry to help men grow in these three areas?

3. How are you doing in these areas of your life? What steps must you take to relight the fire in your relationship with

   God

   your wife

   other men

Men of Identity

In an era when both Russell Crowe toughness and Tom Hanks sensitivity seem limiting, the Bible offers us positive role models and principles that show us what true masculinity is all about. The biblical man is balanced. The biblical man is complete. The biblical man is certain of his *identity*.

You can see men struggle with their identity whenever they gather. Question number one—*What's your name?*—is immediately, inevitably followed by question number two—*What do you do?* As someone so nicely said, male identity in our culture is usually based on one of the four *B*s—brains, brawn, bucks, or beauty.[3]

My wife has a simple equation she uses to describe me. When I start sharing my struggles and what's going on, she'll say, "Steve Sonderman equals numbers."

I know I'm like a lot of men. I'm results-oriented. I love my work. If I don't watch it I start telling myself *I am what I do*. Other guys measure their worth by sales, quotas, and titles. I track how many guys showed up for a meeting. Yet our significance isn't in what we do. In God's system, our identity comes from Christ. There are four biblical principles we can remind our men of right from the start:

We have been created by God for God. In Psalm 139:14 it says, "[We are] fearfully and wonderfully made." We can help our men realize they are unique, specially designed by God. There is no one in the world exactly like them. Their personality, temperament, and physical body are unique. In God's eyes they are important because He created them.

Christ loved us enough to die for us. John 3:16 tells us that God sent His Son to die for us. If our men ever question whether God loves them, we can point them to the cross. It is the greatest definition and most powerful reminder of God's love we can imagine.

Christ lives in me. In Galatians 2:20 we are reminded that if we have been crucified with Christ we no longer live but He lives in us. He is in the process of making men into His image—and what He starts He will finish.

The masculinity of Jesus is our model. The masculinity of Jesus Christ illustrates what *real* masculinity is. He was able to cry and demonstrate incredible compassion. Yet He could be tough as nails. He stood up for what He believed in. He chased guys out of the synagogue who were taking advantage of worshipers with their big business sales and underhanded money changing. Tender, yes, but also tough. He was a man's man. Brawny fisherguys followed him. When people threw a party, who'd they invite? Jesus. He knew how to have a good time and people liked to hang out with Him. Our men need to study the life of Jesus to meet the ultimate man.

We want to develop men who sense what biblically muscular, masculine Christianity is all about. Power under control. Strength clothed in tenderness. As you work with men on this level and use Scripture to reshape their attitudes, they will become all that God meant them to be. Their significance is not in what they do—though there's nothing wrong with that. Their value and identity are in Christ.

POINTS TO PONDER

1. What heroes or leaders do your men identify with? Who are they trying to become?

2. How as a leader are you reflecting the masculinity of Christ to your men?

Men of Influence

After having an incredible coaching career at the University of Oklahoma, Bud Wilkerson responded to a request to head up the President's Council on Physical Fitness. After a year on the job he called a press conference. When a reporter asked why football is good for the country, everyone expected a ten-minute pep talk on the greatness of football. Wilkerson's response was shocking. "Football," he said, "is terrible for this country." Why? "Football is eighty thousand men desperately in need of exercise watching twenty-two men desperately in need of rest." That's just like the church. The church is hundreds and hundreds of men desperately in need of using their gifts watching a handful of guys, weary, exhausted from well-doing, who need a rest.

Take a man who won't settle for the status quo. A man who won't just go through the motions. A man who will leave his comfort zone and say, "I want to stand up. I want to be counted. I want to be a part of what God's doing." That's a man who will get out of the stands and onto the field. That's a man of *influence*.

Part of our goal is to train men to do ministry. And to train men to train *other* men to do ministry. We're not going to settle for just getting together to talk about our problems. We're not meant to be a holy huddle. I don't pay a hundred dollars to watch the Packers huddle. I go to see the Packers line up and butt heads. That's for us too! We have holy huddles. We get together for encouragement and growth and accountability. *Great*. But then we move out in society and do battle.

We're all concerned about changing our world and prevailing over the evils we see in society *right now*. We'll do that. But we also impact our world in unexpected ways—even after we die. We live on in two ways. We live on in eternity with Christ. We also live on in the lives we have influenced, the lives we have invested ourselves in. The first dozen verses of Psalm 78 describe how we as fathers are to teach our children, who in turn teach their children, who will in turn teach their children. What that passage describes is four generations of people being influenced by our actions today. Think about it! We can influence the children of the twenty-second century by investing our lives now. That's the potential of influence.

A man of influence sees the future. He sees the profit his investments will yield many years down the road. And so he pours his time and energy and money into people. Paul shows us how: "We loved you so much that we were delighted to share with you not only the gospel of God but our lives as well, because you had become so dear to us. Surely you remember, brothers, our toil and hardship; we worked night and day in order not to be a burden to anyone while we preached the gospel of God to you" (1 Thessalonians 2:8–9). We loved you so much we shared not only the gospel but our lives. That is ministry. Time and toil invested. The spectacular yield was yet to come.

Walt grew up on the streets of Philadelphia. When Walt became a Christian later in life he went to his church and volunteered to teach Sunday school. The church thought that was fine—but he had to find his own kids for the class. Walt went back to the streets, where he found a bunch of kids playing. He went to the first kid and asked how he'd like to come to his Sunday school class. The kid said sure. He wanted to know what they'd do. Walt told the boy they would have an hour each Sunday to talk about the Bible and spend time together. Then Walt asked if the boy had any friends who would like to come. He pulled them all in. Thirteen guys.

For the next several years Walt stayed with those guys. Every Sunday he met with them, taught them, invested his life in them. He started having them over for dinner, going to their houses for dinner. Took them to the zoo, to a ball game. He started to invest all that he was into those boys.

A few years back, when Walt died, someone checked on what had happened to those thirteen guys. Eleven had gone into full-time Christian service. One was Howard Hendricks, longtime professor at Dallas Theological Seminary—a man who knows what it is to influence men, a man who himself has discipled the next generation of men.[4]

The men we work with are going to live on in the people they invest their lives in. Dietrich Bonhoeffer said it well: "A righteous man is one who lives for the next generation." That's influence.

POINTS TO PONDER

1. Where are most of the men serving in your church?

2. Where is there a need for men to serve?

3. What initial ideas do you have to equip, encourage, and move men into service?

4. How did God work to get you involved in ministry?

See That? That's the Goal

So what's our goal? What are we shooting at? God wants us to build biblical men, men who are fully devoted followers of Christ. That's the goal of our men's ministry. If we fail to produce men of integrity, intimacy, identity, and influence, we have failed to score. We've missed the net. The ball of men's ministry has rolled off the field, out into the street, and been run over by a car. We have missed the chance to follow God and become strong in Him.

So the overall goal is in place, but how do we get there?

Vital Signs of a Healthy Men's Ministry

When you go to the doctor for your annual checkup, he will normally check your vital signs—your heart rate, blood pressure, cholesterol, weight, temperature, etc. Each of these has a bearing on your health. In the same way, we need to ask ourselves what are the vital signs of a healthy ministry. If we are missing some of these, it may be a sign of sickness or immaturity.

The following is a quick overview of what makes a healthy ministry. (More details will follow in the next chapter.) It's important to know that every vital sign will not be evident right away, but they are something to aim for. One of Stephen Covey's main points in *The Seven Habits of Highly Effective People* is to "keep the end in mind." I am continually telling leadership teams all over the world that they need to think in terms of five years to build an effective ministry. There is no way to microwave a ministry; it takes time.

Prayerful Dependence

> I am the vine; you are the branches. If a man remains in me and I in him, he will bear much fruit; apart from me you can do nothing.
>
> —John 15:5

The church will only move forward as it moves forward on its knees. As men, we have a natural bent toward independence and self-sufficiency.

Jesus knew this would be an obstacle to our ministry. He gives us a wonderful picture of what dependent prayer and life looks like with the image of the vine and the branches. The prayer lives of your leadership team should reflect a dependence on Jesus for life-changing powerful ministry.

> Before God has something very great to accomplish for His church, it is His will that there should precede it the fervent prayers of His people.
>
> —JONATHAN EDWARDS

Strong Leadership Team

> From Miletus, Paul sent to Ephesus for the elders of the church. When they arrived, he said to them: "You know how I lived the whole time I was with you, from the first day I came into the province of Asia."
>
> —ACTS 20:17–18

> When he [Paul] had said this, he knelt down with all of them and prayed. They all wept as they embraced him and kissed him. What grieved them most was his statement that they would never see his face again. Then they accompanied him to the ship.
>
> —ACTS 20:36–38

One of the biggest obstacles to a successful ministry is trying to succeed by yourself rather than as a team. Men's ministries that have lasted are ones built around a team of men who share the leadership responsibilities. Both Jesus and Paul modeled for us what ministry as a team looks like. Central to this team of men is a key leader who is passionate about men's ministry and willing to be the point man for the ministry.

Purpose Driven

> Where there is no revelation, the people cast off restraint; but blessed is he who keeps the law.
>
> —PROVERBS 29:18

Leaders are planning lots of events and activities for the men of their church, but the events often lack purpose. An effective ministry is going to have a clear and concise statement of purpose. This statement will give the men direction, keep them focused, and inspire them. Men want to be a part of something significant, something bigger than themselves.

Centrality of the Word

All Scripture is God-breathed and is useful for teaching, rebuking, correcting and training in righteousness, so that the man of God may be thoroughly equipped for every good work.

—2 Timothy 3:16–17

A healthy men's ministry will be committed to the study, teaching, and proclamation of the Word of God. Done in a variety of ways, it will provide the foundation from which men can govern their lives. The Word of God will be used in all that we do, whether it is visiting a man in the hospital, counseling a man who is confused, teaching at a large-group meeting, leading a small group, or meeting a man for lunch.

Male Context

I praise you because I am fearfully and wonderfully made; your works are wonderful, I know that full well.

—Psalm 139:14

To effectively minister to men, we must know who they are and what ministry looks like to them. Men in each church, city, country, and culture are different. It takes a ministry uniquely designed for them in order to reach them.

Pastoral Support

Remember your leaders, who spoke the word of God to you. Consider the outcome of their way of life and imitate their faith.

—Hebrews 13:7

Unless the senior pastor is supportive of the ministry, it will not happen. There are a number of ways to attain his support, but it begins with your leadership team being supportive of him. A healthy men's ministry goes in the same direction as the church.

Built on Loving Relationships

> A new command I give you; Love one another. As I have loved you, so you must love one another.
>
> —JOHN 13:34

Ministry is about people, not programs. It is about helping men build loving, encouraging relationships with those within the body of believers, as well as outside the body. We must help our men reach across social, economic, and racial lines with practical acts of love—with special care for the needy, forgotten, and defenseless. Loving relationships produce unity, accountability, and a powerful demonstration of God's presence within our communities.

Balanced in Its Approach

> So then, just as you received Christ Jesus as Lord, continue to live in him, rooted and built up in him, strengthened in the faith as you were taught and overflowing with thankfulness.
>
> —COLOSSIANS 2:6–7

Jesus was in the "people business," and we should be too. A healthy ministry has a balance between evangelism, establishment, equipping, and empowering. It helps men transform their lives through the work of the Holy Spirit, making it a lifelong process. A successful ministry is not necessarily a bigger or busier ministry, but one that is winning the lost, building believers, and equipping workers.

Intentional Programming

A healthy ministry will be intentional and focused rather than have a number of random events and activities with little or no connection.

It will start small, go slow, and be strategic in what it does. The programs you put in place will assist men in the process of becoming Christlike.

Here's the question now: How do we get men from where they are to where God wants them to be? The rest of this book is going to give you practical ways you and the men around you can build a life-changing ministry to men. Before continuing, though, take a few minutes to do a quick evaluation of your current men's ministry if you have one. This will set a baseline for the work you do in the future.

Evaluating the Vital Signs of Your Men's Ministry

	Weak				Strong
Prayerful Dependence	1	2	3	4	5
Strong Leadership Team	1	2	3	4	5
Purpose Driven	1	2	3	4	5
Centrality of the Word	1	2	3	4	5
Male Context	1	2	3	4	5
Pastoral Support	1	2	3	4	5
Built on Loving Relationships	1	2	3	4	5
Balanced in Its Approach	1	2	3	4	5
Intentional Programming	1	2	3	4	5

NOTES

1. Ron Lee Davis, *Mentoring: The Strategy of the Master* (Nashville: Thomas Nelson, 1991), 102.

2. Kenneth Blanchard, quoted in Touche Ross, Touche Ross & Co., "Ethics in American Business: A Special Report," 37.

3. Patrick Morley, *The Seasons of a Man's Life* (Nashville: Thomas Nelson, 1995), 269.

4. Howard Hendricks and William Hendricks, *As Iron Sharpens Iron* (Chicago: Moody Press, 1995), 14–15.

03

THE CHANGING LANDSCAPE OF MEN'S MINISTRY

Having the opportunity to teach leaders around the world how to start a men's ministry in their local church, and also consulting with churches and denominations, I see the same issues surfacing again and again. In this chapter I want to do a preemptive strike and share some solutions to these common ministry land mines. Each of these solutions will be developed further as we move through the book. Then I'll share some of the promising trends we are witnessing worldwide as it relates to ministry to men.

Land Mine #1: Men's Ministries Based on One Man

The common scenario is that a man comes home from a men's conference, training event, or some other men's gathering and he is all excited about doing something at his church. Because men have a propensity "to do something," he starts with what comes naturally—he plans an event. After the event the men want more, so he starts a small group, then he adds a retreat, then a service project, and the list goes on and on. Unfortunately, he is doing it all. He never takes the time to develop a team of men around him to help carry the ball. So when he burns out, accepts a job transfer, or has a vision for another ministry, the men's ministry he started comes to a screeching halt. What generally happens next is the pastor is forced to take on the leadership duties and spin another ministry plate. This not only puts a sour taste in the pastor's mouth toward men's ministry but it is also a great disappointment to the men of the church if the ministry changes or eventually ends. I cannot tell you how many pastors have told me this very story. So it is understandable when they are reluctant to give men's ministry another try.

Solution: Every effective ministry to men must be based on a *team* approach rather than *one man's* efforts. It is true that one man must supply the initial vision and passion, but that man needs to develop a team of men around him to make it happen effectively. A team-based approach allows for greater use of gifts and mutual encouragement, and accomplishes more to build the kingdom of heaven.

Land Mine #2: Men's Ministry Based on Activities and Events

When I ask a man about his church's ministry to men, he often starts by listing all their past year's events. Usually his eyes light up and his chest sticks out, proud of what they are doing. The problem is, to carry on this type of ministry, the events have to continually be bigger and better. You need a bigger-name speaker, a bigger-name band, or a bigger steak! Unfortunately, when a ministry is based on events and activities, it is not long before the men stop showing up. They've been there, done that, and have the T-shirt to show for it.

Solution: From the beginning, develop a ministry based on relationships rather than activities. This will result in the men getting together not for the sake of hearing another speaker or testimony from some celebrity, but because of the relationships they have forged among them. It won't matter who your speaker is because relationship will be the draw. This is easier said than done, but many ministries have made the transition from activity-based to relational-based. It is done over time. If you are just getting started with your ministry to men, you have the advantage of emphasizing relationships first. I think it was at least a year before we even did any type of event at our church related to men's ministry. In fact, I'm often asked how we do our retreats, and I tell them that we have never had one. They can't believe it!

Having said this, it is important to add that events and activities do have a place in an effective ministry to men. For example, a well planned kick-off event in the fall can really give your ministry a jump start. A kick-off event gives you an opportunity to share with the men of the church the vision of your ministry and how they can be involved. Often men see the fall as a new beginning, and they may be more inclined to attend an event or join a small group. At one kickoff, we gave every man a copy of *Man in the Mirror* by Patrick Morley, along with a schedule of the new small groups using the book. We had tremendous success and saw many men join a small group for the first time. So again, it is not that events and activities are bad, but use them to enhance your ministry to men, not just to keep them busy.

Land Mine #3: Men's Ministry Based on Random Activities

After a man has recited to me his grocery list of events his church is offering to men, I then ask how a certain retreat was related to the Saturday breakfast, how the breakfast was related to small groups, and how small groups were related to the service project. This usually gets me one long stare! Then they ask, "What do you mean?" So I reword the question: "How does everything work together?" In 99 percent of the cases, there is little relationship between the various aspects of the ministry. Most ministries today have a calendar full of activities that in and of themselves are very good, but an overriding purpose and strategy is lacking.

Solution: Intentionality, intentionality, intentionality. In case you missed it, I'll say it again: Intentionality! If you are going to have an effective ministry to men in the context of the local church, you need to see ministry as a process driven by purpose. I try to help leaders understand that everything they do must have a purpose, and various activities need to interrelate with intentional bridges from one aspect of the ministry to the next.

Land Mine #4: Men's Ministry Based on Methods

The church in America is enamored with success and pragmatism. If something is working for someone else, many will pick up that model and try to replicate it in their church. The result? A proliferation of churches trying to mimic what some of the mega churches are doing. This also happens in the men's ministry arena. When I ask leaders why they are doing such and such, they often say it is because another church across the city is doing it that way.

For some reason we are drawn to "better" methods and strategies rather than to the biblical principles explicitly stated in Scripture. Don't get me wrong. I absolutely love what Rick Warren is doing at Saddleback, what Bill Hybels is doing at Willow Creek, and what Mark Driscoll is doing at Mars Hill. I listen to them and others all the time to learn and grow. But I also know they would be the first to say that what they are doing is based on principles they find in Scripture and they are seeking to apply them in their specific context.

Solution: The Bible not only explains the message we are to share with men but also gives us a philosophy and principles for doing ministry. Each church is unique. Its history is unique, its culture is unique, and its personality and philosophy of ministry are unique. And it is safe to say that each church's ministry to men should be unique as well. God wants to develop a ministry that is best for the men in and outside of your church. This means your leadership team will have to study the Bible to discover God's purposes for your church and then seek Him for what He desires for you and your ministry to men. It will not happen overnight, and it will look different for every church in the world.

Land Mine #5: Lack of Pastoral Support

One of the biggest issues I hear about regularly is that the senior pastor is not interested in or supportive of a ministry to men. After talking with hundreds of pastors about this, I have come to realize a few possible reasons:

- He may have had a series of failures in this area and he does not want to pick up the pieces and try again.

- He and the governing board may have other ministries they want to start, and the timing is not right.

- He may be a bit intimidated by the men of the church and cannot envision being accountable and vulnerable to other men.

- He may feel he will be responsible for doing it all.

- He may not have a vision for men and what a fully functioning ministry to men can do for the church and community.

I have found that when you sit down and talk with pastors, they generally see the value of men's ministry, but they are unsure of what it means and how to move forward.

Solution: Spend time with your pastor and find out his vision for the church and how the men can help him accomplish it. I know of many situations where men have come alongside their pastor to encourage and support him, and before they knew it he was fully supportive of a ministry to men. It will be very difficult to undertake a ministry without your pastor's support, so involve him from the start.

Land Mine #6: Lack of Clarity on Roles and Responsibilities of the Leaders

Many leadership teams I consult with share a common problem: having men on the leadership team without clear roles and responsibilities. This can show itself in various ways, all of which are very frustrating for the point man as well as for those on the team.

Sometimes there is no single man on the team taking responsibility to recruit other leaders, cast the vision, divide duties, and keep everyone on task. This normally happens when a few guys get together, decide to start a ministry, and want to do it all together. While this may sound nice, it does not work when it comes to developing and implementing a ministry to men.

A second way leadership teams fall short is when the men on the team do not want the responsibility that comes with a leadership role. Plenty of men like to oversee things, but some are not very good at personally accomplishing tasks. Everyone on the leadership team must be willing to "own" a certain aspect of the ministry and not just be there to give ideas, expecting others to do the work.

A third example is when there are no clear job descriptions, so the men are unsure what is expected of them and who will provide direction. In the end, they get frustrated and ministry is not accomplished.

Solution: Effective leadership teams need a clear-cut leader who is responsible for the team and the overall ministry. After that, for the ministry to achieve its goals, every man on the team must be responsible for one aspect of the ministry, and every team member must have a clear job description that details his responsibilities.

POINTS TO PONDER

1. Is your ministry based on one man, or is there a strong leadership team?

2. Is your ministry based on events and activities, or is it more relational in nature?

3. Is your ministry based on random events, or are you intentional and purposeful in what you do?

4. Is your ministry based on the methods of others, or are you unique in doing what God wants you to do?

5. Does your ministry have the support of the senior pastor?

6. Do you have a clear leader for the team and does everyone have a specific responsibility?

Exciting Trends in Men's Ministry

One of the things that excites me as I look over the last ten to fifteen years of the men's ministry movement is the paradigm shifts that are taking place. This section covers the top trends I see in the U.S. and elsewhere.

1. A Shift From "Men's Ministry" to Ministry to Men

When I first taught training conferences, I would often start by asking, "What is men's ministry?" As mentioned earlier, the answers were usually a long list of activities: pancake breakfasts, golf outings, clean-up day at the church, ushering, a "Men's Sunday," retreats, choral groups, etc. This type of list brings with it the connotation of men's ministry being very programmatic, offering only activities and events. It also wrongly reinforces the idea that men's ministry is just another program—a piece of the church pie, getting a share of the resources, pulpit time, and participants. But this view is very limiting. You will tend to judge your ministry by how many men show up for events and look at ministry only in terms of what happens related to the pie. This view of ministry also leaves your church with numerous ministry silos, with everyone competing for space, money, leaders, and prime time.

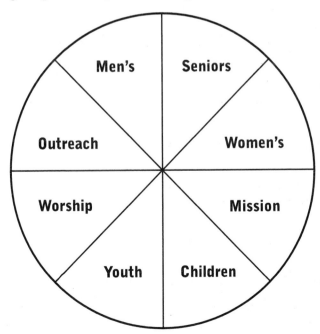

Over the years we have been working to shift mindsets and train men to no longer use the phrase *men's ministry* but instead say and think *a ministry to men*. This may seem like semantics, but it is much more. When we view what we do as ministry to men, it becomes all-inclusive. It is no longer what happens at certain meetings or events, but what happens throughout the church and its overall ministry.

So for example, when you are gathered on a Sunday morning for your regular weekly worship service, you have ministry to men. After all, when and where are you going to get the largest number of men from your church in one place? Seeing your worship as ministry to men will influence the type of music you sing, the environment of your worship center, and the way the pastor preaches. (For further discussion on worship and men, I recommend David Murrow's book *Why Men Hate Going to Church* [Thomas Nelson, 2005].)

Among other things, a ministry to men will include:

- the Sunday school classes

- how your men work with the junior and senior high boys of your church

- how the pastor disciples the elders/deacons at their monthly meeting

Often at our training sessions, a man will say, "Steve, my church isn't big enough to have a men's ministry."

My response usually surprises them. "You are absolutely right!" But then I quickly add that the size of a church never prohibits someone from having *a ministry to men*. I go on to illustrate what it would look like if the questioner called up one guy that week and asked him to lunch, and during lunch asked the friend a series of questions like:

- How are things between you and your wife?

- How are things at work?

- How are things between you and the Lord?

- How can I pray for you this week?

How cool would it be if in the next week you did the same thing with another man, and again the next week, and the week after that. This is ministry to men. No events, no brochures, no committee meetings—just one man walking with another for the purpose of following Christ more fully. You would be doing something just as significant as any large event the church may have!

For someone else, ministry to men may mean simply asking four or five guys to join him in a small group for a year. For that year he pours his life into them, helping them to grow in Christ and preparing them to lead a group of their own in a year or so. That's ministry to men—an organic ministry that takes off further than most imagine.

Another reason we need to view it as ministry to men is the movement to the cell church module. Called different things in different places around the world, these home groups play out generally the same way.

I had worked with a church in Ireland that had been developing a pretty strong ministry to their men when the elders decided to do away with the men's and women's ministries. Instead, everyone would now meet in home groups. The leaders of the men's ministry called me immediately. (I wish they would have thought about the six-hour time difference!) After helping them work through the grief and anger of seeing their three years of hard work seemingly go down the drain, I was able to help them see they were not done; if they truly had a ministry to men, new options were possible. For example, if a home group was going to have a time of prayer each week, why not divide the group every other week with guys in one room and women in the other for accountability, sharing, and prayer time. Another option was to leverage the relationship-building taking place among the men in a cell group with a morning men's time each week or every other week.

2. From Attractional to Incarnational Style Ministry

For thirty years or so churches, particularly in the U.S., have increasingly moved to a module of ministry that says "come to us." In other words, "If you build it, they will come." And boy, have we built some big buildings.

The idea behind this style of ministry is that people are interested in religious things and will come to church to have their questions answered and to find God. However, this presupposition is no longer true in our society today. A recent study revealed that only 20.4 percent of the population attend a Christian church on any given weekend in the United States.[1] At the same time, we know that a much higher percentage of people say they are Christians. A recent study done by Trinity College researchers found that 76 percent of American adults consider themselves Christian.[2] So the question is, if all the people who consider themselves Christian aren't in church, where are they? They are at home, at work, at their kid's soccer game, vacationing, and a host of other places other than church. To reach these people, as well as unbelievers, we are not going to do so by offering more programs at the local church. We have to go to them.

The life of Jesus is a great example of what an incarnational style of ministry looks like. John 1:14 says, "The Word became flesh and made his dwelling among us. We have seen his glory, the glory of the One and Only, who came from the Father, full of grace and truth." Jesus left all the splendor, majesty, and glory of heaven to come and live among us. He "pitched his tent" here on earth and interacted with people. His was a life of grace and truth.

Today, we are finding that ministry to men must take place in the community where men live out their lives. We are to be the body of Christ in the world today. We are to be there—at home, in the street, in the marketplace, at school, in the neighborhood—in the places where men live. So instead of trying to get men to come to church, a place many mistrust and are cynical toward, we are to establish beachheads in the community from which we move out. To be incarnational means we first see ourselves as sent to the world. Jesus said in John 17 that in the same way the Father sent Him, he is sending us into the world. We need to see our ministries not as a place to circle the wagons and try to survive but rather as missionaries to the world.

A second aspect of incarnational ministry is to identify with others. This is seen in our willingness to get close enough to people to know their suffering, hurts, and brokenness as well as the joys and victories they are experiencing in life.

Finally, incarnational ministry means having a presence among others. We need to live our lives in front of and with those in our sphere of influence. This is quite opposite from what is happening in so many churches today. Once a person becomes a follower of Christ, he usually cuts himself off from all unchurched people within two years, leaving himself virtually useless when it comes to leaving an imprint on society. Most churchgoing Christians today focus on keeping the church machinery running rather than being Christ to the world.

There are a couple of applications for this point. First, it means helping our men see ministry as relationship-building and teaching them how to make creative connections with men in their sphere of influence. A second application is starting a movement of small groups that meet in the community rather than only at the church. These groups will be open to new men attending and have apprentices ready to birth new groups in the community when a group reaches eight to ten men. These groups will look for ways to serve the community as a whole, and pray for specific men to come to Christ. In short, these groups will see themselves not as an end in themselves, but as groups on a mission to take back contested territory that rightfully belongs to Jesus. Go to the men's section on Elmbrook's Web site for more information on small groups.

3. From Maintenance to Missional

You might have heard the following story—it has circulated for years—but I repeat it because it speaks to where many churches still are today.

> On a dangerous seacoast that saw frequent shipwrecks, there was once a little life-saving station. The building was primitive, and there was just one boat, but the members of the life-saving station were committed and kept a constant watch over the sea. When a ship went down, they unselfishly went out day or night to save the lost. Because so many lives were saved by that station, it became famous. Consequently, many people wanted to be associated with the station to give their

time, talent, and money to support its important work. New boats were bought, new crews were recruited, a formal training session was offered. As the membership in the life-saving station grew, some of the members became unhappy that the building was so primitive and that the equipment was so outdated. They wanted a better place to welcome the survivors pulled from the sea. So they replaced the emergency cots with beds and put better furniture in the enlarged and newly decorated building.

Now the life-saving station became a popular gathering place for its members. They met regularly, and when they did, it was apparent how they loved one another. They greeted each other, hugged each other, and shared with one another the events that had been going on in their lives. But fewer members were now interested in going to sea on life-saving missions; so they hired lifeboat crews to do this for them. About this time, a large ship was wrecked off the coast, and the hired crews brought into the life-saving station boatloads of cold, wet, dirty, sick, and half-drowned people. Some of them had black skin, and some had yellow skin. Some could speak English well, and some could hardly speak it at all. Some were first-class cabin passengers of the ship, and some were the deck hands. The beautiful meeting place became a place of chaos. The plush carpets got dirty. Some of the exquisite furniture got scratched. So the property committee immediately had a shower built outside the house where the victims of shipwreck could be cleaned up before coming inside.

At the next meeting there was a rift in the membership. Most of the members wanted to stop the club's life-saving activities, for they were unpleasant and a hindrance to the normal fellowship of the members. Other members insisted that life-saving was their primary purpose and pointed out that they were still called a life-saving station. But they were finally voted down and told that if they wanted to save the lives of all those various kinds of people who would be shipwrecked, they could begin their own life-saving station down the coast. And that is what they did.

As the years passed, the new station experienced the same changes that had occurred in the old. It evolved into a place to meet regularly for fellowship, for committee meetings, and for special training sessions about their mission, but few went out to the drowning people. The drowning people were no longer welcomed in that new life-saving station. So another life-saving station was founded further down the coast. History continued to repeat itself. And if you visit that seacoast today, you will find a number of adequate meeting places with ample parking and plush carpeting. Shipwrecks are frequent in those waters, but most of the people drown.[3]

Reggie McNeal, in his book *The Present Future,* says, "The church in America has forgotten why it exists. It does not exist for itself; it exists to join God in His redemptive mission for the world."[4] One reason roughly three thousand churches close their doors each year is that they have forgotten their mission. The life-saving station has become a place for people to gather, hang out, tell stories, and talk about how bad things are outside the four walls. In men's ministry, much of the emphasis in the past has been for the already convinced.

Thankfully, not all churches exist for themselves. And the men's movement is shifting from "maintaining" church to being missional, from being consumers to being missionaries, from being caregivers to being equippers, and from having a country club mentality to being a mighty army on the move for Jesus.

The book of Acts gives us a wonderful picture of what this looks like. Early disciples were constantly going from village to village, town to town, and city to city to plant new churches and reach more people. It never occurred to them not to go; they understood that the church existed for mission, not for itself.

In men's ministry today, there is a strong movement to serve the surrounding community. This could be helping widows with their yard work, feeding the hungry, tutoring students in the city, building homes for the homeless, or rehabbing an old school. This notion of being the hands and feet of Jesus to the world really fits with a man's desire to be involved in a cause greater than himself. In his book *Shaped by God's Heart,* Milfred Minatrea says, "A missional ministry is a reproducing community of authentic disciples being equipped as missionaries sent by God, to live and proclaim His Kingdom in the world."[5]

Being an equipping center for men is another aspect of this shift to missional ministry. You and your leaders can provide the encouragement, training (hands-on training in the field rather than just another classroom experience), and equipping that your men need to be missionaries to their community and marketplace.

4. From Parachurch-Based to Church-Based

When I first started working with the men of Elmbrook, I called as many people doing men's ministry as possible. A few months later I attended a Leadership Network gathering at Glen Eyrie, the Navigators headquarters in Colorado Springs. There were about twenty-five men, all involved in some type of men's ministry across the country. In those three days I learned much about men's ministry, but what surprised me most was that I was the only pastor in the group. All the other guys were from parachurch ministries, including Promise Keepers, which was starting to put men's ministry on the map. Through the vision of Bill McCartney and Dave Wardell, thousands and thousands of men came to faith in Christ and were connected to other men through small groups. Not only that, they were the catalyst for what many believe to be at least sixty new men's ministries across the country, and for this we all owe them a debt of gratitude.

In recent years, there has been a move from parachurch men's ministries to ministry to men in the context of the local church. Wherever I go, I see senior pastors catching a vision for ministering to their men, associate pastors being given responsibility to develop a ministry to men, and layleaders being empowered to build teams to reach, grow, and send men. This church-based phenomenon is spreading across the country like wildfire, and nothing excites me more. I think Bill Hybels of Willow Creek Community Church said it best: "There is nothing like the local church when it is working right. Its beauty is indescribable. Its power is breathtaking. Its potential is unlimited. It comforts the grieving and heals the broken in the context of community. It builds bridges to seekers and offers truth to the confused. It provides resources for those in need and opens its arms to the forgotten, the downtrodden, and the disillusioned. It breaks the chains of addictions, frees the oppressed, and offers belonging to the marginalized of this world. Whatever the capacity for human suffering, the church has a greater capacity for healing and wholeness. Still to this day, the potential of the local church is almost more than I can grasp. No other organization on earth is like the church. Nothing even comes close."[6]

5. From Informational to Transformational

For decades the church in the West has been obsessed with learning and knowledge. We firmly believe we can read and discuss our way to spiritual maturity. The scorecard for many churches has been how many people are sitting in the pews on a Sunday listening to a message or how many people are in a Bible study parsing a Hebrew or Greek word. To be honest, I am not even sure what it means to parse a word! We find it easy to sit around and discuss twenty-seven different views of the second coming of Christ and to pray for Aunt Edna's ingrown toenail, but we never get down to discussing the secret sins of our heart! Evangelicals fill our minds with more and more doctrine and Bible facts while the rest of the world is going to hell in a handbasket. As my good friend Kenny Luck, the men's pastor at Saddleback in California, recently said at our No Regrets men's conference, "We are educated way beyond our obedience." And then he challenged the men to "get off their blessed assurance" and do something. I loved it.

What we are beginning to see is a move from spirituality measured solely by what a person knows, to how transformed their life is. Dallas Willard in *Renovation of the Heart* defines spiritual formation this way: "Spiritual Formation for the Christian basically refers to the Spirit-driven process of forming the inner world of the human self in such a way that it becomes like the inner being of Christ himself."[7]

Spiritual maturity is more than just living up to some external expectations. Rather, it is having the life of Jesus formed in us. The transformation process will involve incorporating spiritual disciplines into your life that put you in a place to be touched, taught, and transformed by God. It will involve having people in your life who will encourage you, hold you accountable, and walk with you through difficult times. It will involve a variety of experiences, such as suffering, giving, serving, worship, confession of sin, and others, that God will use to shape and mold you into the image of His Son. Moving from information to transformation will drastically affect how you minister to your men.

6. From Addition to Multiplication

If you want to have fun with your kids at dinner some evening, tell them you have two offers for them. They can either choose to get one million dollars a day for an entire month or get one dollar the first day, double that the next day, and double that the third day, and so on, continuing for an entire month. If your children are like mine, they will go for the one million dollars a day, for a total of $30 million by the end of the month. However, if they took a dollar the first day and then continued to double it each day, they would end up with 2 billion, 147 million dollars. That, my friend, is the difference between multiplication and addition, and unfortunately we are trying to grow churches and ministries through addition rather than multiplication. We are falling way behind the world's growth rate.

In 2 Timothy 2:2, Paul tells his understudy Timothy: "The things you have heard me say in the presence of many witnesses entrust to reliable men who will also be qualified to teach others." Paul is speaking of a process that will involve four generations of people.

In many of our ministries today, we are content with just adding people to the rolls, getting more men to our events or into Bible studies. The needed paradigm shift is to develop a reproducing mentality. That will mean looking at how we can disciple a small group of men, who will then go on and do the same for others. It will involve having small groups that are always looking to birth new groups. It will involve having a ministry that is always looking to birth new ministries and churches that are reproducing new churches.

The church in Antioch (Acts 13), while worshiping the Lord and fasting, heard the Holy Spirit tell them to send out Barnabas and Paul to plant more churches. What makes this so amazing is that these very men helped to start the church in Antioch. They were the best leaders they had, yet the church was willing to give them up. Are we willing to do the same? To give up our best for the sake of the kingdom? To move from adding a few men here and there to building a movement through multiplication?

Hopefully this chapter has provided some warnings as well as some encouragement in reading about the paradigm shifts happening around the world. With all this in mind, let's get started building a team for ministry to men.

NOTES

1. *http://www.christianitytoday.com/ct/2006/april/32.85.html* (accessed 1/08/10).

2. American Religious Identification Survey 2008, *www.americanreligion survey-aris.org/reports/ARIS_Report_2008.pdf* (accessed 11/03/09).

3. Thomas Wedel, *Ecumenical Review* (October 1953), paraphrased by Knofel Staton in "Heaven-Bound Living" (Standard, 1989): 99–101.

4. Reggie McNeal, *The Present Future* (San Francisco: Jossey-Bass, 2003), 15.

5. Milfred Minatrea, *Shaped by God's Heart* (San Francisco: Jossey-Bass, 2004), 12.

6. Bill Hybels, *Courageous Leadership* (Grand Rapids, MI: Zondervan, 2002), 23.

7. Dallas Willard, *Renovation of the Heart* (Colorado Springs: NavPress, 2002), 22.

Developing a
Coaching Staff

Great teams almost always have great coaches. The championship teams I remember from growing up seemed to have one thing in common: a man at the head of the team superbly qualified to motivate and manage players. Players could come and go but the coaches remained the same. The Cowboys had Landry, the Dolphins had Shula, UCLA had Wooden, the Reds had Anderson, the Steelers had Noll, Penn State had Paterno, the 49ers had Walsh, North Carolina had Dean Smith, and the Packers had Lombardi. They were all men who molded other men into winners, who shaped an environment where players worked and won together.

Growing up in Wisconsin, I heard Vince Lombardi bedtime stories. "He treated us all the same," Ray Nitschke used to say of Lombardi. "Like dogs." Defensive tackle Henry Jordon said, "When Coach Lombardi tells me to sit, I don't even look for a chair." No player, no matter how gifted, could upstage Lombardi. "There are planes, trains, and buses leaving Green Bay every day, and you may be on one of them," Lombardi used to say. It wasn't an empty threat. Jim Ringo, the Packers' phenomenal all-pro center, walked into Lombardi's office in 1963 and presented his agent. "Let me get this straight," said Lombardi. "You're his agent?" The hapless fellow nodded. The coach excused himself and walked into an adjoining room, returning a few minutes later. "I'm sorry," Lombardi said, turning to the agent. "You're talking to the wrong man. Jim Ringo is the property of the Philadelphia Eagles."

Lombardi was a coach who made things happen.

The Man Who Knows Where God Is Going

Whenever you start a sports team you start with the coach. He's the man who pulls together a staff, then the team. It's no different in ministry. And in this chapter I will discuss what could easily be the most important aspect of developing an effective ministry to the men in your church. We will look at the issue of leadership, choosing a point person, recruiting a team, and developing that team over time.

In order to reach men, you start with the leadership team—the coaches. More specifically, however, you need to start with one man who is going to head it up—the head coach.

This is a win-or-lose truth: Until you have a man willing to be the point person for your men's ministry, you will have a difficult time making a go of your ministry. Until you have that person, in fact, you may want to hold off on starting your ministry. Richard Elsworth Day, in his book *Filled With the Spirit*, says this about the significance of key individuals in God's plans:

> It would be no surprise if a study of secret causes were undertaken to find that every golden era in human history proceeded from the devotion and righteous passion of some single individual. This does not set aside the sovereignty of God. It simply indicates the instrument through which He uniformly works. There are no bona fide mass movements. It only looks that way. At the center of the column there is always one man or woman who knows God and knows where He is going.[1]

Can you identify the head of your team? He may already be in place. The men of your church may be looking around at each other waiting for someone to take the lead. There's a good chance your leader is the guy holding this book—a man passionate about men's ministry. In this chapter we will look at the characteristics of the men you want leading your ministry and how to recruit them. The man who heads your ministry needs these general qualifications. They're what God expects of any maturing believer. But your head man also needs a clear vision of where God is going and the incredible harvest before us. He also needs some skill at leading, or at least a willingness to learn. Grab a pen and work through *Exercise 1—The Marks of a Leader*.

Exercise 1—The Marks of a Leader

1. Develop a list of ministries and movements of God that started with an individual. Think Bible, church history, revival and evangelistic movements, and significant happenings in your own church. List as many men as you can.

2. Pick five of the individuals you listed. What characteristic(s) made people follow him?

   Person: Key characteristic(s):

   (a)

   (b)

   (c)

   (d)

   (e)

3. What are the characteristics of men you want leading your ministry to men?

   (a)

   (b)

   (c)

   (d)

   (e)

4. Given your church's structure, who decides who will lead your ministry to men? Who's the pick?

Building the Team

It isn't enough to find one man who can sense God's direction and is able to motivate and manage a group of men to get there. You need men serving alongside him. Building that *team* of leaders is the first big step in starting your ministry to men. Until there is a team of men to work with the point man, there can be no ministry. As discussed earlier, the reason so many ministries to men fail is because they don't build a cohesive team.

Ministry happens best in teams. A ministry team sets you up for quality ministry now and positions you for future growth. In his book *The Frog in the Kettle*, George Barna writes that "Leadership will be a key component if the church [or a men's ministry] is going to progress. Churches that grow . . . will be those that have a strong but compassionate leadership team. They will be churches that are focused upon God's vision of ministry for them, and pursue it with passion and excitement."[2]

Aim to develop three to five men who will partner to form your key ministry team. There are six qualities to look for in the men you desire to lead your ministry.

1. *Leaders With a Servant Spirit*

In Mark 10:42–45, Jesus shares with His disciples the key element in spiritual leadership. He tells them the way *up* is *down*. He tells them the person who will lead is the one who will serve. Our society is obsessed with climbing the ladder, upscaling, promotions, and upward mobility. Jesus let it be known that those who will lead in the kingdom of God will be obsessed with descending the ladder, downscaling, spiritual demotions, and downward mobility. Those that lead will be a servant to all.

I have found it exceedingly easy to find men who want to be involved in ministry as long as they start at the top and don't have to do the ordinary, dirty jobs. They want to be up front teaching or around the table making decisions, not in the back making coffee or setting up chairs. Sometimes I get the impression some men feel they are above certain tasks. They import their marketplace position, power, and philosophy and believe it will work in the church.

It doesn't and it shouldn't.

My ears perk up when a man says, "Steve, what needs to be done? Just name it!" A man from our church who owns a huge construction company once asked me if anything needed to be done. I told him we had a bulk mailing—2,600 pieces—to get out yesterday. "It's done," he said. He called a few guys, and they met at the church and went at it. I walked in late that night after another meeting and they were just finishing up. Here's a company president stuffing and licking envelopes. In his company he pays other people to do that. His servant spirit was contagious to the other guys.

That's the type of guy I want leading the ministry. The guy who understands to the core of his being that ministry is servanthood. I look for *FAT* guys. A man with a servant spirit is:

Faithful. Will he follow through on small jobs? Can he be trusted?

Available. Does he offer himself to be used, or are you always pulling him along?

Teachable. Is he willing to learn, or is he arrogant and unbending?

Getting a ministry going creates an enormous amount of work. Some tasks—making calls, compiling surveys, sending out mailings—are repetitive and menial. But they need to be done. One guy on your team who thinks he's above that kind of work breeds instant division.

Have your leadership team study together Henri Nouwen's book *In the Name of Jesus: Reflections on Christian Leadership.* In the book, Nouwen says about servanthood: "Christian leadership in the future . . . is not leadership of power and control, but a leadership of powerlessness and humility in which the suffering servant of God, Jesus Christ, is made manifest . . . a leadership in which power is constantly abandoned in favor of love. . . . Powerlessness and humility in the spiritual life do not refer to people who have no spine and who let everyone else make decisions for them. They refer to people who are so deeply in love with Jesus that they are ready to follow Him wherever He guides them. . . ."[3]

2. Leaders of Character

It isn't how you look, where you work, what you have, who you know, or what you know that counts. It is who you are when no one is looking. It's character that counts.

Real ministry is driven by men of character. One of my favorite passages on leadership is 1 Samuel 16:7. God tells Samuel not to look at the outward appearance of a man, the things that people look at. God looks at the heart. What a key principle for selecting men to lead your ministry! Some additional helpful guidelines are the lists Paul gave to Timothy for selecting elders and deacons (1 Timothy 3:1–13). And 1 Timothy 4:12 makes one of the best measuring tools for choosing leaders. It provides five standards to measure a man's character:

Speech. Does he use his tongue to tear down or to build up? Does he lie or speak the truth? Is he sarcastic and cutting—or loving and kind?

Life. Is there consistency between his behavior on Sunday and Monday? Does he visualize what he verbalizes, behave in accordance with what he believes? There is no room on a leadership team for someone who isn't living faith in the marketplace.

Love. Is his heart interested in the well-being of others? Does he show compassion and tenderness toward others?

Faith. Is he willing to take wise risks and live on the edge? Is he willing to trust God—or does he live purely by human strength?

Purity. Is this man seeking to be morally, ethically, and spiritually pure before God? That doesn't mean he's arrived—but is he striving to do what is right?

When Bill Clinton ran for president against George Bush, he had a sign at his campaign headquarters that read "It's the Economy, Stupid." His campaign team never wanted to lose sight of what they felt was most important. We need a sign at the door of our men's ministry office that says "It's Character, Stupid." Remember what's most important when you select men to be on your leadership team.

3. *Leaders Known for Godliness*

The greatest gift your leadership team can give the men of your church is their personal holiness. There is nothing more important in leading other men to Christ than a vital, authentic relationship with Jesus. Men today want the real thing, not secondhand religion. They want reality, not more ritual. In selecting men to be on your team, start with men you know who are in love with Jesus. Some things I look for are:

Strong private life. Do they spend time with Jesus on a regular basis? When I get together with men, I often ask them what they are learning in their daily devotions. A long stare after that question is a good sign there isn't much happening in that area of their life. Unless they drink from Jesus on a regular basis they will have nothing to give to others. What they are in private with Jesus will directly influence what they do in public with other men.

Obedience. Are they seeking to obey God in all areas of life, or is there an area where they knowingly continue to sin? Are they open to accountability to others for their life and actions?

Worship. Godly men love to worship. They make sure they meet regularly with God's people to worship. If a man's hobbies, golf game, or favorite spectator sport regularly causes him to miss Sunday worship, he's making a loud statement of his priorities.

In short, look for men whose lives point others to God rather than to themselves, who are becoming more and more like Jesus in all they say and do.

4. *Leaders of Passion*

Every once in a while when I least expect it I get a huge bear hug from John. After squeezing all the air out of me he says, "Steve, I just love working with men. I just wish I could do this full time."

That is passion for ministry. To have a passion is to be enthusiastic about what you are doing, to not be able to wait until the next time you get together with your men. It's a love for what you are doing and thankfulness that God has given you gifts and the incredible privilege of serving Him. When I interview men for leadership positions I ask a few questions that help me gauge their passion for ministry: What is your vision for men's ministry? What gets you the most excited about serving? Where do you see yourself fitting in? From these questions and others I can get a sense of whether they really want to do ministry or they are simply motivated by guilt or a feeling that they should do something for the sake of doing it.

5. Leaders Who Are Team Players

Outside our kitchen window is a sandbox, eight feet by eight feet. We inherited it when we moved into the house. We also inherited all the neighborhood kids who came over every night during the summer to play in it. While doing the dishes (yes, real men do the dishes), I would watch the kids playing together in the sandbox, building castles, roads, and so on. Inevitably, one child would end up throwing sand at the other kids or take someone's Tonka truck and go home. Every neighborhood has a few kids who just do not play well in the sandbox. It is not very different in the church! There are a number of men who do not play well in the sandbox. They have a very difficult time handling conflict or checking their pride at the door; they cannot handle constructive criticism or are unable to work with others.

When putting together your leadership team, look for men who are team players, who know how to check their pride and agenda at the door and are willing to put the team first. Ask yourself, can this person:

- handle criticism?
- deal with conflict?
- set aside his agenda?
- share ideas and a common vision?
- work well with people who have different views and ideas?

I once heard Michael Jordan say, "Talent wins games, but teamwork wins championships." It is the same in men's ministry.

6. *Gifted Leaders*

The final quality I seek in a man for my leadership team is giftedness. Every man is gifted, but I want to make sure that a man is gifted for his area of responsibility.

Our natural tendency is to surround ourselves with men just like us—people we want as friends. Men with different gifts think differently. They might laugh at opposite things. They process experiences and emotions in a variety of ways. It can be death to a ministry if everyone on the team is the same. The Packers' head coach, Mike McCarthy, is a great offensive coordinator but is relatively weak on defense. So he surrounds himself with strong defensive minds, men who complement his offensive schemes. In the same way, a leader of men needs to surround himself with other men who complement his giftedness.

As you pull together a group of men, think through the following areas to get a well-rounded team:

Is there someone with the gift of leadership? Many times people lead—even pastors—but do not have the gift of leadership. A true leader has the ability to develop a vision and get others into it. They can mobilize others and get them involved in making that vision a reality. Every team needs one.

Is there a person with the gift of administration? A ministry start-up generates endless amounts of administrative tasks. Find someone who likes administration—keeping ministry details organized and workers on-task and on-time. Any man with the adventurous spirit of a leader needs a guy like this.

Is there a person with the gift of helps? With so much to get done you need to have someone on the team who relishes doing the little things, the behind-the-scene things that make a ministry work.

Is there a person with the gift of mercy? Sometimes a leadership team full of guys who like to get things done leaves a bunch of battered people in their wake. You need someone who can care for the men, be a kinder and gentler example to overeager leaders, and shepherd the other leaders as the team develops.

It isn't a comprehensive list, but these four giftings are keys that keep a team working well. They bring balance to each other. It's possible, though, to have the proper gift mix but still get nowhere. These gifts are different enough that the team needs to work at working well. Each man must bring with him not just a gift but a deep willingness to be a team player.

As you pull together your coaching staff for your men's ministry, keep in mind the words of E. M. Bounds:

> God's plan is to make much of the man, far more of him than anything else, because men are God's method. The church is looking for better methods; God is looking for better men. The Holy Ghost does not flow through methods, but through men. He does not come on machines, but on men. He does not anoint plans, but men. It is not great talents nor great learning that God needs, but men great in holiness, great in faith, great in love, great in fidelity, great for God. Those men can mold a generation for God.[4]

As you build your leadership team, seek men who display servanthood, character, godliness, passion, teamwork, and giftedness. Work through Exercise 2 to see where your team is right now.

Exercise 2—Our Team on a Scale of 1 to 10

1. Each man on the team should take time to rank where he is in each of these areas.

	Excellent				Average			Needs Work		
a. servant spirit	1	2	3	4	5	6	7	8	9	10
b. character	1	2	3	4	5	6	7	8	9	10
c. godliness	1	2	3	4	5	6	7	8	9	10
d. passion	1	2	3	4	5	6	7	8	9	10
e. teamwork	1	2	3	4	5	6	7	8	9	10
f. giftedness	1	2	3	4	5	6	7	8	9	10

2. What are the strengths and weaknesses of our team right now? If there are four key gifts that we need—leadership, administration, helps, mercy—which gifts do we have? Which do we lack?

3. If you are a lone leader at this time, what type of men do you need to complement your gifts?

How to Recruit Your Coaching Staff

It's one thing to know what kind of person you want—even to set your sights on who you want. It's another thing to get him involved. If your church is like ours, 20 percent of the people do 80 percent of the work. All of the church's key people are pulled in many different directions. So when I started doing ministry to men I vowed I wouldn't steal leaders from another ministry. I would instead develop my own from the many who were on the outside looking in.

Here are steps you can take in recruiting men to be on your leadership team:

1. *Pray them out.* In Matthew 9:37–38, Jesus tells the disciples that the harvest is plentiful. That's true in our day as well. But what was the first thing He told them to do? Hire a headhunter? No! The first step is to ask the Lord of the harvest to send workers for the harvest.

Someone shared this verse with me back in my seminary days. It has prompted me to keep a list of men in my journal who aren't currently involved in any ministry. Whenever I see someone at church that isn't involved—but who should be—I put his name on the list. I regularly pray through this list, asking God to thrust these people into the harvest, maybe in the men's ministry, maybe in another area. I pray that God would bring just the right position for this man, based on his giftedness, passion, and availability.

Make a list. Start praying for men right now who can be part of your leadership team.

2. *Develop relationships with them.* One principle I will bang home throughout this book is that ministry happens best through friendships.

Do things with potential leaders in order to know them. Take them out for breakfast or lunch. Within these informal settings you can begin to see where they are at. Before you ask them to put their hands to the plow, you want to get to know their heart.

3. *Meet them one-on-one.* The best way to ask someone to be involved is in a one-on-one setting. I usually meet him for a meal, or in his office or mine. I try to connect face-to-face before I settle for a phone conversation. To begin, I tell him that I have been praying about his involvement in the men's ministry and that I feel it's time to talk about a certain area. I then share our vision for the ministry and where we are going—the big picture. I work to recruit men to a vision, not a program. Once they grasp the big picture, I share more specifically about the area I see them getting involved in. It could be heading up the small groups or leading a small group, doing publicity for the ministry, or a hundred other things. I let him know my perspective of why I think he is the right person for the job and how he would fit on the team.

4. *Share a job description.* At this one-on-one meeting I then share a straightforward job description for the specific area where I would like him to help. It helps to have a copy of this in writing to make everything as clear as possible, though you will first cover it verbally. The job description tells him specifically what I expect of him. It includes:

    a. what he would do—the ministry responsibilities
    b. how much time it takes to do it
    c. whom he reports to
    d. the term of service
    e. what the men's ministry leadership team and the church will do to support him in his ministry
    f. the qualifications necessary for the job

After walking a guy through the job description, I ask him if he has any questions about the ministry opportunity. (I have included a sample job description at the end of the chapter.)

5. *Ask for a commitment.* I finish the conversation by asking my prospective leader to pray about the opportunity and, if he's married, to talk to his wife about it before making a commitment. I give him

a specific time frame of when I need a response, usually a week, two weeks maximum. If I don't hear from him, I'll call him to see what he's thinking. If he agrees to join the team, great! We start the process of incorporating him into the team. If he says no, I ask if there is another area of ministry he would like to get involved in.

I will never forget what Bill Hybels said at the Leadership Summit years ago: "Nothing in the kingdom of God gets done unless someone asks." Whether it is asking someone to come to church with us, to join a small group, to attend a men's event, to commit their life to Christ, to join a mission team, to give, or to help on the leadership team, we need to ask. Leaders are forever praying and asking men to join them in the work of the ministry. Men, nothing gets done without asking.

The steps above can be used in recruiting any leader for your ministry. Right now we are simply talking about getting your ministry started, and again, all you are looking for is three to five men who will form your main ministry team. If there are two or three of you already, then you need to decide how many guys you want on your team and who should talk to whom about coming on board.

Exercise 3—Choosing Leaders

1. How many do you want on your ministry team? What types of men do you need on your team to bring a balance of gifts, personality, race, ethnicity? Ask God to help you think beyond your buddies to men who can broaden your ministry and genuinely help in your efforts.

2. Make a list of men from your church who are potentials for your Ministry to Men Leadership Team.

   (a)

   (b)

   (c)

(d)

(e)

3. After spending time in prayer about it, whom do you want to ask to be a part of the team? Who is going to ask them?

Building Your Leadership Team

Just gathering a committed group of leaders in the same room around one table does not make a team—or a ministry. It takes time to become a team and to prepare for the work ahead. I generally tell new leadership teams to think in terms of eight to twelve months of preparation time before launching their ministry. It's an old but true saying: "By failing to prepare, you are preparing to fail." The Bible is full of men who, when called by God to minister for Him, took a great deal of time to prepare themselves for effective ministry.

- Nehemiah was called to rebuild the walls of Jerusalem and prayed for four months before he went to the King to ask permission. He talked to people to gather information and rode around the city examining the walls. He waited—vision comes to those who wait. He set realistic goals on what needed to take place, and he put together a timeline. He then built a team of workers, shared the vision with them, put the plan into action, and trusted God. A careful study of the book of Nehemiah can serve as an outline of developing a ministry to men as well.

- Moses was called by God to deliver His people from slavery in Egypt to the Promised Land. He had spent forty years in the desert caring for sheep, preparing for this God-sized assignment.

- Jesus spent thirty years in preparation for three years of public ministry.

- The apostle Paul was called by God to reach the Gentiles on the road to Damascus. He, too, found himself in a prolonged time of preparation before starting his public ministry.

For the remainder of this chapter and into the next several, I will walk through what needs to be done to prepare a solid foundation for years of effective ministry to men. A very popular saying among those involved in the National Coalition of Men's Ministry (NCMM) goes like this: "Let's become to one another what we want the men in our church to be." I am not sure where it originated, but I like the idea and use it as a motto in our groups. That is your goal during the next several months with your leadership team. You want to become a group of men who love each other, are growing in Christ, being accountable to one another, encouraging one another, comforting each other, and living life together. Your leadership team will become a model of what you want every man in your church to experience. The following diagram will help you see the preparation.

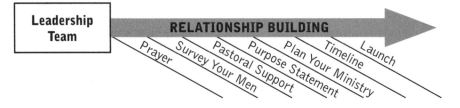

Why Take the Time to Build the Team?

A common question I get is "Why should we take all this time to build relationships and prepare? We know what we want to do and we just want to get started." Allow me to share a few reasons why it is so important to spend this time building the team and doing the preparation work.

1. *A small group is the best way to develop leaders.* Leadership development takes place best in the context of relationships and community. It cannot be accomplished in a classroom a few times a year. In a small group, rough edges can be smoothed, skills can be honed, encouragement provided, and a safe place developed to share life. Wise leaders invest themselves in the things that will have the greatest influence for

the long haul. The development of other leaders is perhaps the most lasting investment a leader can make. Such a focus can leave an influence well beyond you. These are the men who will be leading your ministry, sharing responsibilities, and moving on to develop others for leadership roles.

2. *Provides a healthy small-group experience.* Not only will this group help them develop as leaders, but you will also provide them with a good, healthy experience of what men's small groups are all about. This will be very useful in the future as they lead their own small groups.

3. *Builds a sense of community.* In this group, they can share life together and learn what a biblically functioning group looks like. They will serve arm-in-arm in the future, so it is important they know each other well and can work together. When things get tough, they will stick together. They become the example for the men of your church. If I have said it once, I've said it a hundred times: "Ministry flows from relationship."

4. *Lays the foundation for your men's ministry.* As you move through the year, you will be able to build your prayer team, prepare your survey work, develop your purpose statement, plan your ministry, and gather pieces to start the work of the ministry.

5. *Growth in Christ.* This is the bottom line. As a group you will be able to sharpen each other and help each other become more and more Christlike. The optimal place for spiritual growth is in a small group.

There are various meeting routines for building a team. In some churches the leadership team meets every week for study, sharing, and prayer time, while one meeting a month is devoted to business items, such as writing a survey to learn more about the men of the church. Other teams meet for study and sharing every week, and then add an additional meeting each month for any business at a separate day and time. Other routines can work as well, but the most important thing to keep in mind is that you are building relationships, not simply checking off items on an agenda.

Now let's work through each of the steps in the preparation phase, as you continue to build relationships with one another.

The God Who Makes Things Happen

First, you need a point man to make things happen. Then you need additional men to form a leadership team, because men's ministry isn't a one-man show. But you will need to move ahead with the certainty that *God* is the supreme head over all you do. You can make your plans and ask God for His rubber-stamp approval . . . or you can invite Him to guide and empower you in all that you do.

How do you know God is leading your ministry? Pray. It's the undergirding for the rest of your ministry. Ask God for His help. Express your dependence on Him. Humbly invite God to act.

Before you flip to the next chapter to look for more "How-To's of Men's Ministry," consider these words of S. D. Gordon from his *Quiet Talks on Prayer:*

> You can do more than pray after you have prayed. But you cannot do more than pray until you have prayed. Prayer is striking the winning blow at the concealed enemy, service is gathering up the results of that blow among the men and women we see and touch.[5]

Once you have a leader in place who has the vision, passion, giftedness, and character to lead your ministry, and as you're starting to build your leadership core, your next step is to pray diligently as a group. For a ministry to move forward and bear lasting fruit, it must move forward on its knees. Unfortunately, in many churches today prayer is only given lip service. We talk about it, we sing about it, we read about it, but rarely do we *do* it. You may have heard the story of Charles Spurgeon and his famous "Furnace Room of Prayer":

> An American couple visiting England a number of years ago decided to take a tour of Charles Haddon Spurgeon's Baptist Tabernacle, one of the most famous churches in London. Thousands came each week to hear Dr. Spurgeon, and every week scores were converted. The couple arrived at the church an hour before worship began, and as you might imagine, there was no one yet in the sanctuary. They looked around for a few minutes trying to figure out what to do, when a bearded gentleman came up to them and asked, "May I help you?"

"Yes. We're visiting from America," they explained, "and before the service starts we would like a tour of the church."

The man said, "Well, I'm a member of the church. I'd be glad to give you a tour."

They thought that would be wonderful, but the man offered something quite out of the ordinary. "The first thing I want to show you," he said, "is our furnace room." The couple took pains to be polite but they really didn't want to see the church's furnace room. But when in Rome . . .

So they followed the man down the winding stairs of the Victorian building to the basement, then to the sub-basement, the sub-sub-basement, and the sub-sub-sub-basement. As they went deeper and deeper into the ground it got danker and danker and darker and darker.

The American couple protested: "Well, you know, you don't need to take us any farther," they said. "We know what a furnace room looks like."

But the man remained firm. He said, "No, no. It's very important that if you're going to come to our church that you see our furnace room." So down to the final sub-basement they went, into the coal room, where coal was piled everywhere. It was, of course, how the church was heated. The man indicated a huge oak door, bound by iron clasps and iron handles, and said, "This is our furnace room."

And they said, "Well fine, thank you very much. Now, may we see the rest of the church?"

"No, no, you haven't been in the furnace room yet!"

"Well, we don't really want to go into the furnace room."

He insisted. "But you must."

They relented. The man opened the huge door and they looked into the massive room with its boilers and furnaces. To their surprise, the room was filled with hundreds of people on their knees, praying the hour before the service.

The couple looked at the bearded gentleman, then back at the hundreds of people praying on the floor. When they turned to him again, he smiled and said, "Well, I've had my little joke with you. Yes, I am a member of this church and, in fact, I'm the pastor. I'm Charles Spurgeon. People come from all over the world to this church to see what God is doing, and He is doing incredible things, but they think it's because of me that God is doing all of this. I'm not the reason it is happening. The reason things are happening here is that every Sunday morning, from ten until noon, when I'm finished with the service, hundreds of people gather here in the furnace room. They pray for the service, for my sermon, for my ministry. They pray for conversions, for Christians to be fully committed to Christ. That is why God does the ministry He does at Baptist Tabernacle. It isn't because of me."

Every ministry needs a furnace room where men are committed to pray for both leaders and participants. The only way that I was willing to do men's ministry was if other men would pray for me and for the ministry on a regular basis. I found it vital to start a prayer ministry first. It's the place where the real work gets done. Here are five steps to making it work at your church:

Step One—Find a small group of men who will commit to pray regularly for you and the ministry. You can find these men through a number of means. You can make a list of fifteen to twenty men and send them each a letter and a commitment card to return to you if they accept the challenge. You can run a bulletin announcement letting the men of your church know you are developing a prayer team.

I asked the men to pray and fast for the ministry every Wednesday noon. Some of the men had other meetings on Wednesdays, so they had to do it another day. We didn't gather to pray; each man prayed individually wherever he was. For an example of the type of commitment we ask for, look at the end of this chapter for "Elmbrook's Prayer Ministry for Men."

Step Two—On a regular basis send the requests for your ministry out to the men. I send a prayer card before the first Wednesday of the month so the men can pray specifically. These cards usually have new requests, both personal and for the ministry, as well as answers to prayer. See the "Front Lines Prayer Requests" card at the end of the chapter.

Step Three—Get the men together. During the course of the year we have a breakfast for the entire prayer team. We get to know one another and have a couple guys share testimonies of how things are going. We talk about struggles as well as victories.

Step Four—Keep the men informed. This happens in two ways. First, I use a monthly newsletter to instruct the men on prayer. I encourage them to read and to be growing in prayer. One year we read through *What God Does When Men Pray*, by William Carr Peel (NavPress, 1993). Other years we read *Too Busy Not to Pray*, by Bill Hybels (InterVarsity Press, 1988), and *Revival Fire*, by Wesley Duewel (Zondervan, 1995). Some other books on prayer you may consider are: *Prayer*, by Philip Yancey (Zondervan, 2006); *Prayer That Works*, by Jill Briscoe (Tyndale House, 2000); *Prayer Coach*, by James Nicodem (Crossway, 2008). The second way I keep them informed is to let them know how God is answering prayer. I did an awful job of this the first year. Men kept asking how my talks went. How the events went. They had prayed. They wanted to know if anything had happened. It told me that if I asked men to pray I had better watch for answers and pass them on to the men. There's no greater motivation for prayer than to see and hear about answers to prayer.

Exercise 4—Building a Prayer Team

1. Make a list of five men you could ask to be on your prayer team.

   (a)

   (b)

   (c)

   (d)

   (e)

2. What are you going to ask them to pray for?
   Personally

   (a)

   (b)

   (c)

For the Ministry

(a)

(b)

(c)

3. How are you going to keep these men growing in prayer and informed of answers to prayer?

As you begin to develop your leadership team I would suggest you find one person to be responsible for the prayer team. Our prayer coordinator collects all the requests and gets them to prayer team members. It takes the responsibility off you and helps another man to grow!

In the next chapter we will talk about "scouting." A team can't win if they don't know who they're working with. We will look at finding out more about who men are and how to survey them to find out their needs, their vision, and what they want from your ministry to men.

Other Resources for Prayer:

How to Develop a Prayer Partner Ministry, Injoy Ministry, 1530 Jamacha Road, Suite D, El Cajon, CA 92019. Phone: (619) 444-8400, 1-800-333-6506.

The Complete Works of E. M. Bounds on Prayer, Baker, Grand Rapids, MI, 1990.

Mighty Prevailing Prayer by Wesley Duewel, Zondervan, Grand Rapids, MI, 1990.

Churches That Pray by Peter Wagner, Regal, Ventura, CA, 1993.

Prayer by Philip Yancey, Zondervan, Grand Rapids, MI, 2006.

Prayer, the Great Adventure by David Jeremiah, Multnomah, Sisters, OR, 1997.

NOTES

1. Quoted by Ravi Zacharias from the book by Richard Elsworth Day, *Filled With the Spirit*, in a message given at the 1988 Elmbrook Missions Conference.

2. George Barna, *The Frog in the Kettle: What the Christian Community Needs to Know About Life in the Year 2000* (Ventura, CA: Regal, 1990), 148.

3. Henri Nouwen, *In the Name of Jesus: Reflections on Christian Leadership* (New York: Crossroad, 1989), 63–64.

4. E. M. Bounds, *The Power of Prayer* (Grand Rapids, MI: Baker, 1972), 269.

5. S. D. Gordon, *Quiet Talks on Prayer* (Uhrichsville, OH: Barbour, 1984), 16.

ELMBROOK CHURCH MEN'S MINISTRY JOB DESCRIPTION

JOB TITLE: Top-Gun (TG) Instructor

REPORTS TO: Top-Gun Coordinators

MINISTRY RESPONSIBILITIES:

1. Go through the training program for TG instructors.
2. Prepare the lesson each week for the meeting.
3. Facilitate the discussion each week of the Bible study.
4. Meet with the men in an informal setting two or three times throughout the year.
5. Dialogue with the co-leaders on a regular basis regarding the well-being of the group.
6. Participate in the services during the course of the year.
7. Pray on a regular basis for your group.

LENGTH OF SERVICE: Nine-month commitment to the ministry. September for training; the groups run October through May.

TIME REQUIRED: Average of four hours per week.

IN-SERVICE SUPPORT:

1. Training sessions before you start.
2. Periodic in-service meetings.
3. Shepherd from TG Leadership Team to pray for you on a regular basis and to be available to you at all times to talk.

QUALIFICATIONS AND SPECIAL SKILLS:

1. Elmbrook church member.
2. Must have gone through TG Basic Training.
3. We expect regular church attendance at Elmbrook.
4. We expect you to make your personal devotion time a priority.
5. We expect you to attend all training sessions.
6. We expect you to be prepared for each session.

PRAYER REQUESTS

NO REGRETS MEN'S CONFERENCE

- For the selection of the 70-plus seminar speakers and contacting them
- For a couple of additional men on the team
- For the keynote speaker two years from now

BREAKFAST OF CHAMPIONS AT THE COUNTRY INN, WAUKESHA

- For the keynote speaker and man giving his testimony as they prepare their talk and testimony
- For the men of the church to have boldness in inviting friends to hear a clear gospel presentation
- That men would be drawn to Jesus

GENERAL

- Wisdom in the development of the small-group plan for the men
- Praise for a great year of Quest in which a number of men came to Christ
- Praise for the fruitful ministry trips to Angola Prison to help build a chapel
- Pray for the planning of the fall kickoff in September
- Pray for the new small-group material being written by Todd
- Pray for some new team members for the following ministries: Soul Purpose, Quest, and Fall Kickoff

STEVE'S PERSONAL REQUESTS

- Discipline in writing of new book *Mobilizing Men for One-on-One Ministry*
- Preparation for ministry trip to the Philippines in the fall
- Pray for our family as we vacation together in June

ELMBROOK'S PRAYER MINISTRY FOR MEN

We are constantly on a stretch if not a strain, to devise new methods, new plans, new organizations to advance the church and secure enlargement and efficiency for the gospel. . . . Men are God's method. The Church is looking for better methods; God is looking for better men. . . . The Holy Ghost does not flow through methods, but through men. He does not come on machinery, but men. He does not anoint plans, but men—men of prayer.

—E. M. BOUNDS *THE PREACHER AND PRAYER*
(NOW *PURPOSE IN PRAYER*)

One of the greatest sins the church in America needs to confess is the sin of prayerlessness. What is needed for the church to get back on track is prayer. The Frontlines Ministry is a group of men who are dependent on God and express this dependence in a life of prayer, which will in turn effect changes in themselves to be men of integrity in their home, church, and workplace. We are looking for men who will commit to be men of prayer. The commitment is as follows:

- It is for one year.
- It is to pray every Wednesday noon (or another day of the week if necessary) wherever you are, for the Men's Ministry, its leaders, and its purposes.
- To individually work through a selected book on prayer/worship and be prepared to share what God is teaching you in your study.
- Fasting is optional this year, but we think you will be too busy praying to eat.
- Participate in the various prayer retreats and meetings that will be scheduled throughout the coming year.
- Consistency in spiritual disciplines and physical workout schedule

If you are willing to move the church ahead on your knees, sign the card and return it to Steve Sonderman at Elmbrook Church, 777 S. Barker Rd., Brookfield, WI 53045. When you sign up, we'll send you the first set of prayer requests, book syllabus, and more information. If you have any questions, call Steve Sonderman.

‒ ‒

✁

COMMITMENT CARD

Name _____

Address _____

City _____ State _____ Zip _____

Signature _____

‒ ‒

✁

Several years ago Willow Creek senior pastor Bill Hybels made this clear-sighted remark: "In order to effectively minister to people . . . we must not only be able to exegete the scriptures, but society."[1] It is crucial that you base your ministry to men on a clear understanding of the society or culture you work with—the men you want to reach and their roles in this world.

It isn't enough to understand the Bible. God intends for His Word to connect with men's daily lives. That won't happen if the person doing the connecting doesn't know the men he is leading. Before you build a ministry to and for your men, you need to know them.

Too often local fellowships copy programs from other churches in other cities, then are surprised when the latest, greatest fail-proof model meets with little success. Churches are different. People are different. The men of each church have different interests, pressures, schedules, incomes, and needs. They aren't likely to accept a ministry developed without their input, however well-intentioned their leaders are. That great theologian and international diplomat Bobby Knight still takes that foist-my-way-on-them approach. When a guy goes to play basketball for Coach Knight, there's only one way to play the game: Bobby Knight's way. Knight recruits young men to fit his mold, his style of play. When it comes to basketball, it's his way or the highway.

That doesn't fly in the church. Every group of people is different. They expect different ministries. And ministries for them must be developed with them in mind.

Getting to Know Your Men

I obviously can't tell you everything about the men in your church. This chapter is going to give you tools to effectively find out who your men are and identify their needs. We will look at how to interview and survey your men and how to keep your pastor involved in the process. I will wrap up the chapter by looking at men's ten most common needs— some of the issues you will probably uncover in your surveying. But the information *you* gather will likely be the most valuable thing you bring to the next stage of building a men's ministry—developing a game plan and structuring a program to meet real needs.

With these general characteristics in mind and a point man and leadership team of three to five men in place, your next step is to interview and survey the men of your church. Are you sitting down? This process can take several months, though it can happen a little faster. If that sounds like a time-consuming project, consider these benefits:

You discover the needs of the men in your church. This is the only way you can get an accurate picture of *your* men in *your* church.

You avoid striking off in a wrong direction—blazing a trail for your men to follow and seeing no one follow. Men's ministry isn't for the leaders. It's for the men. It's meant to meet their expressed needs and deeper needs that may go unsaid. Surveying your men avoids needless work. I have a close pastor friend who began his working life as a builder and contractor. One of his favorite sayings: "Measure once, cut twice. Measure twice, cut once."

You will give the men of your congregation ownership of the ministry. They get in on the ground floor because the ministry is being developed with their awareness and input.

You will grow interest in the upcoming ministry, using this lead time to build anticipation.

Choosing Men for One-on-One Interviews

I suggest you start with individual interviews. Meeting one-on-one enables you and your team to target specific men in the church to spend time with. One big thing to remember: Make these meetings more productive by going as a listener. Don't go to share ideas *you* have.

How many men you meet with is far less important than *who* you meet with. I met with sixty men because our church is large and being the men's pastor is my full-time job. Consider the size of your church, but figure that your leadership team will do well if they meet with ten to sixteen carefully chosen men. When you set up your schedule of whom you want to meet with, you will want as much variety as possible. Keep the following categories in mind:

- Married men and singles

- Men in their twenties to men in their seventies

- Men with children and men without children

- Men who are working and men who are retired

- Professionals and nonprofessionals

- Men who travel often for work and men who don't

- Men who have been involved in men's ministry and men who haven't

- Men of different races, ethnic groups

- Men interested in sports and active outings and men who aren't so inclined

- New believers and mature believers

- Men on the inside of your church and men on the periphery

In other words, try to get a good cross section of the men of your church. The natural tendency is to meet only with those you know and feel comfortable with. You can avoid this by setting up a grid with age and some of the key characteristics across the top, running names down the left-hand side. Think through and mark which men fit which characteristics—it's a good visual way to ensure you get a mix of men from your church.

Connecting With Your Men

Once your team develops a list, divide up the names, call the men, and make appointments with them. Schedule a time to meet with your pastor as well—and check out the following guidelines. Here is a list of things to mention on the phone to your men:

1. Explain what you are doing and promise to take only one hour of their time. Schedule your meeting at a time and location that works for them. Remember they are doing you a favor.
2. Tell the men that being interviewed doesn't constitute making a commitment to the men's ministry. All you want at this time is their input.
3. When a man says his opinion isn't worth anything because he doesn't know much about men's ministry, tell him that you don't either—and that being a male is the only qualification he needs. Once I let the men know there were no stupid responses, I didn't have a single man tell me he didn't want to do it.

Meeting With Your Men

When it's time to meet with your men, keep these things in mind:

1. Give them a set of questions ahead of time so they can think about them.
2. Call a day ahead to confirm the meeting.
3. If you don't know the man you are interviewing, introduce yourself and explain once again what you are doing.
4. Get right into it. Guys like to get to the business at hand.
5. Listen, listen, and listen. There's no substitute for listening to what a man is saying. Work at making him the expert on men.
6. Write everything down. I took notes on each of the conversations so I would not forget anything.
7. Stick to your agenda. Be flexible enough to take the conversation in different directions if you need to, but try to cover the questions

your team decided on. You can use Exercise 1 (below) to develop the list of questions you want to cover in your time together.

8. Close by thanking the man you interview for his time, energy, and input. Ask him if he would like to see the results of the survey when they are tabulated.

Exercise 1—Interviewing Your Men

1. Your questions will be different from the ones I used because your church, men, and culture are different. But consider these as starters and modify them as needed:

    (a) What has been your involvement in men's ministry in the past? What do you see as its strengths? What do you see as its weaknesses?

    (b) Describe what you think are men's needs today. What are their main stresses, anxieties, and pressure points? What are four or five characteristics of men today? What do men want?

    (c) How can the men's ministry minister to men at [your church] and outside of [your church]?

    (d) Based on what you have told me about men today, what type of ministry will best cover the following: evangelism, establishment, equipping?

    (e) What are your visions for men's ministry at [your church]?

2. What questions would be most helpful for you to ask a number of men in your church? What do you really want to know from them?

    (a)

    (b)

    (c)

(d)

(e)

(f)

(g)

(h)

(i)

(j)

Getting More Information

Get together with your leadership team after the individual surveys are completed and tabulated. Ask yourself the following questions: What are some of the common themes? What are some of the common needs of men in our church? What type of ministries do they envision? What would be most effective in ministering to them based on what we have heard? I can tell you right now, you will be amazed at the things you hear. You may have been thinking of going a certain direction with your ministry to men, but these conversations may open your eyes to something completely different.

Based on what you now know, put together a survey for all the men of the church. This survey provides you with the opportunity to take the general ideas that came from the individual surveys and ask specific questions. If the men say they are very interested in being in small groups, for example, you can ask in the all-church survey, "When is the best time for small groups to meet?" "Where should they meet?" "What do you want to study?" "Are you willing to lead a group?" and,

"Are you interested in being part of a group?" This survey will allow you to drill down on the specifics and logistics to effectively plan your ministry. Here are some ideas to keep in mind when you put together the survey:

1. Ask your pastor for permission to do the survey. Show him what you have done so far and explain why you want to survey all the men. Ask him if the survey could be done during the service or if he would rather have it done afterward. Another option available today is Web-based surveys. A number of resources on the Web make this very easy. We use Survey Monkey at Elmbrook, but there are others as well.

2. Make sure the survey can be done in five minutes or less.

3. Design questions so they can be answered with a check mark.

4. Have a few men read the questionnaire ahead of time to make sure the questions make sense. Is each of the questions helpful for the development of the ministry? You may not get to do another all-church survey for years, so get all the information you need NOW.

5. Arrange with the ushers how the survey will be collected. If you put the survey in the Sunday bulletin, you might want to have a well-marked drop-off box at each exit of the sanctuary.

6. Prepare ahead of time how you will tabulate the results.

7. Let the men know the results. Put out a special handout showing the results, or if your pastor is agreeable, list them in the bulletin. (At the end of this chapter, I have included the survey we used as well as a handout that presented our findings.)

Surveying Other Churches

One last thing you can do to generate ideas is to contact other churches in your city, state, or even across the country and find out what they are doing in men's ministry. Not to duplicate what they are doing, but to get some ideas. I spent many hours on the phone talking to men already doing men's ministry in their church or through a parachurch organization. I asked *what* they were doing, *how* they were doing it, and *why* they were doing it. The more people I talked to the more ideas I had for what we could do for our men.

There's a great shortcut that gives you information from many churches all at once. More and more states are hosting training sessions sponsored by Man in the Mirror, Iron Sharpens Iron, Top Gun, or other organizations, and these conferences are great places to network. As more churches start men's ministries, networking gets easier.

Involving Your Pastor

Regardless of the size of your church, you will need the support of the senior pastor. You should not move forward with your planning without his support. No matter what, you will always be able to have a ministry to men individually, but programming will be very difficult without the pastor's support. I have been a pastor for twenty-five years, so I fully appreciate the love-hate relationship pastors have with new ministry ideas. Pastors are excited—*someone else is grabbing hold of ministry!* At our church the best ministries started at the grassroots level. Pastors are also nervous—*where is this thing headed?* Pastors look at the big picture of the whole church and wonder what additional demands they will face to keep one more ministry going. They can also interpret a ministry start-up as a slam that they aren't doing an adequate job to meet the needs of the congregation. Here are some steps you can take to help the situation:

1. *Include your pastor.* Meet with your pastor early in the process. Before you even get started make an appointment with him to share your vision and ideas. Ask if he has any plans for starting a men's ministry and what they are. Ask him when it would be a good time to get something started. You might hear that the church is already starting a couple of other ministries this year and that he wants you to wait a year. Accept that as time to build relationships with your men and to fine-tune your understanding of what the men need.

Your pastor may ask you to speak to the church board, or put you under the supervision of an elder or deacon. If he does, work hard to include that man in your planning in the same way you would include your pastor.

2. *Interview your pastor.* As I mentioned earlier, get together with him when you do your survey. The time I spent with our senior pastor and other associates was highly profitable, and I am sure it will be for you as well.

3. *Inform your pastor.* Send him copies of the minutes from your meetings as well as the results of the survey. It will keep him from feeling you are a loose cannon. Keep him involved in the process by scheduling your planning meetings when he can make it—*if* he wants to be there. Ask him if he wants to be there or just be kept informed. Don't pressure him to attend.

4. *Intercede for your pastor.* You can give your pastor no greater gift than your prayer support. A church in Madison, Wisconsin, has a group of men that meet in the pastor's office each Sunday morning to pray for the pastor before he goes into the pulpit. What an encouragement that must be! Call your pastor and ask him how you can pray for him and his family that week or month. Ask if you can pass on his prayer requests to your prayer team.

5. *Invite your pastor.* Make sure you invite him to the events you sponsor. Ask him to speak at some of your events as well. Pastors enjoy the opportunity to get out with the guys and talk with them, hang out with them, and bring teaching. Don't take it personally, though, if your pastor doesn't show up for every event. He could easily be at meetings every evening of his life if he said yes to everything. He does have a family, and he needs his downtime too!

6. *Encourage your pastor.* (Sorry—I couldn't come up with a sixth *I* word.) Make sure the men of your church encourage him in the work he is already doing. Drop him a note or give him a call to let him know how much he means to you and the church. As a leadership team, ask your pastor how you can serve him and his family. It may be helping with the spring cleaning, sending him and his wife on a weekend getaway, or any number of other things. There is no greater feeling for a pastor than knowing the men of the church stand with him.

At the end of the day, the pastor may say he does not want a ministry to men in the church, and this is more common than you think. Over the years I have heard many reasons:

- The timing may not be right. The church board may have a list of priorities and new ministries they are trying to start, and men's ministry is not one of them. In this case it may mean waiting a year or so.

- He may be uninformed. There are many pastors who don't know what a ministry to men can do for the church. You will have to share with him the many positive effects a men's ministry brings to the church.

- He may have had a bad experience in the past. Many pastors have been burned by a ministry based on one person, and when that person left he had to keep it going. Now he has too many responsibilities and may not want to chance it again.

- He may be afraid. Some pastors find a men's ministry intimidating. He may not want to become vulnerable in a small group, because then he may have to be real with others. He may be intimidated by confident men. He may be afraid of losing control once it starts, and there are a host of other reasons.

In the end you will have to respect your pastor's and the board's decision on whether or not to proceed with a ministry to men. But as I said earlier, if they don't approve one, it is still possible to have a personal ministry to men in your sphere of influence.

Drawing Some Conclusions

By this point, if you are going to proceed, you have the information you need to begin to pray over the results and discuss what type of ministry will best serve the men of your church. You have interviewed a variety of men in your church, and you have surveyed the men in your church. You have incorporated your pastor's goals and ideas. It's time to get your team together. Exercise 2 will take you through a series of questions designed to help you critically analyze the information you have gathered.

Exercise 2—Pulling It Together

1. After looking through the surveys, what major themes stand out?

2. What are the top three expressed needs of the men in our church?
   (a)

   (b)

   (c)

3. If the biblical man is a man of intimacy, integrity, identity, and influence, where do our men seem to excel? Where do they need the most help?

4. What are the top three practical issues our men want to learn about?
   (a)

   (b)

   (c)

5. What type of ministry is going on already? What are its strengths and weaknesses? Where are our men involved in the church?

6. What type of ministry do our men want (retreats, small groups, monthly large group, other)? How well do their desires match the

hopes and expectations of our pastor and other church leadership? If they are significantly different, how will they be reconciled?

7. You have spent a lot of time talking to and about the men of your church and what you have learned about them. In this next exercise I want you to think about men in general. Specifically, what do we know about men that influences how we minister to men?

For example: Men are looking for relevance, and that means we have to answer the questions they are asking and dealing with.

Men are looking for action, and that means we will need to incorporate opportunities for them to do things in the community.

	What We Know About Men	How This Influences Ministry
1.		
2.		
3.		
4.		
5.		

6.		
7.		
8.		

Putting It All Together

Interviewing, surveying, working with your pastor, discerning needs—it can all feel tedious. But it's well worth the time and effort. For a sports team to be successful, the coaching staff must spend hours and hours looking at game films and watching players in order to decide how best to approach game day. It's no different in the ministry. To have a successful ministry you must take time to know the men of your church *before* you think about putting together ministry plans. In the next chapter we will outline the process for developing a game plan for your ministry. Every team forms for a purpose, and unless you take the time to develop a compelling purpose statement, it will only leave you frustrated and without direction.

NOTES

1. Bill Hybels, speaking at the Willow Creek Leadership Conference, February 1986.

MEN'S MINISTRY SURVEY

The Men's Ministry of Elmbrook Church desires to help men be the men God created them to be. Take a few minutes of your time to help us plan and develop a ministry best suited to your needs. Please return this survey to an usher or to the Info Center, or by mail to: Elmbrook Church, Attention Steve Sonderman. Thank you for your time and input on this vital ministry.

BACKGROUND INFORMATION

1. Age: ☐ 18–24 ☐ 25–29 ☐ 30–39 ☐ 40–49 ☐ 50–64 ☐ 65 +

2. Marital Status: Single_____ Married_____ Number of Children_____

3. Type of work _____

4. Which of these issues are most important to you?
   (check two most important)

   a. ☐ Finding a job   f. ☐ Parenting skills
   b. ☐ Relationship to wife   g. ☐ Retirement
   c. ☐ Job security   h. ☐ Reaching other men
   d. ☐ Male roles and identity   i. ☐ Spiritual life
   e. ☐ Balancing work, home, and
        ministry

A MAN AND HIS FAMILY

5. Would you be interested in a monthly meeting on family issues?
   (parenting, relationship to wife, etc.)   ☐ Yes   ☐ No

6. When would be the best time for you to attend that meeting?

   a. ☐ Saturday morning
   b. ☐ Weeknight   Which night? _____
   c. ☐ Sunday night
   d. ☐ Sunday morning

7. What topics would you like to see addressed? (check two)
   a. ☐ Keeping the romance alive in your marriage
   b. ☐ Disciplining your children

c. ☐ Surviving the teenage years

d. ☐ Being the spiritual leader at home

e. ☐ Handling conflict

f. ☐ Communicating with your wife

g. ☐ Other _____

MEN IN THE MARKETPLACE

8. How can we best help you integrate your Christian faith into your job?

    a. ☐ Monthly meeting with a speaker

    b. ☐ Weekly small group meeting to discuss the issues

    c. ☐ Monthly small group meeting to discuss the issues

    d. ☐ 3- to 5-week seminar on ethics, relationships on the job, etc.

9. Best time for these small groups or seminars:

    a. ☐ Weekday morning

    b. ☐ Weekday evening

    c. ☐ Saturday morning

    d. ☐ Sunday evening

10. Topics I would like to hear addressed: (check top 3)

    a. ☐ Handling stress

    b. ☐ Changing careers

    c. ☐ Relationships on the job

    d. ☐ Sharing your faith with work associates

    e. ☐ Balancing home, work and ministry

    f. ☐ Keeping your ethic/edge sharp

    g. ☐ Coping with failure

    h. ☐ Mentoring

    i. ☐ Planning retirement

    j. ☐ Resisting sexual temptations

    k. ☐ Avoiding the success obsession

MEN AND THE WORLD

11. Would a short-term missions trip be of interest to you?

    ☐ Yes   ☐ No

12. What type of short-term missions trip would interest you the most?

    a. ☐ Construction project

    b. ☐ Athletic trip (i.e., basketball in the Philippines)

    c. ☐ Business trip (i.e., giving seminars in eastern Europe)

    d. ☐ Medical trip

13. What would be a good length of stay for such a trip?

    a. ☐ weekend

    b. ☐ 1 week

    c. ☐ 2 weeks

    d. ☐ 3 weeks

    e. ☐ one month or more

RETREATS

14. If we would begin to have retreats as part of the ministry, would you be interested? ☐ Yes ☐ No

15. What type of retreat would interest you most?

    a. ☐ Teaching type

    b. ☐ Adventurous type (canoeing, camping, fishing, etc.)

    c. ☐ Spiritual and personal renewal

    d. ☐ Networking with other men

16. And the length of the retreat?

    a. ☐ One night   b. ☐ Two nights

17. How far would you be willing to travel for a retreat?

    a. ☐ 30 minutes   d. ☐ 3 hours

    b. ☐ 1 hour   e. ☐ More than 3 hours

    c. ☐ 2 hours

MAN TO MAN

18. Are you currently attending a men's Bible study group?

    ☐ Yes ☐ No

19. If you are not in a group, would you be interested in attending a men's small group? ☐ Yes ☐ No

20. What would you like to see happen in that group? (check two)
   a. ☐ Study the Bible
   b. ☐ Talk about problems at home and work
   c. ☐ Pray for one another
   d ☐ Discuss how you integrate your Christian faith and your work and family life

21. Which would you prefer for meeting?
   a. ☐ Every week for one hour
   b. ☐ Once a month for three hours
   c. ☐ Every other week

22. When would you prefer to meet?
   a. ☐ Early morning before work
   b. ☐ After work in the evening
   c. ☐ Lunch hour
   d ☐ Over the weekend

MEN'S CONFERENCE

23. What type of seminars would you like to see at the Men's Conference? (check three)
   a. ☐ Parenting
   b. ☐ Masculinity
   c. ☐ Relationship to wife
   d ☐ Work ethics
   e. ☐ Changing jobs
   f. ☐ Dealing with retirement
   g. ☐ Balancing work, home, and ministry
   h. ☐ Finances
   i. ☐ Evangelism
   j. ☐ Growing as a Christian
   k. ☐ Other _____

MEN'S MINISTRY

24. Would you be willing to assist in Elmbrook's Men Alive ministry?

☐ Yes ☐ No

a. ☐ Publicity

b. ☐ Organize events (retreats, golf outings, etc.)

c. ☐ Work in the kitchen

d ☐ Lead small group

e. ☐ Do telephoning

f. ☐ Work with work projects

g. ☐ Marketplace ministries

26. What do you or would you personally like to accomplish through your involvement in Men's Ministry? (check two)

a. ☐ A closer walk with God

b. ☐ Fellowship with other Christian men

c. ☐ An outlet to vent problems or frustrations

d ☐ More involvement in the church

e. ☐ A chance to meet other men

f. ☐ Other (please specify): _____

27. When the entire men's program is determined, I would like someone to contact me so I can become more involved or receive more information.

☐ Yes   If yes, Name _____

Phone # Days_____

Eves_____

Address_____

City_____Zip_____

☐ No

Please list additional comments about the Men's Ministry you may have in the space below. You may optionally include your name, mailing address, and telephone number. Thank you very much for completing this survey.

MEN'S MINISTRY SURVEY RESULTS
QUICK FACTS

WHAT ISSUES ARE MOST IMPORTANT TO YOU?
1. Balancing work, home, and family
2. Relationship to wife

A MAN AND HIS FAMILY
Would you be interested in a monthly meeting on family issues?
> Survey says: Overwhelmingly "YES"

MEN IN THE MARKETPLACE
How can we help you integrate your Christian faith into your job?
1. Monthly meeting with a speaker
2. Monthly small groups to discuss the issue

What topics would you like to hear addressed?
1. Balancing home, work, and ministry
2. Sharing your faith with associates
3. Keeping your ethical edge sharp

MEN AND THE WORLD
Would a short-term missions trip interest you?
> Survey says: 60% YES

RETREATS
If we held retreats as part of the Men's Ministry, would you be interested?
> Survey says: 75% YES

SMALL GROUPS
If you are not already in a small group, would you be interested in one?
> Survey says: 55% YES

I want to thank every man who helped by filling out a survey. The results will be very useful in planning the full program. I look forward to ministering with you in the coming years.

> Steve Sonderman
> Associate Pastor—Men's Ministry

For NFL players, Tuesday is a playday. It's the day players usually have off—to mend wounds, fish, hunt, or just hang out at home and enjoy their wife and kids. For coaches, though, Tuesday is a workday. It's when the offensive and defensive coaches head to separate rooms and develop their plans for the upcoming game. While coaches do some of this strategic work during the summer, most of it happens on Monday and Tuesday of game week. Coaches view films over and over, study the enemy's weaknesses and strengths, design schemes, and develop plays—all with the purpose of using the talent at hand to its fullest.

We're at the same point in the development of your men's ministry. You have done the preliminary work. Now we're ready to design a game plan for your unique situation. I will outline in this chapter the steps you can take to write a purpose statement, develop a strategy, and lay out a timeline for your ministry. You leadership types will shine. You administrative types will eat this up.

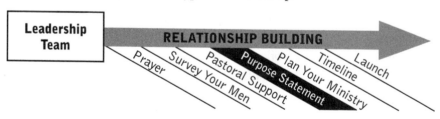

There's no getting around the fact that to do serious planning you need a place and time where you can concentrate. This is too important to the development of your ministry to hurry through the exercises. It takes time to do your planning right. It takes more time to do it wrong. Try one of the following options to make quality *and* quantity planning time happen:

Option 1: Weekend Retreat. You might choose to take your leadership team to a local retreat center where you can spend Friday evening through Saturday evening working through the material. You probably have plenty of retreat centers around, but scout out the following to make the best use of your time:

a. A spot *close to home* so you don't spend all your time driving.
b. *Food prepared* for you so you don't spend all your time cooking and cleaning up.
c. A *quiet meeting room* where you can relax, talk, pray, and work through the material.
d. *Decent sleeping facilities* so you get a good night's sleep.
e. A *flip chart* for writing down all your ideas and thoughts. You may come back to something you thought of at the start of your time together.
f. Allow for some *free time.* You won't be able to keep working at an intense level for hours on end. Plan into your weekend time to take walks, go swimming, or just hang out.

Option 2: Four Evenings. If you can't free up time for a retreat, try four consecutive Monday evenings. It gives you the same amount of work time, just spread out. One benefit of this option is that it gives you in-between think time. Make sure you still seek out a spot that is quiet and removed from any distractions—a home where the kids are gone for the evening or a room at church might work. I know of one leadership team that rented a conference room at a local hotel so they would have a sense of work while they did their planning.

Option 3: Two All-Day Saturdays. These are a little tougher to plan because most men make Saturdays family day. You could do one Saturday, and then wait a month to meet a second Saturday. Again you get in-between time to run your ideas past other people.

Brainstorming

You might think of other ways to structure your planning time. But no matter where or when you decide to meet, there are several steps you can work through to put together your game plan. You might not find each part of the process necessary to your situation, but each is designed to help the process along. Before you do anything, make sure to take time to pray as a group. Seek God and ask for His wisdom and direction as you start.

The first step—brainstorming ministry ideas—may be the most exciting and rewarding for you as a leader. Having tabulated all the surveys and culled some general themes, you can get down to business and bring focus to the ministry. Brainstorming is how you take general ideas and begin to make them into something that begins to look like a ministry.

You can limit this activity to the small group of men on your leadership retreat, but it's even better to do it with a larger group of men *before* you go. It's a way to give men *ownership* of the ministry and *excitement* for the ministry. I built our larger brainstorming group two ways. First, once I had completed all of the individual surveys, I notified those men that we would meet in a few weeks to share the information gathered and to brainstorm further on the issues they raised. Of the sixty men interviewed, forty showed up to continue the process. What I saw was that the time I had taken to personally involve these men through the interview process had already raised their stake in the ministry. Second, I invited all the men who had indicated on the churchwide survey that they wanted to help with the men's ministry.

I began the meeting by sharing the results of the survey. I then broke the men into random small groups for brainstorming, giving them five areas to discuss for ten minutes each. These were five areas that had stood out during our survey work—we talked through, for example, how to get men into small groups, what to do once the men are plugged in, and how to train leaders. Your top five concerns may be totally different from ours.

At the end of the brainstorming time, each man ranked on a 3 x 5 card his top three ideas from all the ones recorded. Each man then shared his rankings with the rest of the group, so that in the end each group produced three or four ideas they ranked the highest. They did this for each of the areas I wanted them to discuss. Then they came back to the large group with their three top suggestions for small groups—and what an incredible time that was. It was one of the most exciting hours of my life to hear each group stand up and share their ideas, visions, dreams, and plans. We passed on all of the men's 3 x 5 cards of ideas and suggestions to the leadership team for tabulation—so we didn't waste any ideas. I can look back almost seventeen years at the notes from that initial brainstorming session and see there in basic form what we are doing today.

To sum up, here are some general guidelines you should share with the guys before they break into their groups:

1. Accept and record all ideas.
2. Don't comment on anyone else's ideas during the brainstorming process.
3. Save time at the end to discuss the ideas and refine the suggestions.
4. Don't start to draw conclusions—this meeting is for generating ideas, not setting forth plans.

Here's an overview of the process we used:

1. All ideas within a group are shared and written on a chalk board or flip chart.
2. Individually the men write on a 3 x 5 card their top three choices out of the many suggested.
3. Each man around the circle shares his number-one choice. That pick gets three points. His second choice gets two. His third choice gets one.
4. The numbers are totaled up and the top three or four ideas move on to the larger group.

Settle on a Purpose

Not everyone who took part in the brainstorming process joined our leadership team. But many did. To have so many guys involved in the brainstorming session really generates an infectious enthusiasm and excitement.

With your brainstorming complete it is time to move on to the most critical step in the whole process—defining your purpose. Pinpointing the goal of your ministry isn't something you can do in a large group—this is definitely a task for your planning retreat or meetings.

Without a clear and concise purpose it will be very difficult for your ministry to stay on track. It is very easy to plan a lot of exciting meetings and activities and not have a purpose. There are three related reasons why you need a purpose statement for your ministry:

1. *A purpose statement keeps you from taking on more than you can handle.* Every time I go to a leadership planning meeting I find myself saying the same thing: "How does this fit into our purpose?" At noon today I met with two coordinators from our ministry. They told me all of the things they wanted for next year—great ideas, but I had to pop the big purpose question. *What is our purpose for the men's ministry? And what is the purpose for your part of the ministry?* The discussion that followed got us back on track. It is your road map for the ministry.

It's too easy to do activities for the sake of activity. You can always revisit your purpose statement. It can evolve over time. But having a purpose statement that is short and sweet keeps what you do fitting within the big picture.

2. *A purpose statement helps you make decisions.* When someone has a new idea for a ministry, there are two questions I always ask: (a) *Who is going to lead it?* and (b) *What is its purpose?* Without a purpose statement, deciding for or against a ministry can be tough. With a purpose statement, you aren't deciding on the basis of egos, slick presentations, or what happens to sound fun at the moment. Because everyone has signed on knowing our purpose statement, it's the one fair way to determine which ideas work for us and which don't. Our coordinators' meetings are much smoother when we keep in mind the overriding purpose of the ministry.

3. *A purpose statement keeps you focused.* It allows you to make decisions on what to do and what not to do. You can do many things. But what have you decided is the *best* thing? Most ministries try to do too many things. It's better to start slow and simple. Reach one group of people and minister to them effectively before you move on to another group. A well-designed purpose statement keeps you on task.

4. A purpose statement inspires. It has the ability to create energy and give life. There is absolutely nothing more discouraging than to be on a team that does not know where it is going. This statement should get you out of bed in the morning and keep you going late at night.

5. A purpose statement reduces the drain of leadership succession. Your statement will outlive your present leadership team and maybe even you as the point man. The statement is not based on one leader but on the Word of God and what God wants to do in your midst. We have had a number of leaders come and go over the years, but our purpose and vision remain the same.

A well-written purpose statement is a brief, concise statement expressing current thinking about the reason we exist. Why has God brought us together? What role does God want our ministry to play in His greater purpose for the Great Commission and Great Commandment?

It would be easy to swipe someone else's statement, and I have been tempted to do that many times. But the real benefit of working through your mission yourselves is *ownership*. In the end you may end up with a statement identical to another group's. That's fine. You know that you went through the process and determined what God has put in your own hearts.

You can start the process of writing your purpose statement by having the leadership team read as many passages of Scripture as possible that are relevant to your ministry's mission. You can come prepared with some, and have the group share some as well. (For example: Matthew 28:19–20; Ephesians 4:11–12; Colossians 2:6–7; Acts 1:8; John 13:34–35; Acts 2:42–47; Ephesians 3:10–11; Mark 12:30–31; 2 Timothy 2:2; Colossians 1:28; Hebrews 10:24–25.) This exercise will help you focus on where you believe God is leading your ministry.

Exercise 1—God's Purpose and Your Purpose

1. Make a list of verses that have to do with God's purpose for your ministry.

2. With these in mind, pull out themes that highlight what you believe God could be calling your ministry to. You will find it helpful to write down some of the key phrases or words that come from the verses you read and study (for example: *equip men, evangelize men, mobilize men for service, build disciples, engage the community, demonstrate compassion to those less fortunate, build leaders, reconcile men to . . . , instruct men in . . .*). Make the list as long as you can.

3. Get ahold of your church's purpose statement and write it on the board. You want to make sure that what you are doing as a ministry is consistent with where the church is going as a whole. Think and talk about the following questions:

   (a) What are the major themes in this statement?

   (b) How does this fit with where we are thinking of going as a ministry?

   (c) What do we need to incorporate into our men's ministry statement?

Exercise 2—Defining Your Purpose

1. Taking time to talk and pray, narrow your list from the second question in Exercise 1 to phrases you believe give direction to your ministry.

   (a)

   (b)

(c)

(d)

(e)

(f)

2. After looking at all the verses and statements, individually and as a team answer these questions:

   (a) Why does this ministry exist?

   (b) What are we to be as a ministry?

   (c) What are we to do as a ministry?

   (d) What are some action words we can use to communicate that vision?

3. Write a rough draft of your purpose statement. You might want to start off your statement with something like "Our ministry exists to glorify Jesus by . . ." Remember, what you write will tell you and others what the main business of your ministry is.

4. Refine your purpose statement. Here are some questions to ask yourselves:

   Is it clear and concise—not more than one sentence?

   Could it be easily understood by a twelve-year-old?

   Does it state what we are about as a ministry?

Is it easy to communicate to the leaders and men of your church?

Does it empower us as leaders?

Is it consistent with who we are as a church?

Can it be recited by memory (at gunpoint!)?

5. Once you have settled on a purpose statement, take time to evaluate it. Pray over it; work on its grammar and phrasing. Share it with others and get their input. As a leadership group, come back to it in a month and see if it is still what you want. Make notes here of changes you need to make.

Down the road it will be important to have a purpose statement for each ministry you develop within the men's ministry. Just recently our small-groups team met regularly on Friday mornings to develop its own mission statement that flowed from the overarching one. As an outside observer, it was exciting and gratifying to see these men wrestle with what their part of the ministry is to be about. With the purpose statement in hand, they have a greater sense of mission and ownership in the ministry.

You're probably curious as to what the purpose statements of other men's groups look like. This was ours when we first started:

> The purpose of the Elmbrook Men's Ministry is to encourage and equip men to evangelize the lost, establish them in their faith, and equip them for service in Milwaukee, Wisconsin, and the world.

About five years ago we went through the process again to make sure we were doing what God wanted us to do, and we came up with this:

> The men's ministry of Elmbrook Church exists to call every man to:
> Become a fully devoted follower of Christ
> Serve Christ in the context of the local church
> Be connected to other men through a small group

Another ministry says it this way:

The Men's Ministry exists to make disciples who will build a movement of multiplying groups to bring Christ to all of [our city] and beyond.

Here are a few other purpose statements I have collected over the years from churches around the world:

- To help men be a disciple and to make disciples.

- To empower men to know Christ and to make Him known.

- To build men into fully devoted followers of Christ.

- Assist men to be Great Commission and Great Commandment men.

- To build men into contagious followers of Christ who live distinctly and love dynamically, and whose lives make a difference.

- To empower men to build authentic relationships in Jesus Christ, inspired by the Holy Spirit to become godly influences in their world.

- [Our church's] Men's Ministry is dedicated to creating opportunities for men to develop vital friendships, personal integrity, and profound Christ-centered growth.

Recommended Reading: One book I have found very helpful when it comes to writing a vision document for your church or ministry is *Church Unique* by Will Mancini. It is a Leadership Network Publication.

Planning Your Ministry

You need to know *what* you want to do. But you also need to decide *how* you are going to do it. In this step you will determine as a leadership team how you will plan and structure your ministry to accomplish your mission.

This isn't an easy step for most people. Our natural tendency is to do ministry the way it's always been done, or to grab an idea from a book or magazine or conference. But to develop a life-changing ministry, you need programs that work best for *your* people in *your* congregation. For some of you it may be a monthly Saturday breakfast. For others it may be a once-a-quarter evening rally. For others a Sunday school class just for men—and maybe only part of the year. Every situation presents different needs. Every situation holds different opportunities. So every situation demands a different approach. Remember, every church is different and its ministry to men will also be different! Do not be concerned about what other churches are doing. Focus on this question: What does God want you to do?

Now is your time to identify the best place for you to start. As you work through the following exercise, think long-term. Give yourself time. Start wondering what programs you can put in place over the next *five years* to accomplish your mission statement. Don't forget to draw on all of the information you have gathered—from interviews, surveys, meetings with your pastor and other church leadership, and your brainstorming sessions.

Exercise 3—Structuring Our Men's Ministry

1. Tell what you know about the men of your church and your area:

   What are their top five needs?

   What do their friends need?

   When are they available?

   Where are they involved in the church already?

   Why do they need their own ministry—what can you provide that the rest of the church doesn't?

2. Tell what you know about effective ministry to them:
Where will they likely come to a meeting?

What types of special events are consistent with who they are?

What topics are they interested in?

How do they build relationships with other men?

How much time do they have to offer?

How structured should it be?

3. Tell what you know about your leadership team:
What is your greatest strength?

What is your greatest weakness?

If you had to do a men's event tomorrow, what could you do well?

4. Tell what you know about your church:
What types of ministries have been successful in your church? Why?

What expectations does the church leadership have for what you do?

5. Given your answers to the questions above, what elements would you like to include in your ministry to men? (evening small groups, weekly large group, monthly large group, quarterly large group, other).

6. Use your purpose statement to filter through these ideas. Which ideas help you reach your goals? Which ideas should you set aside because they don't directly help you to reach your goals?

7. Where should you start? What *one* program would be most effective and relatively easy to initiate within the next year?

8. What additional programs do you want to see happen over the next several years? In what order?

Time-line the Ministry

Once you have decided where to start, your next step is to plan exactly how to make it happen. To project managers out there this will sound very familiar—and even those of us who don't manage timelines day to day can use some of the great software designed to help this process. Whether you plot your ministry on-screen or on paper, what you want to do is *put things in order*, because some things can't happen until other things take place first. And you need to *break the jobs down* into manageable tasks with manageable deadlines. Developing an entire men's ministry can be utterly overwhelming, but looking at small steps along the way feels much more achievable.

When I began our men's ministry, for example, I knew I had to do two things the first year: raise the identity of the ministry and develop leadership for the ministry. I was committed to this for the long haul, and for the ministry to grow I needed solid leaders. So the first ministry we started was Top Gun, a nine-month leadership training program designed to encourage and equip men to lead in their home, workplace, church, community, and world. My sole purpose was to develop a small number of leaders who would be responsible for the ministry in the future. Of the twenty-four men who went through the program the first year, eighteen hold key leadership roles for us now. Those two steps were small enough to handle, yet big enough to get us on the right path.

Three points to remember here. First, think long-term and go slow! I can't say it enough. You won't develop your ministry overnight. Even if you put in place one or two straightforward programs, what you do needs ongoing evaluation and innovation to stay fresh. When I consult with churches, everyone wants a big men's ministry right away. It just doesn't happen that way. A well-rounded, full-blown ministry takes years to happen. Second, you need to choose one area to work on: leadership development, small groups, a men's retreat. It is more important to do one ministry well than to do a bunch poorly. When men sense you are doing things with excellence and purpose they will be drawn in and pull others in with them. Each year you can add one or two more components to the ministry, taking strategic steps you outline in your five-year plan. And third, what works in one church may not work in another. There is no magic formula for doing ministry. One of the scariest things about putting this material in print is that someone might think that what we do at Elmbrook has to happen everywhere.

Use the following exercise to set a timeline for the major ministries you want to see happen over the next five years and to list what needs to happen to ensure the program is established and completed.

Exercise 4—A Timeline for Ministry

1. When do we want to start the various components to the ministry?

Year One

Year Two

Year Three

Year Four

Year Five

2. What has to be done in the first year for each of the major ministries we want to start?

Ministry

Task

When done?

Task

When done?

Task

When done?

Ministry

Task

When done?

Task

When done?

Task

When done?

3. Step back and consider: Are the goals you have set for each year of your ministry realistic? Measurable? Open to evaluation? Flexible?

Divide Up Responsibilities

This is the easy part. When you have a list of everything to be done for your first ministry, assign people to do them. We'll look in detail in the next few chapters at what kind of help you need to make your plans happen, but at this point you might want to work on a list of other people to help you. Go back to Question 2 in the last exercise and jot down the names of men who may be able to help you with each task.

Wrapping Up Your Retreat or Planning Sessions

When I coached high school football, we spent Saturdays watching film from the night before and putting together our game plan for the next week. The room where we met had a sign in it that said *K.I.S.S.* When I first started I had to ask one of the other assistants what *K.I.S.S.* stood for. I should have known: *Keep It Simple, Stupid.* It was a principle we reminded ourselves of every time we drew up a game plan.

It's not a bad slogan for ministry as well. It's easy to come up with great ideas and schemes—but if your people can't execute them they aren't much use. What you have accomplished in your planning retreat or planning sessions now needs to be evaluated over the course of time by your leadership team and the men of your church. Take what you have done and let it simmer for a few months. By giving yourselves time you will be able to pray over your plans, think through them, refine them—and boil them down to what you can actually do. To be honest, this is the most difficult part of the process. I know several ministries that have taken up to a year to work through all of this.

So take your time. And keep it simple.

Exercise 5—Revisiting Our Plans

Give yourself at least a month after your initial planning sessions before your leadership team considers the following questions.

1. Are your plans realistic? Are there any ideas that seemed good during your initial planning that you need to reconsider?

2. What obstacles do you see to your plans? How can you overcome them?

3. Refine your decisions. What changes do you need to make to your plans?

DREAMING OF
THE BIG WIN

After a particularly disappointing midseason loss to a team the Packers were heavily favored to beat, Coach Lombardi gathered his players in the locker room. It was deathly quiet as the players realized they were about to receive another tongue-lashing from their coach. Lombardi slowly turned to face the team. In a stern voice he said, "Men, in all my days of coaching and playing I have never witnessed such a poor exhibition of football. We did not tackle, run, throw or catch the way you have been taught. Starting right now we are going to begin with the basics." With that he pulled out a football and held it in front of them. "Men," he said, "this is a football."

After a couple seconds of silence, all-pro middle linebacker Ray Nitschke raised his hand. "Coach," he said, "could you go a little slower?"

Sometimes I feel like Lombardi. In men's ministry it's easy to get caught up in a thousand plans and plays and fine moves and to neglect the basics. We have already looked at who men are these days and at the spiritual man or biblical man—the guy we are aiming to develop. We talked about recruiting a leadership team and together finding out what your men need and want. Before we go any further, I want to hold up the ball and say, "This is a football." I want to look deeper at the basic principles of an effective ministry to men, some of the things that can and should happen.

No matter what your ministry ends up looking like, no matter what the size or location of your church, certain principles apply across the board. You want to develop a principle-centered, purpose-driven ministry, one that avoids weaving to and fro with every fad that hits the church or men's movement. You will gain benchmarks to measure all you are doing. And you will be able to ask yourself as a leadership team whether or not you are accomplishing your goals.

Principle #1: A Life-Changing Ministry Is Relationally Driven

Ministry happens best in the context of friendships. Let me say it again: Ministry flows from friendship. We have a saying on our leadership team: "Become friends and change the world." It starts with our leadership team and then flows out to everything we do as a ministry.

As we have grown our ministry we have had to battle to stay people-centered rather than program-driven. Energy and excitement and numerical growth push any ministry to spin out another program, to devise another string of events. You need programs. But you also need to guard against letting planning and executing programs become so consuming that it robs time from building relationships. Authentic ministry happens when one man gets close to another man and develops a relationship with him. It's impossible to do ministry from a distance.

Some of you may be thinking at this point that your church is too small to have a real men's ministry. Or you may have no pastoral oversight. Or you honestly don't see a lot of men in your church interested right now. Those are valid concerns. But remember, you can still have a ministry to men, because it is rooted in relationships. Those can happen anywhere! Even if you're the only man in your church trying to make a difference, you can have an informal but effective ministry simply by building relationships with the men of your church. All it takes is time and a listening ear.

An article in *Christianity Today* recounted the faithful and effective ministry Richard Halverson had as chaplain of the United States Senate. "When one might expect to see the chaplain only on the Senate floor for the morning prayer, his presence is everywhere," Senator Hatfield stated. Halverson brought with him a lesson he had learned years earlier about the importance of simply being available to people at their convenience and in their time of need. In his book *The Living Body*, Halverson recalls that as a young minister he asked God to direct him to people in his congregation he should work to befriend. He felt God's Spirit lead him to contact a dentist he had seen in the pews. The dentist invited him to lunch. The dentist was shocked to reach the end of their time together to find that the pastor had no hidden agenda and wanted no money for the church but simply wanted to get to know him.[1]

What an incredible ministry you can have by building relationships with men in your sphere of influence, both believer and non-believer. I cannot tell you how many times this no-frills approach has opened doors for me to minister. I call a man and ask him to meet for breakfast or lunch—most of my meetings involve food. His inevitable first question: *Why?* What did I do wrong? What do you want? Where do you want me to serve? What are you trying to recruit me to do? I answer that I just want to talk and have a chance to get to know each other. They can hardly believe it!

Here are some basic guidelines you can use to build relationships with men:

1. *Walk with them.* One of the older and wiser associates on our staff gave me some advice when I started working with the men. He said, "Steve, when you meet with men, it is on their time schedule, their turf, and their agenda." You build relationships with men by showing up in their world and walking with them. Go to where they live and work and see firsthand what their life is like.

2. *Listen to them.* When I meet I talk news, sports, and weather for a while, then move on to deeper, more personal questions like the ones mentioned earlier in this book.

How are things between you and your wife?

How are things between you and your kids?

How are things with your job?

How are things between you and your Lord?

I rarely get through all of these because the talk usually flows into many related issues. My main goal in all of this is to work hard at just listening to what the man is going through in life and then seeking to understand him. If he asks for advice I give it, if I have any. More often, though, I just allow him to speak. Many times small talk gradually leads to more significant talk.

3. Love them. John 13:34–35 says we are to love one another just as Christ loved us. Men today are starved for love and encouragement. The old adage is true: "People do not care how much you know until they know how much you care." People aren't going to be impressed by all the theology you know or what great programs you run. What stands out is your love and concern for them. So during these meetings I look for practical ways we can be helping in men's lives. I work to encourage them in how they are parenting, serving at church, or seeking to live as a Christian in the marketplace.

4. Pray for them. I end our time together by asking the man how I can pray for him in the coming weeks. Sometimes it's appropriate to pray for him right there. If not, I promise to pray for him when I get back to the office.

Whether you have a church of fifty or five thousand, ministry to men starts with relationships. Taking time to develop friendships with men in the church is the best type of ministry you can have.

Exercise 1—Relationally Driven Ministry

1. What are some of the barriers to developing relationships with other men?

   (a)

   (b)

   (c)

   (d)

2. What can you do as a leadership team to ensure that your ministry is built—and continues to be built—on relationships?

3. What are some things you can do to build relationships—formally and informally—with the men of your church?

Principle #2: A Life-Changing Men's Ministry Is Done by the Men

Two years after I became a Christian I was thrown into my first ministry opportunity. I was in college, and I was asked to lead a Bible study for students from my old high school. When I arrived the first night, thirty students were waiting for me in the basement of one of the student's homes. I began by asking them what they wanted to do on Wednesday evenings. They said they wanted a meeting where they would feel comfortable bringing their friends. They wanted to reach their school for Christ.

I told them I could never pull that off by myself. We started to divide up tasks. Treats (eats are important for high school ministry). Slides to illustrate my talk (I guess that kind of dates me!). Greeters, musicians, and discussion-group leaders. Before we left that first evening, everyone in the room had an assignment for the next week. They not only knew they were into something much bigger than themselves but they also felt important—everyone was vital to the ministry. The results were staggering. This small group of thirty students quickly grew to over one hundred fifty within a couple of years. I learned a major lesson in ministry. The church works best when everyone does his or her part.

Men's ministry is effective when it is done by the men themselves. Ephesians 4:11–12 states the principle: We are "to prepare God's people for works of service. . . ." The word *prepare* means "to set a broken bone," "to mend a frayed fishing net," "to restore something to its original condition," or "to condition an athlete." The only way a church will come to maturity, Paul says, is if people are deployed into service.

The first Reformation put the *Word of God* into the hands of God's people. Today we are in the middle of a second reformation that is putting the *work of God* into the hands of God's people. For many years most men have settled for ushering and maintaining church buildings and grounds. Men can do so much more. You will severely hinder your ministry's development if you try to do everything yourself. The task of the leadership is to give away the ministry to other men. Always be looking for men who can take responsibility. Again, to use the illustration of a coach: It isn't your job to play the game. It's your job to prepare your players to play. You train them. You develop their skills. You motivate them to work hard. In the same way the job of your leadership team is to train, develop, and motivate men to serve both inside and outside the church. The one place where this analogy breaks down is that in a game only certain people play and some sit on the bench and watch. In God's economy there is no such thing as sitting on the bench. I tell our guys all the time that every man is a starter for God and they need to get off the bench and into the game. The principle I have tried to lead by is this: Your ministry will only grow as fast as leadership is developed.

A couple of questions to ask yourself:

What am I doing that someone else could be doing? Maybe someone else can do it better. Maybe they can't. Give the job away and give a man a chance to learn. As our senior pastor says, "Anything worth doing is worth doing badly."

Which men aren't serving in the church who should be serving? I am not interested in stealing men away from serving somewhere else and signing them up to serve in my ministry. I look for guys sitting on the sidelines who need a little encouragement to get into the game.

And some thoughts to remember:

Don't start a new ministry until you have a leader lined up. It's easy to dream up great programs you could start for the men. But without leadership recruited and ready, the job will fall back to you and your leadership team. If someone has a great idea for men, I listen. And then encourage *him* to start it. I provide support, training, and prayer. I won't do what another man can do. God seems to work this way: If He gives a man the vision He's probably giving him the ministry.

Make service opportunities known. Just this month we were wondering how we were going to start a new Outdoors Ministry. Finally we listed our need in the bulletin. Five men showed up to be on the committee. If we hadn't made the need known we would still be agonizing over whom to ask rather than allowing men to be guided by their God-given interests.

Start your ministry right by giving it away from the beginning. Your leadership team has to make widespread involvement in doing ministry a core value right from the start. It's easier to talk about Ephesians 4 than to actually do it. It may be hard for some on your team. They worry the job won't be done well. They're probably right that it's easier to do it themselves. That isn't the point. Constantly ask your leaders who they are getting to help them on whatever project they do.

Exercise 2—Ministry by Men

1. As a leadership team, make a list of the benefits of having a ministry where men actively serve.

   (a)

   (b)

   (c)

   (d)

   (e)

2. Make a list of places within your ministry where you need men to help right now (examples: men to collate surveys, handle publicity, staff registration tables, lead small groups, organize a retreat, other).

3. If your ministry is already up and running, where could you open up more places for men to serve?

4. Make a list of potential men from your church who could serve in your ministry.

Principle #3: A Life-Changing Ministry Shows Balance

Over the last several years I have spent more and more time studying the life of Jesus, not only for personal growth but also to catch something of the DNA of His ministry. I have come to the conclusion that Jesus was the best men's ministry pastor of all time. In His ministry we see a wonderful picture of what it means to minister to men. He ministered to all types of men, from all walks of life, facing different issues and struggles. One lesson I have learned is that an effective ministry to men must be balanced and incorporate what I consider five biblical mandates: prayer, evangelism, establishment, equipping, and missions.

It's easy to grow a ministry that gets so caught up in one biblical mandate that it ignores the others. The men of your church become muscle-bound in one area and ninety-eight-pound weaklings in another. It is possible, for example, to pour a great deal of energy, money, and time into seeing unbelievers come to know Christ but then to spend little time grounding them in the basics (establishment) and helping them become fully devoted followers of Jesus. Your attendance will be great but your men's maturity level dismal. It's possible, on the other hand, to spend so much time perfecting your care for one another that you never bother to reach out to those outside the faith.

The practical point is this: From the outset you want to plan a balanced ministry. I will be candid: This isn't easy. The trend today even in whole churches is to move toward one area or another.

As you develop your plan, keep the following five biblical mandates in mind. I'm not saying that you will be able to address each of these the day you start your ministry. Rather, these are things to aim at as you move ahead.

Prayer

Your ministry will only develop properly through prayer. Oftentimes we ask God to bless our plans and to direct our steps long after we have put the plan into action. It is obvious from the life of Jesus that prayer was not a *part* of His life, it *was* His life. Christ taught and modeled prayer in at least forty-five sections of Scripture and thirty different occasions during His ministry. He began His life in prayer and ended His life in prayer. He prayed in private and He prayed in public. He prayed about the common things in life, as well as the complex. Prayer permeated His life. Prayer was such a significant part of Christ's life that his disciples requested, "Teach us to pray" (Luke 11:1). Even the slow-learning disciples recognized that the uniqueness and strength of Christ's life was based on his walk with his heavenly Father in prayer. It should permeate ours as well.

Jesus, our example:

> Jesus often withdrew to lonely places and prayed.
>
> —LUKE 5:16

> One of those days Jesus went out to a mountainside to pray, and spent the night praying to God.
>
> —LUKE 6:12

> One day Jesus was praying in a certain place. When He finished, one of His disciples said to Him, "Lord, teach us to pray, just as John taught his disciples."
>
> —LUKE 11:1

Not only did Jesus pray often and consistently, but the early church caught the vision from Him and continued in prayer. When the people of the early church prayed, their meeting place shook. They prayed and an earthquake rocked the prison walls. When they prayed, doors opened and thousands trusted Jesus. Their prayers and faith carried all before them. They were like an army of invincible warriors. Nothing could stand before them. Nothing could stand in the way of the church and her great mission when armed with the power of prayer. The whole power of imperial Rome, the mistress of the world, proved unable to resist the power and influence of their intensified prayers.

Several years ago I was asked to go to the Middle East to help lead a leadership training conference for underground pastors, evangelists, and church planters. One evening an Arab man gave an incredible talk on intercessory prayer, after which we were supposed to go to dinner. Before going to eat, someone suggested, "Since we just heard this talk on prayer, why don't we pray for every country here?" A man from Iraq stood up and shared several requests for his country and we prayed for Iraq. Then a man from Jordan stood up and shared some requests for his country and we prayed for Jordan. On we went through all ten countries that were represented. An hour later we were about to head for dinner when another man said, "Since there are about twenty-five countries in the Middle East, why don't we pray for all of them?" By now my stomach was saying, *Enough!* But we took a map off the wall, put it in the middle of the floor, and all 120 attendees lay on the ground and began to weep and pray over the Middle East. We prayed for dictators, kings, relatives, from one side to the other. We prayed that the strong arm of Islam would be lifted from the Middle East. This experience became a life lesson for me. More Muslims are coming to faith in the Middle East today than any other time in history. Why? Because in the Middle East they do ministry in a novel way—they pray and they pray and they pray.

The only way the hard hearts of men are going to be softened and the blinders removed is if we pray. If your ministry is going to move forward, it must be on its knees! Here are a couple of principles to keep in mind:

Every leader, a pray-er. It starts with leadership. The leaders have to believe to their core that God will only work and fruit will only be born if they pray. They will guard their prayer times and take everything to the Lord. A prayerful man is a fearful weapon in the hands of a Holy God.

Every men's ministry has a prayer team. There is power in numbers, and it will be important for your ministry team to enlist men and women who will pray regularly for your ministry.

Evangelism

Jesus made it clear that He came to seek and save the lost. His life was about building relationships with people. If one does a careful study of Jesus, it's clear that Jesus was in the "people business," and the hearts of people were of utmost importance to Him. Jesus was a friend of sinners and spent a great deal of time with them. As a matter of fact, the New Testament records more than fifty occurrences of Jesus being with those in need of a Savior.

- The calling of Matthew (Matthew 9:9–13)
- The invitation to have dinner with Zacchaeus (Luke 19:1–10)
- The conversation with the woman at the well (John 4:4–26)
- Jesus is at home with tax collectors and sinners (Mark 2:15–17)
- From one town and village to another (Luke 8:1–3)

Jesus clearly modeled the priority of evangelism. Later in His ministry, after a ministry team was developed, He challenged them to become "fishers of men." He taught them the same process He followed earlier in His ministry—a relational process of proclamation. Jesus' primary goal was to help His disciples succeed at becoming "fishers of men."

In Mark 16:15, Jesus gave His disciples the mandate to go into the world and preach the good news of the gospel. Archbishop William Temple has a great definition of what Jesus meant. He says, "Evangelism is to present Jesus Christ in the power of the Holy Spirit, that men come to put their trust in God through Him, to accept Him as their Savior and to serve Him as their King in the fellowship of His church."[2]

More than five billion people on earth don't know Jesus Christ as Lord and Savior. Most of the men you have in your ministry are surrounded daily by people who make up this category. Part of your ministry needs to be designed for those in your community who are without God, without Christ, without hope. Here are a few brief principles that will help you develop a ministry that reaches out to non-Christian men:

See evangelism as a process. Many people see evangelism as a Tuesday-night mugging session. There's a reaping mentality that says you have blown your job if men at your meetings don't immediately pray a prayer to accept Christ. But in John 4:34–38, Jesus likens evangelism to farming. Some dig up the hard ground, others plant the seeds, still others water and weed, and in the end someone gets to harvest the crop. Evangelism is the same way. You make your presence known in the community through lives that are pure, holy, and loving. You proclaim the gospel in verbal witness. In time you help nonbelievers step over from a life separated from Christ to a new life with Christ.

Think beyond the walls of the church. Encourage your men to see their sphere of influence as the places where they spend most of their time—likely their workplace and neighborhood. A survey conducted in Chicago's downtown loop asked four hundred business people whom they would most likely talk to about spiritual things. Given four options— a priest, an evangelist, a family member, or the person working in the office next to theirs—more than 90 percent said the person working in the next office. That person would best understand their stresses. You can help your men see the need to develop relationships with those immediately around them.

Supplement their personal evangelistic efforts. While your men are busy building bridges with those around them, start to plan activities throughout the year that supplement their efforts. Plan events designed for men to bring other men. That's why we do our Breakfast of Champions each spring. The event has one purpose—to proclaim the message of Jesus to the guests our men invite. As a leadership team, think hard about what you can do that is specifically evangelistic.

Train your men. Most men haven't been trained in one-on-one evangelism. Not only are most men unsure how to explain their faith point by point to another man, most men aren't able to share their own testimony with another man. Build events into your ministry that aim to teach all the men in your church how to share the gospel. You could accomplish your goal through a special Sunday school series. We include it in our Top-Gun program. Bill Hybels' book *Just Walk Across the Room*[3] is an excellent resource, as is Paul Little's book *How to Give Away Your Faith*.[4]

See evangelism as a team effort. One of my favorite passages to preach from is the story in Mark 2 of the four men and their friend who is a paralytic. When Jesus comes to town, the man has no way to get to Jesus, but his friends go and pick him up, literally, and lower him on his mat through a roof and into the presence of Jesus. Verse 5 says, "When Jesus saw their faith, he said to the paralytic, 'Son, your sins are forgiven.' " This man's life is completely transformed because four men were willing to work together to bring this man to Jesus. What a picture of evangelism today. Men in our society need to hear the gospel message and see it lived out in numerous lives before they will trust Jesus. We need to help our men catch the vision that every man has a "mat" and needs to be brought into the presence of Jesus so their lives can be changed.

Evangelism will happen in different ways. In the last few years I have had the privilege of doing a number of training events for pastors with my good friend Kenny Luck, the men's ministry pastor at Saddleback Church. Kenny regularly tells the pastors that he sees evangelism happening in four ways, and I have seen the same thing.

1. *Through a cause*—Men want to be involved in a cause greater than themselves, and we can use that to expose men to Christ. We have found that most men want to see this world become a better place, so when invited to help build a home, or go on a rehab project to New Orleans, or tutor youth, they are more than willing to help. This side-by-side type of work often leads to face-to-face conversations and eventually a deeper understanding of who Christ is and what He has done for us.

2. *Through a need*—As you well know, there are so many hurting people in our society today, whether it is a result of unemployment, addiction, marital issues, the loss of a loved one, or a whole host of other issues. These men are looking for help and healing, and your

ministry to men can be the place they find it. Our support groups, small groups, and one-on-one counseling all have been a refuge for many men where they can find true healing.

3. *Through fun*—Men are looking for a place to have fun, to be with other men, and to laugh together. There is nothing wrong with building into your ministry opportunities for men to get together and have fun. This may mean going hunting, fishing, golfing, or to a ball game. Maybe have a game night or share a meal together. One of the false caricatures about Christianity is that Christians can't have fun.

4. *Through relationships*—It should not surprise you that year after year, when people are surveyed on how they became a Christ-follower, 85 to 90 percent came to Christ through a relationship. Our men need to be released into the world in order to win others through relationship.

Establishment

Much of the first half of Jesus' public ministry was spent developing relationships with men who, in the future, would become the leaders of the church. His strategy of impact was relational. He invested relationally in people who could invest in others, who could in turn invest in others. Jesus said, "As the Father has sent me, I am sending you" (John 20:21). His goal was to assist men in becoming rooted, established, and built up in the faith. He desired for these men to have a solid knowledge of Him and know what it was to obey Him, trust Him, and follow Him for the rest of their lives. One such example of this is the Sermon on the Mount (Matthew 5–7), where Jesus teaches about kingdom living and what life looks like when it comes under the gracious rule of God.

Men not only need to commit their lives to Christ, but need to be grounded in that relationship. In Colossians 2:6–7 Paul writes, "Just as you received Christ Jesus as Lord, continue to live in him, rooted and built up in him, strengthened in the faith as you were taught, and over-flowing with thankfulness."

Most men aren't well grounded in the basics of Christianity even after years of church involvement. They can say and do the right things, but there's little vitality in their relationship with Jesus Christ. Many men in our churches who are in their forties, fifties, and sixties are still babies in the faith. They are talking like babies, thinking like babies, acting like babies, and making baby messes all over the place. We need to help them grow up into spiritual adulthood.

In the "establishment" area of your ministry you can help men to be what they have positionally already become in Christ. It's a process of grounding them in the basic spiritual disciplines of prayer, Bible study, solitude, and memorization. It's here where you give them skills to walk with Jesus the rest of their lives, so they aren't dependent on others for their growth. It's here where they learn what it means to be a disciple of Christ—to obey Him, learn of Him, follow Him, and become like Him. Some principles to keep in mind for this area of your ministry:

Use natural bridges. If a man in your church leads another man to Christ, he may be the best person to do the follow-up work. He could use a tool like the Navigators' *Operation Timothy* or *Discipleship Essentials* by Greg Ogden (InterVarsity, 1998) and meet with the man for several weeks to cover the material.

Use small groups to build men. Later we will spend a whole chapter talking about how to develop a network of small groups in your ministry. For now let's just say that small groups are an unbeatable way for men to grow in their relationship with Jesus. Small groups are where men can be encouraged, challenged, prayed for, and held accountable. It's where the flames of faith can be fanned. As a leadership team, ask yourself how you can get small groups going in your church and get every man in your church in one.

Don't overlook the basics. With the wealth of men's material on the market today, it's easy to study topics like parenting, being a better husband, or getting along at work—and never deal with the issue of Christian growth. Keep in mind that your goal isn't just to mold men into better dads and husbands. You want men to learn to love Jesus Christ and obey Him in every area of life. The recent men's movement is compartmentalizing men—even despiritualizing them. It isn't a good trend. Within your curriculum for both small groups and large groups you want to include material that grounds men in the basics of Christianity as well as in men's issues.

Teach how to learn and apply Scripture. God's Word was central to the life and ministry of Jesus. He referred to the Old Testament more than ninety times and quoted from more than seventy different chapters. He knew the Word and used it regularly. The goal is to get our men into the Word and not just under the Word. Lives are transformed by interaction with God and His Word. The men will need to be taught how to study, memorize, and apply Scripture.

Equipping

After Jesus had gathered a group of disciples around Him and they began to understand who He was, He began to train them. At first Jesus told them, "Follow me." But then He said, "Follow me and I will make you fishers of men." In a very intentional way, Jesus prepared them for service in the kingdom.

- Commissioning the twelve and sending them out to minister (Mark 6:7–11)

- Banquet at Matthew's home, an experience in evangelism (Luke 5:29–32)

- Commissioning the expanding team and sending its members out to minister (Luke 10:1–16)

- Spending more time with the few (John 2:12; Matthew 14:13–14, 17:1–8)

We don't want to raise a bunch of human sponges who attend our meetings solely to take in what they can. To get men out of the stands and into the game, equipping is necessary, the fourth part of a balanced ministry. Help your men discover, develop, and deploy their spiritual gifts. Help them find areas in the church where they can serve. Help them not only to understand but also to practice good stewardship of time, energy, and money. In short, help them become contributing members of the body. Some principles to keep in mind:

Provide ongoing training. As with evangelism, most men haven't had teaching in the area of spiritual gifts and servanthood. This is something you can build right into your small-group curriculum if it isn't offered on a church-wide basis. Christian bookstores have many gift assessment books; a helpful one is *Discover Your Spiritual Gifts the Network Way* (Zondervan, 2005). Another tool that looks in depth at how talents, spiritual gifts, values, passions, and personality fit together is *LifeKeys* (Bethany House, 1996).

It's important when you use gift assessments to talk with each class participant to discuss what he found and where he wants to serve. The crucial point is to connect men with service opportunities—and to let them try something else if their first shot isn't a good fit.

Pair men with mentors. Most men prefer to learn by watching and doing rather than sitting in never-ending classes. Keep *all* your training opportunities active and practical. Give special attention, though, to pairing new men with experienced leaders in your church. Whatever the ministry skill to be learned, the time should be both educational and encouraging. What men need from a mentor:

- Example—of what it is like to minister for Jesus
- Encouragement—in the work of ministry
- Experiences—in a variety of settings
- Accountability—for what he is doing and learning

Form men in teams. Throughout our church we have groups of friends that serve together. Some areas of our youth Sunday school, for example, are run by teams of singles or young marrieds. Other classes are taught by pairs and trios of men. Give your men away and let them impact your church *together.*

Sent Out

Jesus' final words to the disciples were *to go*, and boy did they go. Read through the book of Acts, and it becomes obvious that they took the words of Jesus seriously. They were sent out from village to village and city to city. They went to the Jews and the Gentiles. They went to those who were educated and those who were not. Our being here today is proof that they went, and Jesus calls us to do the same.

Mission is the final piece of a balanced ministry. Nothing is more exciting than to see men involved in Christian Businessmen's Committee (CBMC), prison ministry, sports ministries, or missions. The fact that the church exists to take the whole gospel to the whole world is something to continually keep in front of your men. Around our place we call it becoming a "World-Class Christian." One criteria you can use down the road to evaluate your ministry is how many men you train and send to serve in ministries that reach non-Christians. Keep in mind the following:

Encourage "vacations with a purpose." These two-day to two-week trips allow men to experience a culture different from their own. Your men can take a construction trip, business trip, prayer trip, sports trip, or medical trip. Whatever their task, it's a great way to expose your men to what God is doing around the world. Pre-trip training and the trip itself teach the men what missions is all about.

Men who have gone on our trips to the Philippines, Romania, or South America have all said the trip was instrumental in their growth as a Christian and in their involvement in world missions. They come home knowing that "we are to be global Christians, with a global vision because our God is a global God," as John Stott puts it.[5] Mission trips help men realize they are part of something enormously bigger than themselves—that they can help every nation, tribe, and people come to know Jesus. In a later chapter I will discuss how to plan and carry out a short-term mission trip with your men.

Profile missions in your ministry. Because some men aren't anywhere close to going on a cross-cultural trip, you need to bring missions to them. You can have missionaries on furlough share at your large-group meetings. You can spend time praying for the missionaries your church supports. During our annual church-wide missions fest we throw a special men's breakfast for all the visiting missionaries. They get to eat with the men, share what they are doing, and tell how the men can pray for them. It's a highlight of our year. You can also feature at your meetings men who are getting ready to leave on short-term trips. Have them explain what they will be doing, why they are going, and how the men can pray for them. All of these things build excitement for world missions.

Include missionaries in your ministry. When missionaries are home on furlough they need places where they feel encouraged and loved. Ask your pastor if there are any missionaries in the area that you can invite to join a small group—not to lead but to simply be one of the guys. It's an excellent way you can minister to them.

Highlight parachurch ministries. Many wonderful ministries need your men. Periodically you can feature one of these ministries not only to let the men know what the group does but to advertise ministry opportunities. You could feature ministries such as the Gideons, Athletes in Action, Fellowship of Christian Athletes, Prison Fellowship, or the Christian Businessmen's Association. These and many more are worthwhile ministries.

Make compassion "ministry central." I cannot encourage you enough to build into your ministry opportunities for men to be released into your community to be the hands and feet of Jesus to those who are marginalized, unloved, and uncared for. Whether it is feeding the hungry, tutoring high school students, going to prisons, or providing job training, all done in the name of Jesus, it will make a huge impact in the lives of those serving and those being ministered to.

It could be easy to be overwhelmed as you read through these five keys to a balanced ministry. Let me say it again: these won't all be in place from the beginning. You need to go slow to develop a solid foundation. But as you grow, keep these five areas in mind so as to develop a balanced ministry.

Exercise 3—Balanced Ministry

1. As you have grown in your relationship to the Lord, which of these five mandates do you naturally migrate toward?

   - Prayer
   - Evangelism

- Establishment
- Equipping
- Sending

2. In developing a ministry to men, what are some steps you can take to keep your ministry balanced?

If you have a ministry already:

3. How do you see each of the above five components represented in your ministry?

4. What "bridges" have you put in place to move men along? How well are your own men using these?

5. What are you doing that is different from what you originally set out to do? Have you been sidetracked?

6. Take time as a leadership team to brainstorm what you could do under each of the aforementioned five areas in your ministry.

Principle #4: A Life-Changing Ministry Happens in Manageable Pieces

Leading men has as much to do with *how* we do ministry as *what* we do. The good news is that when you read through the New Testament—and more specifically, through the book of Acts—there isn't one "right" way to do ministry. It doesn't say anywhere that when you have a ministry to men you have to do specific things. What we see instead are principles that span the ages, principles still relevant to how we do ministry today. In this last section we will look at a number of basic principles to keep in mind as your leadership team shapes how you will do ministry in your specific setting. The key question to ask is: *How* are we going to reach the goals and objectives we have set for our ministry? The "funnel" diagram (at the end of this chapter), for example, shows how our ministry works to move men to maturity. It gives these principles a shape. It suggests how programs accomplish certain goals. Keep in mind that a men's ministry is a *process based on principles to accomplish a purpose.*

1. *Start ministry with relationships.* We have already discussed this point at length, but remember that all effective ministry starts with men building bridges with other men within their sphere of influence.

2. *Start small.* Remember that numbers are not important. They were not important to Jesus, so why should they be important to us? If Jesus had been judged on numbers, He would have been considered a failure. Stick to the Master's plan. Work with a small group of men who in turn will minister to the masses. Take this group of men and teach them what it means to fall in love with Jesus. And remember, only start a new ministry when you have the right person in place.

3. *Make ministry a progression.* If faith is a process of growing into Christlikeness, then ministry should likewise be a *process* of growing men. Men's ministry isn't an isolated event but an intentional series of steps that help men become fully devoted followers of Jesus. It's easy to fall into the trap of providing any number of unrelated activities for the guys at your church. Whenever you plan an event or a new ministry, ask yourself how it fits into your philosophy and purpose. Does it help you reach your goals and objectives—or just take up time and energy?

4. *Provide a variety of entry points.* Small things can make it difficult for men to become a part of your ministry. A number of years ago part of our college ministry met at a home on Monday evenings. When our leadership team thought about the situation, we realized we had made going to the study unnecessarily difficult. The home was in an out-of-the-way neighborhood and hard to find at night. Parking was limited. And students had to walk up to a stranger's house all alone. Not an optimal arrangement for new people. Don't count on your men

being any more brave or persistent than my college students. Work hard to spot any hassles: out-of-the-way meeting places, inconvenient times, awkward first moments, lack of opportunities to mix and become part of the established group.

Ask yourselves not only how easy it is to get involved, but also if you have created enough ministry entry points. Different men are attracted to different things. Some want sports. Some like speakers. Some hate to sing. Others love it. Some like large groups. Others prefer small groups. You won't be able to provide a lot of options all at once, but as you grow make sure you provide a good mix.

5. *Blaze a path for growing commitment.* As you move up the funnel, the level of commitment increases. All it takes for a man to take part in our special events is for him to show up and listen. At our monthly large groups they come, listen, and discuss the material presented—but not at a deep personal level. In our small groups there is minimal homework but the sharing goes deeper. Men at the Top-Gun level meet many more expectations.

As you plan your program, ask whether or not you are making opportunities for the men to grow in commitment. Make the next step clear—not to exclude anyone, but to tap into men's love of challenge. Again, when you start you won't be able to provide the full range of commitment levels. When we began, for example, we had a shortage of leadership. We started with Top-Gun groups, with the specific goal of developing leadership for the ministry. A couple of years later we were able to backtrack and add some of the less demanding ministries.

6. *Build bridges to the next level.* Related to the previous thoughts on commitment, it is important never to do anything in your ministry without building a bridge to the next part of the process.

Building Bridges to the Next Level

Special Event
- Golf Outing
- Retreat
- Men's Breakfast

Introductory Bible Study

For many years we have offered a monthly breakfast as an entry point for men who haven't yet connected to ministry. The topics I address and the environment we have developed is conducive to new men taking their first step. After I speak, we allow twenty to thirty minutes for table discussion about the topic. Men get a chance to make application to their lives and it gives them a brief small-group experience. When our time concludes, I announce that if anyone wants to join a small group, a new one would be starting that week based on the topic they just discussed. Over the years we have started a new small group almost every month. These entry-level groups are an introduction to Jesus and to small groups. Our very best leaders are in charge of these groups, because we know we may only get one shot with these men. After five weeks the leader will ask if the men are enjoying the time and want to continue with another topic for eight to ten weeks. We have found that almost 85 percent of the men stay with it. Once you get them in a small group, you've got them! This process continues until they join our Top-Gun training groups where they are prepared to serve Jesus somewhere in the church, and the process continues. Everything has a purpose and everything is linked to the next step, not leaving it to chance whether a man takes the next step. I would encourage you to do the same.

7. *Root your ministry in culture.* Like every community and city, every church is different. Don't take a model from another place and spring it on your church! Pay attention to your survey results and the characteristics of your men and your church. Those are the factors that weigh heavily in deciding how to minister to your men. Fight any temptation to be like everyone else.

8. *Take time to build.* I need to say it again: Move slowly! Ministry is not a hundred-yard dash but rather a marathon. If you want to build a ministry with staying power, take your time. We tend to want everything now. The current enthusiasm for men's ministry creates a temptation to do events for the sake of events. But real ministry will attract men anytime. I can't bang the drum any louder. Don't hurry. I normally tell churches to think in terms of five years to get a basic foundation in place.

9. *Decentralize.* Women seem to have a herding instinct that makes them want to gather in large groups all the time. I have found that men's

ministry happens best out where men are—on their own turf. While you will need to do some ministry at your church, like monthly or quarterly breakfasts or meetings, most of what you do happens best in homes and in the marketplace. Moving out of the church helps men realize the church isn't a building but a group of people who care for one another. As you measure your ministry, look at how much is church-based and how much is marketplace-based.

10. *Open a variety of service opportunities.* In the same way that you need several points for the men of your church to enter your ministry, so you will want to develop a number of ways for men to serve. Some service options make minimal demands. Others carry a much greater commitment.

Not only is there a variety of commitment levels to accommodate, but also a variety of gifts. Each man is gifted and has a place where he uniquely fits. List ways men could serve and make that list available to your men. Try not to stereotype or pigeonhole men into just a couple of traditional service options. Notice that the funnel is open-ended. A funnel isn't designed to hold water but rather to channel it in the right direction. It's the same with ministry. It shouldn't be designed to trap men but to train, equip, mobilize, and send them out into the church and the world.

11. *Take advantage of affinity groups.* A hot trend in reaching non-Christians today is "affinity group evangelism." It says that lawyers are most likely to reach lawyers; teachers are best able to reach teachers. God wants us to reach beyond our comfortable boundaries, but affinity group evangelism recognizes that reaping is often easiest among people with shared concerns. As you strategize, think about how this principle might influence small groups and evangelism—who is in them and where they meet. You might want, for example, to have a small group for doctors. They are on similar (crazy) schedules and face similar pressures. By being in a small group together they can share their stresses and shepherd younger doctors just entering the fray. This of course applies to any occupation.

12. *Take what society gives you.* In these days, society is giving us innumerable opportunities for ministry. For example, with the sudden economic downturn, men are vulnerable, fearful, and looking for answers. Now is the perfect time to provide a support group for those

unemployed or underemployed. It is a chance for the church to shine brightly. Men today want help with their finances and work situation. In the midst of helping them with these very important issues, we can tell them of the God who knows them, loves them, and wants the best for them. You can use such topics as sports, finances, parenting, marriage, and work to your advantage when it comes to ministering to men.

13. *Center on the Word of God.* Last, and most important, give your men the gift of the life-changing Word of God. It's God's revelation of himself. It sets forth His guidelines for living. As I tell our guys, it's their playbook for life at work, at home, and in the world. Whether in the teaching in your large groups or discussions in your small groups, focus on the Word of God. The Word is what will change men's hearts, minds, and lives. Just meeting together won't do it.

It's possible, of course, to present the truths of Scripture in many creative ways—and in many not-so-creative ways. Here's a principle we live by that may help: We "give them what they need in the guise of what they want." You can give them what they want—a seminar on parenting, for example—to give them what they need: basic principles straight from Scripture that teach them *more* than how to get their kids to behave. You can show them how to motivate their kids to follow God from the heart.

These thirteen principles aren't exhaustive. But they are key principles to keep in mind as you move forward in developing and evaluating your ministry.

Exercise 4—Looking At All the Pieces

You probably came to this book with ideas of what your men's ministry should look like. You heard more ideas as you surveyed your men. In the next chapter you will start to sketch a plan for your ministry. But do some evaluation of your current ideas as well as programs you might already have in place.

1. If ministry is a progression, does everything you do fit into that progression? Does it accomplish what you are trying to do? Is there anything you need to get rid of? What are you moving your men toward?

2. How difficult is it for men to get started in your ministry? How many easy, non-threatening entry points are there into the ministry? Where can you swing open some more doors?

3. How do you plan to grow the men from where they are when they come in? Can the men identify these step-by-step growth opportunities?

4. How well does your ministry fit the culture of your church and the men who attend the church?

5. Are you allowing ministry to happen in God's timing or are you trying to force things to happen?

6. Do your men have a wide variety of ways to serve in the church? What limits do they face?

7. Is your ministry church-based, marketplace-based, or a balance of the two?

8. What affinity groups do you see among your men that may be natural bonds for evangelism or small groups?

9. How are your men being taught to feed on the Word of God for themselves? In what ways do you see them settling for scraps from others?

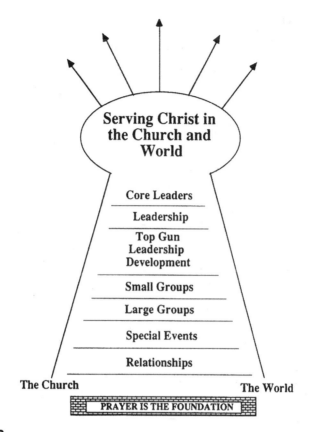

NOTES

1. Karen M. Feaver, "The Soul of the Senate," *Christianity Today* article on Richard Halverson (January 9, 1995): 27.

2. Archbishop William Temple, *Archbishops' Committee on Enquiry on the Evangelistic Work of the Church,* 1918, 25.

3. Bill Hybels, *Just Walk Across the Room* (Grand Rapids, MI: Zondervan, 2006).

4. Paul Little, *How to Give Away Your Faith* (Downers Grove, IL: InterVarsity, 1966).

5. John Stott, "The Living God Is a Missionary God," *Perspectives on the World Christian Movement* (Pasadena, CA: William Carey Library, 1981), 18.

After hours of lifting and running, months of preparation and practice, there's nothing like Game Day. Everyone senses something big is about to crash in. The band plays, the fans cheer, the air is electric. Everybody knows this is no scrimmage. This time the score at the end of the game counts.

It's no different in ministry. You have spent months planning, praying, and preparing. Now it's time to do it. You Type A's have surely struggled with all my planning talk. The next few chapters of this book are for you—the doers. In this final section of the book, I will move through different aspects of a ministry and get practical about how a ministry to men happens. In this chapter I will outline how you can carry out special events and monthly meetings. Still to come are chapters on small groups, leadership development, "Special Teams" play (short-term missions and evangelism among men), and finally, being a leader who lasts.

Options for Launching Your Ministry

There is no single right way to get started with your ministry to men. The most important thing is to spend time in prayer seeking God and what He wants you to do.

Before getting into specifics, here are a few ways churches have launched their ministry. Each option has been mentioned earlier in the book.

A special event. A natural time for introducing a new ministry is a special event early in the fall or in January. At your special event you can share the vision of the ministry, connect men to small groups, and outline ministry opportunities for the men. (I will outline how to plan that event.)

Small groups. A second way to start is for each member of your leadership team to form a small group with five to eight other men from the church. This is a little more under the radar and does not have the hype of a special event. The advantage of doing this is you are developing small-group leaders for the future and also building the ministry on relationships.

Leadership development. A third way to start is to spend your first year developing a small group of men who will become your leaders in the future. As I have said before, there is no movement of God without leaders, and if you want to sustain the ministry for the long run you may want to go this route.

A series of meetings. Some churches I have worked with planned three special meetings for the first year—one in the fall, one in the winter, and one in the spring. They centered on key issues men are facing, and provided opportunities for men to take the next step and join small groups.

There are certainly other ways to launch a ministry to men. But be purposeful and intentional in what you do. Don't do something just for the sake of doing.

Special Events

I am starting with special events because they are the easiest way to get a men's ministry going. Besides that, you can stretch and reshape almost anything you do—a retreat, barbecue, sports outing, rally night, or something else—to serve a specific purpose within your ministry. If you look at the diagram at the end of chapter 7, special events are on the bottom of my funnel illustration. So what do they accomplish?

Special events raise the identity of your ministry. If you are just starting your ministry, special large gatherings let men of your church hear about the ministry and its plans. I use these events to paint with broad strokes our vision of the ministry, or to detail some new program we will start in the near future. Some churches do two major events for their men during the first year of their men's ministry, using these events to spark the men's interest and to convey to them plans for the upcoming year.

Special events can be a safe place for new men or to bring other men. You can plan most special events as entry points into your ministry. They can be places where a man is encouraged to simply come and listen— and not feel compelled to talk in front of a group, share his feelings, or discuss his deepest sins. Rather he can simply receive ministry and have an opportunity to fellowship with other men from the church.

Special events are a chance for men to be gently encouraged to go deeper. We do special events fully knowing new men will attend. So we often have a testimony from someone in a small group. At the conclusion of the event, we give men the chance to take the next step beyond our large, relatively anonymous events and join a small group. Most of our small groups have grown out of special events.

Special events develop leaders. Many of the key leaders in our ministry are men who started on one of our special event committees. Activities pull men into service. As leaders we spend considerable time thinking of all the things that need to get done for an event to really cook—and then think of all the men we can draw in. Men love activity, so we usually find many who are open to help run an event, especially since these events have a defined start and finish so the commitment isn't long-term.

Special events give men time with other men. Special events allow men to just hang out. Often the parts of our ministry become segregated, with some men active in one area and others active in another. At a special event all the men come together and hear what is going on with men they normally don't see or talk to.

Special events are a great way to kick off a new year. Special events give your leadership team a platform to explain what the upcoming year looks like and to sign men up for the activities. At our fall special events we set up publicity tables for each aspect of our ministry in order to make them all visible. Men can find something that interests them and sign up for the year. Many ministries find it helpful to have a fall men's retreat.

It brings men together, gives them a taste of small groups, and gives the leadership an opportunity to share their vision with the men.

I hope it is obvious by now that I love special events and strongly believe they do a lot of good in a ministry to men. We used them in a big way the first couple of years to get our ministry going. Just doing events shows men a ministry is up and running.

Events are safe. They don't require men to go deep. Unfortunately, some men equate only activities with ministry. Some men's ministries are being planned and orchestrated so guys can jump from one activity to another without ever going further than showing up. Special events are vital to a well-rounded men's ministry, but you can't base your entire ministry on them. It's tempting to overdo them. They're great to build numbers. But if you don't move your men into individual ministries, you will do them a gigantic disservice.

In appendix B of this book I present a list of sixteen potential special events—from breakfasts to golf events to trips and retreats—with a word or two on what to keep in mind for each. But in the rest of this chapter we will look at overall strategies that make a special event work.

Your Special Events Planning Team

To pull off an event without you or another leadership member burning out, you will want to build a team of men to work together. This will not only spare your sanity, it will give other men a chance to grow in leadership.

I won't start without a coordinator, or better yet, *co*-coordinators. We have found that *co*-coordinators work well in spreading around responsibility and building accountability. With my help these co-coordinators recruit the rest of the team members. It's important when they recruit men for the team that they detail what each man will be doing. Men want to know what tasks they're getting themselves into—and how long the job will take. They won't offer to help next time if you pop too many surprises on them.

For the sake of discussion, I will look at how you could pull together what you need for a fall ministry kickoff to happen on a Friday evening. The purpose of the get-together is to let men of your church know what will be happening in the men's ministry in the coming year and give them a chance to come together to worship, fellowship, and receive some general teaching on being a godly man. The event will happen at church on a Friday evening in early September.

The following is a list of the team members you will want for a kickoff and their job descriptions. This may look rather intimidating— possibly nine guys to recruit. However, there are at least five reasons to work hard at recruiting as many men as you can to help. Getting more help . . .

1. Spreads out responsibility and cuts down on burnout
2. Gives more men in the church ownership of the ministry
3. Fosters a team spirit
4. Develops more leadership for the ministry
5. Provides more resources for ideas and contacts

Keep in mind, though, that depending on the size of your group and the type of event you plan, some men might be able to handle two areas of responsibility. Then consider this your special event to-do list.

Chairperson

1. Recruits committee members with the help of the men's ministry leadership team.
2. Organizes committee meetings.
3. Keeps the leadership team up-to-date.
4. Serves as a resource for committee members.
5. Develops the timetable for things to be accomplished.
6. Prays for the committee members.
7. Coordinates the evaluation process.
8. Encourages committee members in their tasks.
9. Makes sure committee members get things done on time.

Publicity Coordinator

1. Designs, writes, and reproduces brochure or flyer (see end of chapter for some ideas).
2. Mails brochure to individuals in the church, with cover letter from leadership team—may include the ministry's general brochure for that year as well.
3. Makes posters for the event and has them placed around the church one month before the event.
4. Talks to pastor about having an announcement from the pulpit a few weeks before the event.
5. Coordinates e-mail blasts to the men in the congregation.

Budget Manager

1. Sets a deadline for budget requests.
2. Helps chairman set a budget for the event and price (if any) to charge men—covering expenses for food, publicity, honorariums, materials, facility use, and rentals or transportation, if needed. It's best to set a budget that covers all possible costs, even if you end up with a modest turnout. Any extra goes toward next year's event.
3. Networks with registration coordinator to get money into proper account.
4. Ensures all bills are paid.
5. Provides change and collects proceeds from on-site registration at the event.

Registration Coordinator

1. Recruits team of volunteers to sell tickets on Sunday mornings and handle mail-in registrations.
2. Enters registrations into computer. (Keeping track of attendees will help you plan future events—as well as provide a list of potential helpers.)
3. Coordinates prepaid and walk-in registrations on the day of the event.
4. Recruits team to register people at the event.
5. Coordinates with budget person to get money into proper account.

Facilities Coordinator

1. Recruits team of volunteers.
2. Reserves rooms for the event—prayer room, fellowship hall, kitchen, chapel.
3. Recruits team to help move equipment on and off stage, as needed.
4. If books will be offered for purchase, makes arrangements with Christian bookstore.
5. Coordinates with church facilities person for setup (chairs, registration tables, publicity tables, etc.).

Hospitality Coordinator

1. Recruits and trains ushers for the event.
2. Recruits greeters for the event.
3. Recruits team to serve refreshments after the event.

Program Coordinator

1. Recruits team to handle the event's logistics.
2. Plans the program with the help of chairperson.
3. Works with technical people on visuals, lighting, sound, and lyrics if there will be singing.
4. Contacts the people involved (worship team, special music, testimonies, speakers, emcee, prayer team) to make sure they know what is happening.

Food Guy (Don't forget the food guy!)

1. Recruits men to help prepare the food.
2. Puts the menu together and orders the food.
3. Gets everything together necessary to cook.
4. Oversees preparation and serving of food on the night of the event.
5. Cleans up the facilities when finished or sees that it gets done.

Prayer Coordinator

1. Obtains prayer requests from the various coordinators on a monthly basis.
2. Distributes prayer requests to prayer teams from the church.
3. Mobilizes a team of men to pray during the event.

Death by Committee

The last thing you want is for your committee meetings to mimic the boring meetings most men endure at work. After recruiting your working committee, your next step is to call a planning meeting to accomplish two major tasks: team building and decision making. Spend the first hour of your meeting getting to know one another through team building and discussion exercises. (Have a barbecue. After sharing and prayer for the first thirty minutes, break the committee into groups of three. Have each man share how he became a Christian and why he wants to be on the committee. Or have the men share their most embarrassing moments.) Then spend time in prayer for the event—*before* you make your decisions.

Some of the major decisions you need to work through in your first few meetings:

What is the purpose of the event? You must decide this early on. Don't just *do* an event—know *why* you're doing it. Is it an evangelistic outreach, instruction for believers, a time of fellowship, worship, or something else? Should it cover a specific issue like finances or parenting, or is it going to be more general? Most events fail because of a lack of focus.

Who is it for? Is it for the men of your church only or for the community at large?

When is it going to be? Friday evening, Saturday morning, Sunday evening, or another weeknight? What is the best time for the men of your church?

Where should it be held? At the church, at a retreat center, at a local banquet hall? This will be tied in to the purpose of the event. If it is an evangelistic breakfast, for example, you might want to move it out of the church and onto men's turf—such as a banquet room of a local hotel.

What will you include in the program? A few options include a speaker, testimonies, video of past events, drama, small-group discussion, prayer time, worship time, and vision sharing.

Will you serve food? Is it going to be a burger cookout or coffee and rolls; catered or you-cook-it; or simple refreshments?

Committee Meetings

For a large event your working committee probably needs to meet monthly. Learn to run these meetings allowing for on-task planning and for God's spontaneity. Start and end on time. Evening meetings that are done in two hours might follow this format:

7:00–7:10: Catching up

7:10–7:20: Devotions

7:20–8:15: Committee reports (program, budget, facilities, publicity, hospitality, etc.). Each committee member takes time to bring other members up to speed on what he has been doing in his area as well as to get input on any decisions he needs to make.

8:15–8:30: Prayer for event and any other issues raised during the reports

8:30–9:00: New business

A Special-Event Timeline

Once you have decided what you want to do and when you will do it, put together a timeline for all the things you need to complete. You may be able to stage events in much less time than we do. If you know you can do it, adjust this timetable to your own schedule. You can't get around doing some things—like facility reservations—far in advance. But consider this as a model of how to give you and everyone else enough time so as not to put undo strain on anyone:

Nine Months Ahead

- Co-coordinators recruited for the event
- Committee pulled together by the co-coordinators

Seven Months Ahead
- First committee meeting
- Team members get to know one another and pray together
- Decisions made on what the event will look like
- Dates set for future monthly meetings
- Letters sent out to speakers
- Rooms at church reserved (gym, kitchen, fellowship hall, and chapel)

Six Months Ahead
- List of committee members distributed
- Timeline put together and job descriptions finalized
- Committee members recruit men to serve with them in their areas
- Committee members secure prices for their specific area (the food people, for example, determine how much it will cost per person for the dinner portion of the event)

Five Months Ahead
- Budget developed for the event and ticket price determined
- All participants for the event are contacted and secured (for example: worship leaders, men who will give testimonies, drama team, and emcee)
- Work begun on the brochure or flyer for the event
- Accommodations reserved for guests

Four Months Ahead
- Rough draft of brochure examined and any changes made
- Date of event is included in men's ministry mailings
- Leaders recruited for follow-up small groups

Three Months Ahead
- Brochures and posters printed

- Sound people contacted and given preliminary outline for evening

Two Months Ahead

- Mailing sent to all men of the church and to any other local churches involved
- Final program defined and timed out (see example)
- Music selected, overheads or computer presentation made, and copyrights obtained
- DVD created to introduce program
- Posters put up around church
- Registration table staffed on Sunday mornings to take registrations and handle questions
- Training for small-group leaders takes place
- Bulletin announcements placed with church office
- Men assigned to care for any special guests (seminar speakers, keynote speakers, musicians, etc.)

One Month Ahead

- Program for the evening finalized
- Material printed
- Name tags purchased
- Evaluation forms prepared and printed
- Small-group sign-up sheets prepared
- All speakers contacted for any special requests
- Food ordered
- Room setups coordinated with church custodial staff
- Date set for evaluation meeting by working committee

Week of Event

- Final head count sent to the food coordinators
- Signs made to direct men around church (if needed)
- Honorarium checks cut for the guest speakers, others

The Big Day

It's easy to forget details on the big day. Use this sample schedule for starters:

12:00 p.m.—Setup begins

- Gym: tables set up with chairs, decorations
- Registration tables set up
- Grills set up
- Sanctuary set up: screens, worship band, sound system
- Ministry tables set up

5:30 p.m.—Begin to serve food in the gym

6:30 p.m.—Concert in the sanctuary

7:00 p.m.—Program begins

- DVD intro (2 minutes)
- Welcome by the emcee
- Overview of the evening (5 minutes)
- Crowd breaker (10 minutes)
- Worship: Men's Worship Band (10 minutes)
- Overview of upcoming ministry (10 minutes)
- Testimony by man influenced by men's ministry (3 minutes)
- Worship (10 minutes)
- Drama (5 minutes)
- Speaker (35 minutes)
- Wrap-up: thank people and speaker, remind about refreshments afterward and that they can sign up for a small group.

8:30 p.m.—Reception in Fellowship Hall

9:30 p.m.—Cleanup

Keys to a Successful Special Event

Good special events don't just happen. Some of this might be review, but here's what makes a special event successful:

1. *Specific purpose.* Early on in the planning process you agree on the purpose of the event so you aren't all trying to do different things. Be specific, and know that one event cannot meet all the men's needs.

2. *Give away responsibility.* While one or two men could probably do an event by themselves, it isn't beneficial to them or the men of the church. Special events are opportunities to get others involved and serve. We will never allow an event to happen unless there is a team of men to do it.

3. *Timing.* Plan your event with the whole church calendar in mind. It's easy to play a maverick in the ministry, but you're a part of the church. Make sure you don't hinder other ministries by the timing of your event. Case in point: Don't plan a men's retreat the weekend after a couple's retreat, or plan a men's event on Valentine's Day or Mother's Day—yep, it's been done.

4. *Plan.* It is one thing to have a plan; it is an entirely different thing to have a plan to make it happen. The plan will include: your timeline, responsibilities, and resources needed.

5. *Evaluate.* If an event is worth doing, it is worth evaluating for the next time. Give the men time at the event to evaluate the event and to make suggestions for the future. After the event, hold an evaluation meeting where you can go over the evaluations and suggestions and plan for the future.

Evaluations work best when done both by participants and by the men who organized and carried out the program. After an evangelistic outreach luncheon with Frank Tanna, former Detroit Tigers pitcher, I sent a letter to ten men who attended the luncheon and who also brought a friend. I asked questions like the following:

1. Was the setting where we met appropriate for what we were trying to do?   Yes ☐   No ☐
2. How was the service at your table?
   Poor ☐   Average ☐   Excellent ☐

3. Was the food hot when it reached your table?

   Yes ☐   No ☐

4. Was the message clear?   Yes ☐   No ☐

5. Did the program allow for follow-up of the discussion after the meeting?   Yes ☐   No ☐

6. What should we change the next time we do an event like this one?

7. What should we do the same?

8. What recommendations do you have for the planning committee?

With these evaluations in hand, the working committee does its own evaluation. Have an evaluation meeting a week or so after the event, while everything is still fresh in people's minds. Go through each aspect of the event and ask the tough questions. For example, in terms of publicity: Was the flyer/brochure out in time? Was the brochure clear to both those who invited others and to those who were being invited? Did we use every means possible to get men to the event? What could we do differently next time?

This can be a grueling, even painful process. But it will help your men learn and prepare for next time—even if next time is a completely different program or event. The kind of evaluations you do will depend on the event. Some need only a quick ten-minute meeting after the event. Others need a full evening of discussion. I'll say it again, though: If anything is worth doing, it is worth evaluating!

Monthly Large-Group Meetings

In the same way special events held a couple of times a year have an important role, so do monthly meetings. In the grand scheme of things, these involve a little more commitment by the leaders—and a little more involvement on the part of the men. There are a lot of reasons for having a regularly scheduled meeting. It *provides an opportunity* for your church's men to gather regularly for fellowship. It *creates a place for new men* in the church to get involved in the men's ministry with a modest time commitment, in a non-threatening environment. It *builds a springboard* for men to get involved in small groups. It *serves as the hub* for all your men's ministry activities. With men involved in various small groups, committees, and ministries, this is their chance to come together and share what God is doing in their lives and in their ministries. It *establishes a place* where the vision of the ministry can constantly be shared and upcoming events discussed. It *provides a place for leadership* to develop. You can train future small-group leaders by having them lead discussion groups at the meeting.

Here's what you need to begin a monthly large-group ministry:

1. *Develop a leadership team.* You will want *co-coordinators*—they call the meetings, develop the team, make sure every man on the committee is doing his job. *Publicity*—to place bulletin announcements, to get information in the church newsletter, to send reminders. *Cooking*—to prepare the meal or refreshments for each meeting. *Program*—to line up speakers, music, testimonies, emcee, multimedia. *Table talk*—to recruit discussion leaders, make sure the speaker has questions for discussions that are related to his talk. *Greeters*—to meet the men when they arrive and give them name tags. This committee can meet right after the meeting to evaluate and go over any details for the next meeting.

2. *Develop a purpose statement.* Don't shoot me—but here I go again: Your team needs to develop a purpose statement. Our men wrote this: "The Saturday GameDay Breakfast exists to provide an opportunity for the men of Elmbrook to have fellowship and find encouragement on a monthly basis." Allow your team time to think through and discuss why they want to meet and how it fits into the big picture.

3. *Decide on a structure.* There are many ways to do what you want to do. Everything depends on your specific church situation and when your men prefer to meet. Below are two formats very different from each other—but each works well in various churches:

Monthly Saturday Breakfast
7:30–8:00 Welcome, and eat breakfast
8:00–8:10 Announcements
8:10–8:30 Worship
8:30–9:00 Speaker
9:00–9:30 Table discussion

Monthly Wednesday Evening
6:30–7:00 Worship, and announcements
7:00–7:35 Speaker
7:35–8:15 Refreshments

4. *Line up speakers.* There is no magical way to do this. Wherever you find your speakers, schedule them as far in advance as possible. Some churches I work with use outside speakers exclusively. By using leaders from sports, business, and the church at large they let their men and their guests hear from a wide variety of men. Other places—like Elmbrook—use just one person to provide a series for the year. In my case our meetings are the one opportunity I have to address the men on a monthly basis. The consistency is helpful. You might want to ask your pastor if he would like to speak at these monthly events. If you use outside speakers, make sure to provide an honorarium and travel expenses. If he has to stay overnight, be sure to provide lodging for him. Whether he stays at a hotel or at someone's home, give him time for rest and preparation.

5. *Develop a theme for the year.* By picking a theme for the year, you tell your men you are serious about these meetings and have thought out what you want to accomplish. In the past we have had themes such as "Running Like a Champion," "Tackling Men's Toughest Questions," "Becoming a Man of Purpose," and "Unlocking the Masculine Soul." All of my talks, as well as the testimonies and everything else we do at those meetings, have focused on that one theme.

6. *Use your meetings as a bridge.* If you remember from a couple of chapters back, one of the keys to ministry to men is moving men along in their commitment to Christ. Include things in the meetings that

provide the men an opportunity to take the next step. You can announce new small-group start-ups, for example, so men can join. Or you can announce a service opportunity at church. I continually ask myself this question about all we do: *How can I use this to move men forward?*

7. *Follow up on newcomers.* One of the old principles for evangelism is to go where the Spirit leads. If a man comes to your meeting for the first time, he showed up for a reason. Maybe he wants fellowship, or encouragement, or guidance. Have your leadership team call these new people and ask them how they liked it. Ask what they would change—that makes them the expert—and what they got out of it. This personal follow-up is a means to help the men feel cared for and counted on. It may blow open doors to really minister to a man. It isn't uncommon for the guys on our team to end up in profound conversations as they make these calls.

8. *Plan your meetings carefully.* When you put together your meetings you will want to keep in mind the following:

Are there smooth transitions from one part of the meeting to the next? Does the meeting flow—or is it awkward and choppy?

Are there breaks in the meeting so the men can stretch?

Is there a chance for the men to just talk with other men? It is possible to overly structure the meeting so the men can never meet this simple need. If you have a table discussion after the message, make sure your table captains are trained to facilitate discussion and not teach.

Do the components of the meeting fit together?

If you do music, are the screens or song sheets easy to read? New people will feel out of place if you sing songs without printed words. I would also recommend that you use music that most of your men would feel comfortable with. This is not the time to experiment.

Are the seats comfortable for the men to sit on for an extended time? The heart only hears what the seat can stand.

Is a sound system necessary for the room you are using? Does it work properly? Don't use a sound system that would make an angel blaring from heaven sound like a squawking duck.

Is the message practical and relevant—meeting the men of your church where they are? Does it have points for the men to apply? Is it biblically based? Do you have a handout so the men can take notes, with some potential resources listed on the bottom?

Do you have tables set up for resources, small-group sign-ups, service opportunities, and events?

Another type of large-group meeting that can be very effective at ministering to men on the fringe, looking for a first step, is Men's Fraternity. The DVD-based study offers some great material developed by Robert Lewis at Fellowship Bible Church in Little Rock, Arkansas. You can go to *www.mensfraternity.com* to get more information. The first year is called "The Quest for Authentic Manhood," and it's a 24-week study on topics such as the wounds of a man, the biblical definition of manhood, and relationships to his family. Each session includes a 45-minute video by Robert, followed by 30 minutes of small-group discussion time. We have used the material as a large-group experience for the past several years and have found it to be extremely helpful for our guys, and a number of men have come to Christ though it.

There are a wide variety of ways to do large-group meetings. They are a marvelous opportunity to minister to the men of your church. Large-group meetings may be all you choose to do in the first year of your ministry. You can also choose to use other methods in your first years and add a large-group meeting later, as we did.

Advertising Your Ministry

One thing you don't want men to say about your ministry is "I didn't even know you existed." In some congregations the men's ministry is the best kept secret in the church. Once you have worked at framing a basic program for the men, you want to press hard to raise the identity of the ministry and ensure that everyone knows what will soon take place. And when you do something, make sure you do it with excellence. It's better to do fewer things and do them right than to do a lot of things shabbily. If a man comes to a well-orchestrated event he will tell his friends—and before you know it you have a movement. Let me wrap up this chapter with some ways you can get the word out about your ministry:

A ministry brochure. You can do a brochure in a variety of styles, but create one piece that can be mailed to all of the men in the fall as well as made available to newcomers and visitors to your church.

Bulletin spots. Make someone in your ministry responsible for getting events into the bulletin at least three weeks ahead of time.

E-mail blasts. Much of our communication is done via e-mail these days. Of course, the toughest thing about this is keeping the e-mail address lists up-to-date. We also found that because of the volume of e-mails most people deal with, we have to be careful not to overload them with our e-mails.

Direct mailing. As a result of e-mail, we send less and less snail mail. We usually mail the yearly brochure to all the men in the church and make brochures available in kiosks for those attending church on weekends. If we are running a major event, we may send a card or flyer, but not often.

Reminder cards. Send postcards to smaller groups of men to remind them of upcoming events. We send everyone who has attended one of our Saturday GameDay Breakfasts a reminder card one week before the next GameDay Breakfast.

Women's ministry. If you want the men to come to an event, go through their wives. We work hard at getting the women on our team. We are fortunate to have a thriving women's ministry in our church, and they allow me or one of my leaders to regularly announce upcoming events and pass out registration forms at their events. I know the wives go home and tell their husbands.

Newsletter. Any sort of a periodic newsletter is a wonderful tool to share what is going on in the ministry. The downside is that newsletters are a ton of work. We send an e-mail newsletter to all our leaders every other month that includes a letter from me, prayer requests for the ministry, recommended small-group resources, and upcoming events.

Testimonies. Ask your pastor if you could periodically have someone from your ministry share on a Sunday morning what God is doing in his life as a result of your men's ministry. If you send a group of men to an Ignite Conference in the summer, for example, check to see if you can have a couple of guys share when they get back.

Bulletin board/kiosk. Ask your pastor if there is a bulletin board somewhere in the church that your ministry could share or even have full time. Work with someone to keep it up-to-date with upcoming events and activities.

Flyers. Make up flyers not only for the men already in your ministry but to insert in the bulletin or pass out as people leave the church after a Sunday service.

Word of mouth. The best of all. As men see their lives changing they will talk up your ministry.

There are bigger, splashier ways to get the word out—media, drama, music. But these are some straightforward ideas. I have to admit that I have come to appreciate the need for publicity to enable a ministry to happen. Don't be afraid to spend energy and money on marketing, if I can call it that. The money you use to get men to your activities puts them in a position to be changed through your ministry—and that is what it is all about.

Special events and monthly meetings are only a small part of what can happen in your ministry. With that base laid, let's move on to look at small groups—the places where men can meet to be encouraged, confronted, comforted, held accountable, and fan the flames of faith.

09

Huddles: Starting Small Groups for Your Men

In the prologue to their great book about the Vietnam War, *We Were Soldiers Once . . . and Young,* Hal Moore and Joe Galloway write:

> Another war story, you say? Not exactly, for on the more important levels this is a love story, told in our own words and by our own actions. We were the children of the 1950s and we went where we were sent because we loved our country. . . .
>
> We went to war because our country asked us to go, because our new president, Lyndon B. Johnson, ordered us to go, but more important because we saw it as our duty to go. That is one kind of love.
>
> Another and far more transcendent love came to us unbidden on the battlefields, as it does on every battlefield in every way man has ever fought. We discovered in that depressing, hellish place, where death was our constant companion, that we loved each other. We killed for each other, we died for each other, and we wept for each other. And in time we came to love each other as brothers. In battle our world shrank to the man on our left and the man on our right and the enemy all around. We held each other's lives in our hands and we learned to share our fears, our hopes, our dreams as readily as we shared what little else good came our way.[1]

It's always been that way. Real men need a Band of Brothers. It was that way in Vietnam in 1965, and it is that way today.

Allow me to tell you about my Band of Brothers. Eighteen years ago I asked two friends if they would like to meet regularly to share what was going on in our lives and to pray for one another. Never did I imagine how we would grow together. As we began to meet for an hour a week or every other week, some things started to happen:

Our group became a place where I could be encouraged. Hebrews

10:24–25 tells us that believers aren't to neglect meeting together—and that when we do meet one key purpose for being together is encouragement. That's a big piece of what I gained. When one of us took a step of faith or said no to sin, the other two cheered. We covenanted never to let the others walk through the valley of death by themselves. Shortly after we started getting together I found myself in the hospital with a blown-out knee. Hardly life threatening, but within an hour both men were there.

Our group provided a place for accountability. Men are icebergs. People only see a tenth or so of our lives—almost always the beautiful part. What's below the surface, however, is where our real lives happen— lives often hidden from the scrutiny of other Christians. The jagged subsurface edges of my secret life often ripped open relationships and damaged my spiritual life. When my friends probed my hidden side they offered an accountability that exposed those jagged areas of my life and allowed me to be healed.

The group fanned the flames of faith. Proverbs 27:17 says that "as iron sharpens iron so one man sharpens another." Our small group was a place to talk about ways to improve my prayer life and my devotion to Christ. It helped me discover whether I was serving in the right area and if my gifts were being used.

Through the last eighteen years I have changed ministry focus and faced personal challenges. It is the small group that has helped hold me together. I will always be a part of a small group, and any ministry I oversee will have a small-group ministry at its core. Matter of fact, our ministry to men has thirteen core values, and one of them is "The small group is the optimal place for spiritual growth." Everything we do funnels men toward a small-group experience.

In this chapter I want to discuss how your leadership team can start small groups for the men of your church. To be honest, this may be the most important thing you as a leadership team can provide for your men. It's the stuff that makes disciples. There are a number of great books on how to start and run small groups, and I will mention some of them at the end of this chapter. What I will cover in this chapter won't give you every detail those books can provide regarding running a full-blown small-group ministry. But let me outline some points that will get you started.

Why Men's Small Groups?

While there are many reasons why small groups will benefit your ministry to men, let me mention just a few.

Small groups allow men to share life. In 1 Thessalonians 2:8–9, Paul tells the Thessalonians he came not only to share the gospel of Jesus Christ but also to share his life with them. This principle is exemplified not only in the life of Paul but in the life of Jesus. This life sharing is rare today. Our society is information hungry. We keep a distance from one another through e-mail and voice-mail or answering machines. Small groups break through these superficial, shallow relationships. Men can share what is really going on in their lives.

Who can a man talk to about the troubles he is having with his teenage daughter?

Who can he talk to about the emotional connectedness he feels for a gal at the office?

Who can he talk to about the wounds of his past?

Where can he go to share the joys of leading a co-worker to Christ?

Where can he share his deepest fears as a man?

The answer to all these is *the small group*. It is the biblical means by which men can get together with other men and share life with one another.

Small groups are a place to function as real Christians. A man recently walked up to me and said, "Where do I start?"

I responded by saying, "Start what?"

"Start doing everything the Bible tells me I am supposed to be doing," he said. "I go to a church with three thousand people in the service. I go to the Men's Monthly Breakfast and there are over two hundred men there—but where can I practically love, forgive, accept, and encourage another man?" Great question. There's a great answer as well: a small group. Within the New Testament there are close to one hundred and twenty "One Another Injunctions," such as:

Accept one another (Romans 15:7)
Love one another (John 13:34–35)
Encourage one another (1 Thessalonians 5:11)
Build each other up (1 Thessalonians 5:11)
Carry each other's burdens (Galatians 6:2)
Confess your sins to each other (James 5:16)
Pray for each other (James 5:16)
Instruct one another (Romans 15:14)

Each of these commands can be lived out in a small group. In a group of four to twelve men you can love another, pray for another, carry another's burden, accept others the way they are, and forgive others when wronged. Given our hectic lives, those things are hard to do outside a small group!

Small groups grow men in Christ. In Colossians 1:28, Paul says his goal of teaching is to present every man "perfect in Christ." Not a bad goal for a ministry to men. Within the confines of a small group men can learn what Christianity is all about. By working through a curriculum like *Operation Timothy*, they will be grounded. Or by studying Romans they will learn the great doctrines of our faith. Not only do they discuss what God desires, but men get a chance to apply what they learn—and to be held accountable for areas they want to change. The bottom line is that in a small group men become more and more like Christ in all they say and do. If the group ever loses this component they are finished. Bill Hybels, senior pastor at Willow Creek Community Church in Chicago, says, "No Christian will ever actualize his or her spiritual potential unless they are in a small group. The highest goal of any small group is to grow in Christ."[2]

Small groups offer accountability. One of the failings of much of contemporary Christianity is its emphasis on individualism. Thousands upon thousands of people believe they can make a decision to become a Christian bathed in the glow of their television or amid the crush of a large gathering of people and then never face accountability for their actions the rest of their lives. Christianity for them is a solo sport. But God didn't design Christianity that way. In the same way that it would be suicidal for a quarterback to play offense by himself against eleven defensive players, so it is spiritual suicide to try to live the Christian life without others. Unfortunately, many try—especially men.

In a famous survey of fallen leaders a few years ago, Howard Hendricks, professor at Dallas Theological Seminary, interviewed either over the phone or face-to-face some 242 Christian leaders forced to leave the ministry because of moral failure. One of the questions he asked was if they were in an accountability group. To everyone's surprise, not a single one was. These were good men. Godly men. Leaders who desired nothing but God's best for them. Yet they fell.[3]

I have come to define accountability as giving one or more men the freedom to help you order your private and public life. A small group provides the context where tough questions can be asked week in and week out. Chuck Swindoll has seven questions that give you a taste of what these questions might be like:[4]

1. Have I been with a woman in the past week in a way that could be viewed as compromising?
2. Have all my financial dealings been filled with integrity?
3. Have I viewed or read sexually explicit material?
4. Have I achieved the goals I set for Bible study and prayer?
5. Have I spent quantity time with—and given priority to—my family?
6. Have I fulfilled the mandates of my calling?
7. Have I just lied to you?

These probing questions get right to the point. They rip to the heart of men's struggles. At the end of the chapter I will include a lengthier list your groups can use for accountability.

Small groups maintain the momentum of a large event. Men's ministries face few challenges bigger than shepherding men who attend an Ignite Conference or Wake-Up Call and come home all excited about their life in Christ. Just like high school kids returning home from a retreat, they will lose their fire unless they are put in a position to keep the flames going. If we truly want to bring the fire home to our churches and keep that fire burning, then small groups are the means. One weekend a year doesn't make a man of God. Man in the Mirror and other similar ministries are rightly putting enormous amounts of energy and time into helping men see why they need small groups. We can be there to provide small groups for the men the other fifty-one weeks of the year.

Exercise 1—Why Do Small Groups?

As a leadership team, make a list of the reasons for men to be in a small group.

1.

2.

3.

4.

5.

6.

7.

8.

Types of Small Groups

You are probably asking right about now, *"So what are our options?"* In this section let's look at seven types of small groups you could have within your ministry. This is not an exhaustive list but one that will get you started. In no way am I saying you need all of these or that these seven are your only options. Rather, I want to give you the big picture so you can select and start what is best for your ministry.

Task Groups

Task groups come together to work on a project. They are action-oriented, aiming at accomplishing a specific task—a great way to get men involved.

Fifteen years ago, with one of our church's missionaries, I took three businessmen to Suceava, Romania. We wanted to help a small church get firmly rooted in that city. Our men met with a small group of Christians from the church to talk about economic development—how we could help them start a business to provide enough money to pay the pastor's salary and to run the church. Everyone decided to start a used-clothing store.

To start a used-clothing store, of course, you need clothes. So these guys came back and have been collecting good quality clothes from people in the church and community. Over the years we have sent more than thirty forty-foot cargo containers of clothes to Romania. Some men have traveled back to do business workshops. In order to keep the project going, we meet once a month in my office as a small group. We don't spend time in study, accountability, or extended times of sharing, but we have become a tight bunch and seen God do a marvelous work in our midst. Although our group has a practical bent, these men are practicing the "one anothers." They definitely pass the "I-can-call-them-any-time-of-day-or-night" test. When we meet we talk about the project and what needs to happen to keep it moving forward. Our group has a specific purpose and these men love being a part of it.

Entry-Level Group

Most men cringe when they hear the term *small group*. They would sooner go shopping for a day than be in a small group. It's necessary, therefore, to give men small groups in small doses. I have found that almost any man who gets into a small group grows to love it and will rarely want to leave it.

We use special events to start these groups. I have found it helpful to have groups short in length and high on application. After we had Steve Farrar do a weekend with our guys, for example, we started up eight new small groups. During the event men gave testimony about the importance of small groups, and then we gave men a chance to sign up at the end of the event. The groups were formed to go through Farrar's book *Point Man* and were intended to last six weeks, meeting for an hour a week. The time was split between sharing with one another, praying for one another, and discussing the material. The guys loved it. A number of those groups are still going today. Give 'em a taste and you've got 'em.

Other books we have used to start entry-level groups are *Man in the Mirror* by Patrick Morley, *The Purpose-Driven Life* by Rick Warren, and a little booklet that we have written called "IronMan." You want to use something that is an easy read for men and has high application for their life.

Investigative Bible Studies

Jesus made profound claims about himself that few non-Christians grasp. Investigative Bible studies pull together a number of men seeking to understand these claims. One man I know has spent considerable time building bridges with the men in his office. After a number of spiritual discussions with them, he asked them if they would be interested in joining him for a three-week study of Jesus Christ. The first week they looked at "Who Jesus Is," the second week at "What Jesus Did," and the final week at "What Is Man's Response?" These types of groups afford seekers the chance to ask questions they may not normally ask. It allows them to look at the core issues of Christianity and knocks down false caricatures of Christianity. It is exciting to hear how men have turned to Jesus as a result of this type of small group.

Accountability Groups

The purpose of accountability groups is straightforward—to come together for a short period of time to ask the tough questions, share, and pray for one another. When I meet with my guys it's usually for just one hour. We each take fifteen minutes to share what is going on in our lives, tell the men what we want to be accountable for in the coming week or weeks, and then spend the final fifteen minutes praying for one another. We don't study anything, work on anything, or try to save anyone. This group is purely to sharpen our character and to encourage our souls. Of all the groups mentioned, these are probably the easiest to get going. They can also pay some of the greatest dividends because men seldom find accountability elsewhere in the church.

Study Groups

George meets with eight men every Wednesday morning at a local restaurant. Their table is reserved and the waitress knows them by name because they've been eating in the same booth for the last six years. These guys are committed to one another and to the Word. They spend the first thirty minutes sharing with one another and eating breakfast. Then they break open the real Bread and away they go. They have worked through Genesis, Revelation, Romans, and a host of other books and topics. Surely they have built relationships, but their stated purpose for meeting is to "study the Word." Unfortunately, many men in our society spend a great deal of time *under* the Word of God getting teaching, but not *in* the Word of God digging and living. It's easy to discuss what others say about the Bible and not study it for yourself. Bible study groups allow men to systematically work through various books of the Bible and to allow God to change their hearts and lives.

Support Groups

One group that has been very effective, especially with the recent economy, is our Crossroads Career Network group. These groups are part of a national ministry and are for anyone who is unemployed or under-employed. They meet in a large-group setting once a month and receive training in networking, writing résumés, etc. But then during the next three weeks they meet in small groups to walk alongside men and pray with them. Rarely do men have someone to support them spiritually during this very difficult time in their lives. They're offered the love and support they need.

Top-Gun Groups

Top Gun is our nine-month "men equipping men" program designed to model, teach, and encourage practical application of the biblical principles that build a foundation for living life in Christ. A Top-Gun group is made up of twelve men who meet for two hours a week. They spend the first hour in small groups sharing, praying, and being accountable to one another, and the second hour in the large group discussing the work they did over the course of the week. The modules include "Intimacy with Christ," "How to Study the Bible," "The Man and His Family," "Servant Leadership," "Evangelism," and "Biblical Principles for Work." Each man spends an average of two hours a week in Bible study, Bible memory, and outside reading. The manual has been written by the men of our ministry and is now being used by churches all over the country. Of all the things going on in our ministry, this is by far the most exciting. It's having the biggest impact in the lives of our men. There is information on Top-Gun groups in appendix A.

Friendship Groups

Every Friday morning Paul hosts a group of about ten men in his home. Generally half are from the suburbs and half are from the city. They come from all different denominations, races, and backgrounds. Some are in full-time ministry, others are not. They spend time sharing with one another, fellowshiping, and praying for one another, meeting to break down the walls that exist in our city. There is no agenda, no planning or study—just men getting to know other men and developing friendships. What an incredible thing to see these groups popping up all over the landscape.

Is this an exhaustive list? No. But it does cover a number of the choices for you. Small groups don't have to all be one flavor. As a leadership team you can decide which you want to use or what combination to use. If small groups are anything they are flexible—you can tailor them to your church and your men.

Starting Groups at Your Church

The leaders are recruited. They're trained. They're ready to go. What lies ahead is the process of structuring the ministry and drawing men into the groups. The following tips might be helpful in this process:

1. *Find a coordinator for small groups.* Groups are such an important, integral aspect of ministry you will want one of the men on your leadership team to be in charge of small groups. He should be someone with experience as a small-group leader and have a vision for multiplying himself through others. The two strong gifts that are needed in this area are administration and shepherding. This is why I would recommend that you have co-coordinators if at all possible, because this gift mix is not normally found in the same person. Not only will he be responsible for training leaders but also for getting men into the groups—sharing that task with the group leaders. At times, group organization can be a time-consuming administrative nightmare. His responsibilities are:

- Recruit and train small-group leaders.

- Conduct in-service training sessions.

- Assist small-group leaders in group formation.

- Promote small groups through all means available.

- Establish a system for shepherding the small-group leaders.

- Commit to at least one year.

2. Determine your strategy and philosophy of men's small groups. As a leadership team there are a number of decisions that you will need to make about what your small-group ministry is going to look like. As a leadership team, you will have to decide what types of groups you will have. There are three levels of small groups:

- *Entry level.* These groups normally meet for one hour and have little or no homework. The primary goal is introducing men to Jesus and giving them a healthy small-group experience. At the end of the designated time, the group typically agrees to continue for another eight to twelve weeks.

- *Medium level.* This is your normal Christian men's small group. They would meet one to one and a half hours per week to study the Bible together, pray, and support one another. The purpose is encouraging the men to go deeper in their walk with Jesus, with special emphasis on Bible study, accountability, being transparent, and praying together. These groups also start to develop an outward focus.

- *High level.* These high-commitment groups would serve the purpose of training and equipping men. There would be a possible two hours of preparation and two hours of meeting per week. This is the place where leadership is developed for your ministry and church. Evangelism and discipleship are at the core of these groups. An example of this high-level commitment would be a Basic Training Group.

Other decisions that your leadership team will need to make:

- Who is going to care for the small-group leaders?

- What type of group will we have?

- How are we going to train the leaders?

- What will our criteria be for recruiting leaders?

- Will our groups be open, closed, or both?

3. *Recruit small-group leaders.* When you start a small group you entrust the lives of men to a leader. That being true, you want to ensure your leaders are qualified and trained to lead. You don't recruit these men by "casting wide the net" but by "tapping men on the shoulder." Don't use the bulletin or ask for volunteers at large gatherings of men. Your leadership team or pastor or other church leaders will be the best source of names of potential leaders.

Be careful in selecting men to lead your groups. It would be better to forgo small groups than to put men in charge who aren't qualified to lead. Some qualities to look for in a leader:

- *Godly character.* He takes knowing and loving God very seriously. (1 Timothy 3:1–7)

- *An authentic relationship with Jesus.* His relationship is characterized by obedience and submission to Christ. (1 John 2:3–11)

- *A consistent walk in the power of the Holy Spirit.* He daily yields to God's work in his life. (Ephesians 5:18–20)

- *Spiritual giftedness.* He shows gifts in the area of leading a discussion and engaging others. (1 Corinthians 12:7–10)

- *A teachable spirit.* He is open to learning from others and God. (Job 6:24)

- *A commitment to building and multiplying disciples to reach the world.* He has a vision for the harvest and for building disciples to go into the harvest. (Matthew 28:19–20; 2 Timothy 2:2)

- *He has been in a group already.* Having been a participant gives him the practical experience he needs to lead others. (2 Timothy 4:15–16)

After praying over your list of potential leaders and sensing these men are ready to lead, you can then approach them with the job description. Spell out clearly what you expect, the job they would do, and how long they will need to be involved. Some expectations to include are:

- *He attends church regularly*—all of our small-group leaders are members to ensure that they agree with our Statement of Faith.

- *He makes devotions a priority*—we want their leadership to flow from their relationship with Jesus.

- *He will attend all the training sessions.*

- *He can make a one-year commitment.* This is absolutely necessary unless it is an entry-level group that is only six weeks in length.

- *He will come fully prepared* to each meeting.

- *He will develop a prayer team* for himself as he leads the group.

After a small-group leader has recommended a potential small-group leader to us, one of the coordinators will get together with him and take his spiritual temperature. Some of the questions we ask are listed below. (This is not a complete list and we generally would not ask all of these, but they give you an idea of where to start.)

- Why do you want to be a small-group leader?

- Describe your daily walk with Jesus.

- What has He taught you in your devotional time this week?

- What does it mean for a person to have a relationship with Jesus?

- How did you become a Christian?

- If you have led a small group before, tell us about your experience.

- What are your biggest concerns regarding leading a group?

- What does your spouse think of your leading a group?

- Is there someone you would like to co-lead with?

- When would you be able to start?

4. *Train small-group leaders.* With the leaders recruited, it's time to train them. You will find leaders have a greater sense of confidence if you spend time preparing them for the task you have recruited them to. It's important never to ask men to do something unless you can give them the training and tools necessary to do the job. There are a couple of things you can do to train men to be effective small-group leaders:

Give them a good small-group experience of their own. The best way to train someone to be a small-group leader is to have him first participate in a healthy small group. As we begin recruiting and training, we ask existing leaders who they have in their small groups that they feel would be good future leaders. If someone has seen modeled what it is to lead a discussion, handle a tough question, or tame the guy who talks all the time, he is far better prepared to lead than someone who hasn't been in a group or has been in a dysfunctional group. Start by looking for leaders in your own groups.

Give them an overview of the basics of small-group ministry. You will want to have a time when you cover basic material on how to lead a group. You could have three consecutive Monday-evening sessions, an extended session on a Saturday, or one evening a month during the summer to train the leaders. We have used all three of these schedules. They each have pluses and minuses. During these sessions we have tried to pass on the following information:

- A vision of ministry
- The purpose of small groups
- Expectations of small-group leaders
- The role of a group covenant and how to develop one
- Understanding the stages of small groups
- Small-group dynamics
- Communication skills—listening attentively, stimulating feedback
- How to study the Bible inductively

- How to lead a good discussion—asking good questions, keeping the discussion going, handling conflict
- How to start and finish a group
- How to choose members
- How to lead an effective prayer time
- How to handle difficult people or questions

Training Session Tips

Some things that will help the training sessions:

1. *Give the men a good small-group time.* The training in itself can be one more opportunity for your men to have a healthy group experience. Structure your training to accomplish some of the things you want your leaders to accomplish with their own groups. Give the men a chance to get to know one another and to pray for each other.

2. *Give the men homework.* We had our men read through the *Brothers* book by Promise Keepers over the course of three weeks. We had them do an inductive Bible study and share their results with a small group. We then had them write five questions from that study, and finally had them actually lead a discussion on one of the nights.

3. *Make it practical.* Instead of simply imparting a load of information, we tried to give them on-the-job training, having them apply what they were learning. By having to lead a discussion, they took what they learned in the class and used it immediately. One thing that is helpful—and a hoot—is to have a couple of "plants" in the group—a guy who won't stop talking, and one who asks the most bizarre questions you've ever heard.

4. *Allow plenty of time for questions.* For most of the men, leading a group is something new and they bring some fears with them. Allow them time to ask questions about what you discuss.

5. *Keep it simple.* Most men are bottom-line oriented. They don't care about the history of small groups or intricate theories of how or

why they work. They want to know when to start, what to cover, and how to do it. Stick to the basics. If you don't know where to start, most Christian bookstores have great material on leading small groups and training others to lead. Because of limited space I cannot include our entire training session.

6. *Designate shepherds for the small-group leaders.* It's common for leaders to give to others but feel uncared for themselves. Either the coordinator or someone on his team should take the responsibility of caring for group leaders—praying for leaders often, calling them weekly or biweekly to see how they are doing, and meeting with them a couple of times a year. We have found that a shepherd is able to oversee up to six leaders. More than that is overwhelming. Some of the responsibilities of the shepherds are:

- Pray for the small-group leaders every week.

- Periodically call the small-group leader for updates and progress of the group as well as prayer requests.

- Be available for any questions or problems that may come up.

- Meet with the leader several times during the year to go over the goals of the group, check the temperature of the group, see how the leader is doing and how you can minister to him.

Many small-group leaders believe that once they become a leader they have arrived. We want to help them see that this is where the real leadership training will take place. They are going to learn so much from leading. I will often ask a small-group leader what they are learning about leadership from their experience.

7. *Provide continuing education.* Assemble your leaders once a quarter to provide further training, share and pray for one another, and discuss problems in the groups. A possible schedule would look like this:

- 7:00–7:15 Refreshments and catching up

- 7:15–8:00 Break into small groups to share and pray for one another

- 8:00–8:10 Break

- 8:10–8:30 Discuss any problems coming up in the groups

- 8:30–9:00 Teaching on a topic related to leading small groups

8. *Create windows for group start-ups.* Certain times of the year are better than others for starting small groups. Use some of the highlights of the year to get them going. An obvious time would be after a No Regrets Conference or an Iron Sharpens Iron Conference. At these conferences your men will hear lots of encouragement to get into a small group. You might want to consider having a post-conference event where men can sign up. Another good time would be your fall kickoff. By starting at this time you can publicize nine-month groups that run from September through May. You can use the summer to train leaders and then make a big push at the fall kickoff. One final time to start groups is after a major special event. After a midyear retreat, for example, you will probably find men ready to join small groups. Remember to have those vital testimonies at every major event where a man tells how small groups have impacted him. Over a period of time your men will know when groups are likely to start and can look forward to that window of opportunity.

9. *Encourage your leaders and other men to get into an inviting mode.* Personal invitations are still the best way to get men into small groups. When we train our leaders, we ask them to make a list of prospective participants and to start praying for them with the intention of asking them to join.

10. *Publicize the small groups.* One complaint you may hear from men is "I didn't know about the small groups for men." It really doesn't matter how many times you have said it—some people keep missing it. Your ministry brochure should list current small groups, with the time and place they meet as well as the group leader's name. Make sure you list the name and phone number of the overall person in charge of getting men into small groups so that a man who is interested only has to make one call. Some churches have flyers with all the small groups listed. These lists are great as long as they are kept current.

11. *Stay flexible.* After spending three years trying to match up men

who wanted to be in small groups, we have altered our tactics. We have started telling our men that being in a small group is an option—but that we weren't going to do all the work for them. We told them to go out and form groups on their own. We encouraged them to find men who were similar in maturity, some whom they had things in common with and who shared similar schedules. We provided a small-group starter kit and told them to go to it. We asked only that they let us know when they had a group going.

It's remarkable to hear of all the groups that have started this way. This isn't to say we don't rely on training leaders and starting up official groups. But we realize that many men don't fit into the nice, neat packages we develop, so we allow them to form their own groups, let us know what they're up to, and whether they would like any new people to join them.

12. *Form small groups out of existing ministries.* Another way to start groups is to use what already works for you. Three ideas:

(a) *Committee groups.* Encourage working committees in the ministry to become a small group. I have twelve men responsible for the Top-Gun ministry. These men meet weekly for two hours. Half the time is spent doing small-group things, such as sharing, praying for one another, and studying a variety of materials. The other half of the time is spent in business—developing the business plan for the ministry, setting goals, planning training sessions, and making the ministry happen.

(b) *Monthly meetings.* Many of you already have a monthly meeting for the men of your church. Incorporate into those meetings times to break into discussion groups. Then you can encourage those groups to meet the other weeks of the month on their own.

(c) *Top-Gun groups.* One of the purposes of the Top-Gun ministry is to provide a catalyst for new small groups to start in the church. Every May when the groups finish their time together, churches challenge them to stay together as a small group—a TG II group. They have already spent two hours a week together for nine months. Some serious male bonding has already transpired, so why not stay together? It's a way for us to start about ten new groups each year. Having been in a Top-Gun group for a year, these men are fully convinced of the need to be in a men's small group for the rest of their lives.

13. *Be creative.* I could give you diagrams and charts of how this should all look, but it wouldn't do you much good. The best thing you can do is sit down with your leadership team, take the basic principles described in this chapter and in other books, and develop your own model for small groups. Again, it comes down to what I said in the beginning: Each church is unique and the small-group system will be unique as well.

Seven Small-Group Decisions

Each small group faces seven decisions that determine much of the flavor of the group. Some of these questions you may have settled before you started training your men. Others you may sort through with your new recruits. Either way, your men need answers to these questions:

1. *What is our purpose?* The leader will in some way want to advertise the group. He needs to be able to tell others what type of group he is starting. Is it a task group? An accountability group, study group, support group, or hybrid group? He needs to be clear in his thinking on this one.

2. *Who should be in the group?* Is this group going to be an affinity group, with men in similar occupations to mine? Or will it be a diverse group? There are pros and cons to each. It really depends on what you want to do in the group. If you are looking to start an accountability group, you probably want an affinity group—guys you enjoy hanging out with who are experiencing the same pressures and stresses. Groups seem to jell easier at the start when the members are more or less at the same stage of life and at the same point in their spiritual journey.

3. *Will our group be open or closed?* Once the group is started, will we allow new people into the group? Again, this will be dependent on what the purpose of the group is. Men who want to join a sexual addiction support group need to be filtered through a group leader. Bible

study groups may want to take new members when they reach a break in their material.

4. *When will our group meet?* Weekly? Biweekly? In the morning before work or in the evening after work—or during the Sunday school hour? I have seen that meeting every week helps to keep a group going. If a guy misses a meeting he doesn't have to wait so long to get back into the swing of things.

5. *Where do we meet?* For the group just beginning, a restaurant may be okay. Most restaurants have tables large enough to handle groups of five or more. They may even have private rooms where your group can meet alone. Restaurants, of course, also give the added opportunity for a good meal. Men love that. The downside is the noise and men's self-consciousness about talking through spiritual issues in a public place. It's tough to break into groups to spend a significant time praying and sharing in the middle of a restaurant.

An alternative is to bring in bagels, muffins, donuts, and juice to a conference room at someone's office. Many of our groups meet in conference rooms around the community. Not only are these rooms usually quiet, they put the group on the men's turf. Another possibility is to have the group in someone's home. This works only if there is a rec room or study away from family.

6. *What commitment level do we expect?* Once a group has formed it's a good idea to develop a group covenant—to put down in writing what is expected of the members and what the group is about. Ownership is key. It may take one or two sessions to work it out, but you will find it extremely helpful down the road. I would encourage you to go back to the covenant on a regular basis—every three months—to remind yourselves of why you exist. A sample covenant appears at the end of this chapter.

7. *What are we going to study?* If your group will have a study component, you will need to decide that either as a group or ahead of time as the leader. In order to get guys started in groups, you might need to address some of the hot men's issues, such as parenting, marriage, or balancing work and home, to get them in. Once they're hooked, you

will want to move them to a more well-rounded study that includes studying Bible books and developing Christian disciplines.

Principles for an Effective Group

Finally, here are some points for your small-group leaders to return to again and again to keep their groups sharp.

1. *Keep your focus.* Make sure you decide as a group up front what your purpose is. Stick to it. It will be easy to slide into other things and activities if you don't remind one another of why you meet. Is it to study, to pray, to be accountable, or a combination of these?

2. *Start and finish on time.* One person in the group should be responsible to start the group on time and let everyone know when the time everyone committed to is up.

3. *Focus on people not programs.* It's easy to discuss deep subjects and to debate theological issues and never get to matters of the heart. Start your group with plenty of time for group members to get to know one another. Schedule a night to socialize for this purpose.

4. *Move slowly.* Men don't easily open up the hurts, pains, and frustrations of life. It takes time. For vulnerability to happen in your group, start by developing an environment of love and acceptance, not judgment. In order for accountability to happen, honesty and trust must be in place first.

5. *Take the lead.* Vulnerability is caught not taught. If you are frustrated because no one is sharing, take the initiative. Share what is going on in your life. Most men won't share fears, failures, or feelings because they don't know how. They have never been in an emotionally safe environment. You take the lead.

6. *Live as a body.* Some of the greatest ministry will take place outside your group, when specific needs arise in the men in your group. Make yourselves available to help in times of need, and feel free to call the others in your group for help.

7. *Keep discussions going.* When you discuss a chapter in a book or a section of Scripture, there are three simple guidelines: Wait your turn. Stay on the topic. Keep it brief.

8. *Cultivate small-group prayer.* The *ABCs* of small-group prayer are: *Audible,* so all can hear. *Brief,* so that you don't take everyone else's time. And *Christ-centered,* so you don't spend all your time praying about one personal request. If someone doesn't feel comfortable praying out loud, make sure he knows he doesn't have to.

9. *Avoid the known killers of small groups.* There are at least six ways to kill your group: aimlessness, poor leadership, the wrong mix of men, shallowness, individualism, and competition. Be warned.

10. *Just do it.* Take these guidelines to heart, but plunge in and do small groups. They're the stuff of real Christian faith.

Exercise 2—Sorting Through Small Groups

1. How will you recruit and train men to be small-group leaders? Who are your potential leaders?

2. What is your strategy to get men into groups?

3. What types of groups will you offer?

4. Who will oversee this aspect of the ministry?

5. What are the signs of a healthy men's group?

6. Will all your groups study the same thing or will each group choose what they will study?

7. When is the best time to kick off the small-group ministry?

8. How will you publicize the groups?

9. How will you care for the small-group leaders?

Good Books on How to Lead Small Groups

Brothers! Calling Men Into Vital Relationships by Geoff Gorsuch, NavPress, Colorado Springs, CO, 1994.

Getting Together by Em Griffith, InterVarsity, Downers Grove, IL, 1982.

The Big Book on Small Groups by Jeffrey Arnold, InterVarsity, Downers Grove, IL, 1992.

Transforming Discipleship by Greg Ogden, InterVarsity, Downers Grove, IL, 2003.

TransforMissional Coaching by Steve Ogne and Tim Roehl, Broadman, Nashville, 2008.

The Accountable Man by Tom Eisenman, InterVarsity, Downers Grove, IL, 2004.

Simple Small Groups by Bill Search, Baker, Grand Rapids, MI, 2008.

Leading From Your Strengths by John Trent, Broadman, Nashville, 2005.

Example of a Small-Group Covenant

1. *Total and complete confidentiality.* What you hear here, see here, and say here stays here. I will say nothing that may be traced back or that could be injurious or embarrassing to my group members.

2. *Be as open as you can with your life.* I will be as open with my life at this time as I can. I will show myself to you, letting you know who I am as a person.

3. *Unconditional love.* I will love and affirm you no matter what you have said or done in the past. I will love you as you are and for what Christ wants to make of you.

4. *Voluntary accountability.* I will ask the group to hold me accountable for specific areas of my life. With my permission you can ask me about the goals I set with God, my family, personal life, and world. I expect you to lovingly not "let me off the hook." "As iron sharpens iron, so one man sharpens another" (Proverbs 27:17). On the basis of this verse, I ask you to please share with me areas in my life that do not reflect Jesus, because I want to grow in personal holiness.

5. *Pray for one another.* I promise to pray for the men in my group on a regular basis, to lift up their needs to the Lord.

6. *Sensitivity to where people are in their relationship to the Lord.* I understand every person in this group is at a different point in their walk with the Lord. I will accept you the way you are but encourage you to move on in the Lord.

7. *Come prepared each week.* I will have my work completed and my verse memorized each week when I come to class. I will make every effort to be present at class; it will have high priority in my schedule.

Signed _____

Date _____

NOTES

1. Lt. Gen. Harold Moore and Joseph Galloway, *We Were Soldiers Once . . . and Young* (New York: Harper Collins, 1992), prologue.

2. Bill Hybels, on a tape series entitled *Enlisting in Little Platoons*, Tape 1: "The Purpose of Little Platoons," Willow Creek Community Church, Barrington, IL, 1989.

3. Howard Hendricks, on a tape entitled "The Age of Accountability," given at Campus Crusade Staff Training, Fort Collins, CO, summer 1993.

4. Chuck Swindoll, in a message given at Promise Keepers Conference, Boulder, CO, 1993.

Coaching the Leaders

10

It's a fall tradition in Madison. Coaches walk the lines at freshman orientation, hunting for tall, strong guys who don't play football—men between 6'2" and 6'6", 180 to 200 pounds, with strong backs, legs, and arms, and long endurance. It's a strange way to scout oarsmen for the University of Wisconsin crew team—to build what over the years has become a team heaped with tradition and national championships.

The recruits train constantly. Running miles and miles year-round, rowing in a tank all winter and out on the frigid lake as soon as the ice breaks in the spring. Eight men sit on sliding seats facing the rear of the boat, feet strapped to the bottom of the shell, each manning one oar. There's a ninth man on the team: the coxswain. Usually about 5'4" and hopefully weighing not much more than 100 pounds, the cox sits in the back of the shell facing the oarsmen. Holding blocks of wood attached by ropes to the outside of the shell, he beats out the cadence of the stroke. With these ropes he also works the rudder. Although he has to be small, the main requirement for a coxswain is a strong, deep voice. He yells out the pace, shouting instructions and encouragement to the team. He's the only one who can see where the boat is going and how the competition is doing. His job is to take the boat over the finish line having drawn the very best effort out of every man on the team and having kept them working together with such harmony that the boat nearly flies over the water. Although the cox never dips an oar into the water, and the oarsmen constantly assure him that he is no more than a noisy irritation in the back of the boat, most admit he is the most indispensable member of the team.

Our role in ministry is like the coxswain. When you lead a ministry to men, you need to keep looking ahead, giving direction, setting the pace, measuring the strengths and weaknesses of your team, keeping them pulling together, and cheering them on. We're even more than coach and cheerleader rolled into one. We don't shout advice from the sidelines. We're out in the water with our team, urging them to give their best for the Lord.

In this chapter we will look at how you and I can lead others to the finish. How we coach men. How we lead leaders. How we ride "point." In my mind nothing is more exhilarating than leading. I want to pass on practical suggestions on recruiting, developing, training, shepherding, and releasing others into ministry. At the end of the book I will list some of the best books on this topic. But what I want to do now is share five principles helpful in leading others.

Principle #1: Invest Your Life in Your Leaders

In 1 Thessalonians 2:8, Paul says: "We loved you so much that we were delighted to share with you not only the gospel of God but our lives as well, because you had become so dear to us." Paul clearly says that the *goal* of his ministry was to share the gospel, and in verse 12 he says that the *outcome* of his ministry would be people who live lives worthy of God. But he also says he took great delight in sharing his *life* with the Thessalonians. Paul wasn't so goal-oriented that he lost sight of the real people he sought to impact. Paul realized that when he died he would live on in the men and women he had invested his life in as well as in heaven with God. He understood that ministry was more than speaking a message—even the message of eternal salvation. It was also walking alongside the people God had entrusted to him. The principle I draw from this has become a cornerstone of my ministry among men: *The closer you get to the men, the greater the impact you will have on them—and the greater the impact they will have on others.*

One of the first books I received as a new Christian was Robert Coleman's *The Master Plan of Evangelism*,[1] a book I would recommend your leadership team read together. In this short paperback, Coleman over and over again makes the point that the method of Jesus wasn't to worry about the masses but rather to invest three years of His life in the lives of twelve men. It was these men who in turn would reach the masses.

The principle stills holds today. It's easy to get sidetracked by the masses. But if we are going to be effective in leadership, we have to decide early on that we can only work with so many people and that the best way to multiply ourselves is to pass on what we know and who we are to a few others. The great German theologian Dietrich Bonhoeffer, who spent months in a German concentration camp, penned these words: "The righteous man is one who lives for the next generation." One of my brothers put that statement on a plaque and hung it beside his bedroom door. Every day when he leaves the house he is reminded to pour his life into another.

I am no financial wizard, but my wife, Colleen, and her *Quicken* software keep things flowing along just great. Over the years, however, I *have* picked up a few simple things from friends and newspaper articles—and from my father-in-law. He is constantly handing me diagrams, illustrations, and articles on the importance of packing in our money for the future. One principle he has driven home is the "magic of compounding." It's basically this: If you invest your money early and consistently, the interest you draw will go back into the pot. You earn interest on your interest—and that leads to a substantial growth in your savings. If you give the process time, the investment pays off many times over—like magic (unless of course you have a downturn in the economy; then all bets are off!).

That principle holds true in Christian leadership as well. If early on in your ministry you take time to encourage, listen, teach, and build up another man—and you stick with it over a long period of time—he will take all he has learned from you and multiply it into the next generation. In finances it's called the magic of compounding. In the faith it's called multiplication of life—through investing in others. In 2 Timothy 2:2, Paul instructs his young disciple Timothy: "And the things you have heard me say in the presence of many witnesses," he says, "entrust to reliable men who will also be qualified to teach others." In this passage Paul describes a massive multiplication. He mentions four generations of people being influenced: Paul himself, Timothy, and the other witnesses, reliable men, and the others they teach. An almost unbelievable payback!

Let me share some practical ways you can make heavenly investments in the lives of men you work with.

Demonstrate a Consistent Lifestyle

In the same way that small, consistent investments pay off financially, so the small, consistent influence of a godly lifestyle will pay off in the men you work with. In 1 Peter 5:2–3, it says we as leaders are to be "examples to the flock." In Philippians 3:17, Paul exhorts the Philippians to "join with others in following my example." There is no escaping this truth: One thing our society is looking for is leaders whose beliefs and behavior are congruent, whose actions are consistent with what they articulate, who make visual through their lifestyle what they verbalize with their lips. Nothing is more important for a leader than the life they lead. The way you live will prepare the way for others to hear what you say and follow where you go. Give your men time to see you in the everyday aspects of life:

- How you treat a slow server at a breakfast meeting.

- How you exhibit patience when your little child runs up to you in the middle of a conversation.

- How you honor your wife in front of others.

- Why you go to the Lord in prayer with your daily decisions.

- What you are learning in your daily devotions.

- How you respond to competition in the gym or watching a game.

You want your men to see what it looks like for a Christian man to do business, lead a family, and seek after God. You want them to see you bring Christ into every aspect of your life.

Share Your Time

For a financial investment to grow it needs time. Putting money in a mutual fund for a few weeks, months, or years won't do it. Multiplication takes many years. The same is true of relationships with men: they need time. Having meals together and going to games, retreats, and planning sessions allows you to make small but necessary investments in their lives. It takes time to tear down the protective walls men build up around themselves.

I once heard Howard Hendricks explain that when he can't travel with his wife, he always tries to bring one of his students from Dallas Seminary with him. He said the trips provide an opportunity to just hang out with a young man and talk about everything under the sun. That priority has stuck with me. Whenever I go to speak at a church on a Sunday morning or to do a weekend retreat for another church, I ask one of my leaders to come with me. I have found these travel times yield some of the best fellowship I have ever experienced. Something about being alone with a guy for a couple of hours allows the walls to come down and vulnerable sharing to take place. A number of my most significant discussions with men have taken place in that context.

Include others in what you are doing. Make spending time with men a habit.

Serve Men

The great UCLA basketball coach John Wooden said in his book *They Call Me Coach* that he would never ask his players to do anything he wasn't willing to do. The night before a game he would take his players to a hotel away from the campus so they could get a good night's sleep. But instead of going home to be with his wife, he would spend the night at the hotel with the players.

To serve another man is to invest in his life. It's interesting when you study Jesus' life to note that He, too, never asked the disciples to do anything He wasn't willing to do.

He asked them to pray and He prayed.

He asked them to serve and He washed their feet.

He asked them to love one another and He died on the cross for them.

The disciples learned from being with Jesus. From watching Jesus do the work of His Father. Christianity is contagious, more caught than taught. Christianity is like a fire. People see a fire and they want to be there to watch. They are intrigued by it.

When you are in the trenches serving your men, they will catch your spirit. Remember? Jesus came not to be served but to serve and to give His life as a ransom for many (Mark 10:45). Many are into upward mobility. Jesus and His followers are into downward mobility.

I'm not saying that if you lead a men's ministry you have to be involved with *everything*. In fact, this book gives you tools to enable and empower others to do the work of the kingdom. What I am saying is that leadership isn't barking orders and sitting back and expecting others to do all the work alone. It isn't about "lording it over" people, but rather serving them. Your men will see you serve when you help set up chairs before a meeting, when you help stuff a mailing that needs to get out, when you take a discussion group because a leader can't make it. If you make yourself available you will never lack opportunities to serve your men.

Shepherd Men

As you go along you will find different ways to care for the spiritual needs of your leadership team. We all have different gifts, so how you shepherd your men may look completely different from how other leaders shepherd. But some of the ways you can care for your guys are:

Pray for them regularly. Call them up or find out when you're together how you can pray for them. Let them know you've been thinking about them. I try to pray for two or three different leaders each day, so that over the course of a week I will have prayed for all of the guys I work with personally.

Keep your ears open. I am trying to develop an empathetic ear and heart. If I hear that life is going well for a man or that another man is struggling, I call to see how things are going and find out if I can do anything to help. It's amazing how much you learn when you listen.

Get together with them. Get together one-on-one with your key men a few times over the course of the year just to talk. You may spend some of the time talking about the ministry—problems or ideas they need to talk through. But spend most of the time just asking how things are going. Earlier in the book, I listed a number of questions I ask my leaders, and you have the freedom to go from there.

Send cards. Keep a stash of notes or stationery handy so you will be able to jot off a congratulations for birthdays or wedding anniversaries. If a man or his family is going through a tough time you can send an appropriate card. You're telling the men they are important and what they face is important to you as well. In our age of e-mail, it is easy to send a quick note. However, I still think there is a place for a real card sent by mail.

Principle #2: Train Your Leaders

For many guys a huge roadblock to their serving in the church is their fear that they won't do the job right. Men fear failure, as we discussed earlier. A second key to working with your leadership team is providing the training men need to do what you have asked them to do. You squelch fears when you give men skills, instruction, and resources to do the job properly. Here's the principle: *Never ask a man to do anything you aren't willing to train him to do.*

Training sounds like a weekend of sitting through boring seminar lectures. I have found that most of my effective training takes place in shorter, less formal settings. Here's a list of some ways you can train your men:

Training through one-on-one meetings. There is no getting away from simply meeting one-on-one with your leaders to shepherd and train them. Whenever I meet with a leader, I'll ask a series of questions to help coach them in their development as a leader:

- What are you learning about leadership?
- What are you learning about handling difficult people?

- What are you learning about shepherding men?

- How are you managing to stay spiritually strong while leading?

- What are you reading right now to grow as a leader?

As a follow-up to the last question, I always suggest books to help my leaders grow in the areas they are feeling pressure. Remember that leadership development happens best when they are feeling the pressure to grow in a certain area. I like to call it "just-in-time" training.

I'm not sure who gave me this module for one-on-one meetings, but I have found it very helpful.

E — *Encourage* . . . when they are ministered to

Q — *Questions* . . . asked that give feedback on how they are doing

U — *Understand* . . . learn new skills in order to minister in their sphere

I — *Inspire* . . . moving them on through vision casting

P — *Pray* . . . for them personally and for their ministry

Train through small groups. By far the most effective training I have done has been through our Top-Gun program. Training isn't the main purpose of the program, but throughout the course of the year I was able to share basic leadership principles and slowly drew along a number of guys based on their giftedness.

If you are just starting your ministry, it may be hard to wait to begin small groups or a monthly meeting, but you can't go wrong taking your first year just to develop your leadership. You will set a solid foundation for whatever course you take in the future. And the best way to do that is to gather a group of men around you and meet as a small group. You don't have to use Top Gun. There is an abundance of great leadership books out there that will help you prepare your men. It's unfortunate that we have been deceived into believing that we can train men and women leaders as quickly as we can heat a cup of coffee in the microwave: We think that if we do the right conference or seminar, we can make instant leaders. It just doesn't work that way. It takes time.

Committee meetings. The normal give-and-take of a planning meeting almost always opens opportunities to interject good leadership principles. These are quick minute-or-less lessons. During the meetings I often find myself coaching the men on church procedures—how to reserve rooms, get bulletin announcements, and keep the custodial staff on our side.

Books. Another thing I like to do with my key coordinators is to read a book together, taking time to discuss it when we meet monthly. Some books I have found helpful are *The Master Plan of Evangelism* by Robert Coleman, *Too Busy Not to Pray* by Bill Hybels, *Spiritual Leadership* by Henry Blackaby, *Courageous Leadership* by Bill Hybels, and *The Five Dysfunctions of a Team* by Patrick Lencioni. Studying books together gives all the leaders a common understanding of service and ministry and it keeps them reading—which most men do not like to do. I do love to read and often pass on a good book when I finish it.

Resources. One way you can train your men informally is by providing them with resources. Besides books, you can use periodicals. Ask your pastor to pass on good articles he comes across. Some DVD series make great take-home helps that men can view at their convenience.

Consulting. It's often helpful to bring in an outside person to meet with your leadership team. They can hear what you're doing and provide objective feedback.

On-the-job training. Whenever possible I work alongside another man first before asking him to do a job by himself. Our men do the same. On our special events committee, each member is grooming another man to take his place. These men attend all the meetings and take some responsibilities to prepare them to lead. With our Top-Gun groups, any of the men can lead the group after the first three months if they choose to do so. It's a nice, safe environment in which to grow leadership skills.

Outside seminars and conferences. If you have men preparing to lead small groups, Serendipity Small-Group Studies provides regional training sessions that do excellent training. Kenny Luck at Saddleback does a great training conference several times during the year; the Willow Creek Leadership Summit is also a great conference for any leader. Here at Elmbrook we do several training sessions a year for anyone working with men. Your pastor probably has a handle on what training you have available in your area.

In-church training. This is supplemental to all the other types of training you provide. When you have informal training taking place, these sessions can be job-specific and relatively short. With our Top-Gun program, a man must first have gone through the program as a participant before he can lead a group. Once through the group, he can take a three-night course to get the skills to lead a group with another man. We meet for three consecutive Monday evenings for two hours. We divide the time this way:

- 7:00–7:30   Teaching time—walk through the training manual
- 7:30–8:00   Small-group discussion of the material
- 8:00–8:10   Break
- 8:10–8:40   Teaching time
- 8:40–9:00   Small-group discussion of the material

If you are training men to lead small groups, there are many ways to divide up your time. But keep the following points in mind:

1. Provide plenty of time for discussing the material.
2. Provide time for sharing and prayer.
3. Give them homework to read and complete between sessions.
4. Provide time during the sessions for men to lead what they are being trained to lead.

Principle #3: Create a Winning Environment for Your Leaders

I know even less about gardening than I do about finances. My personal gardening motto is this: I've never met a plant I couldn't kill. Nevertheless, every spring I go with my wife to the greenhouse to help pick out flowers. (She wants me to have a say in what I spend my summer killing.) For me, the best part of that trip is the greenhouse. I love going inside and seeing those plants sprouting with incredible speed. The reason they grow so fast, of course, is that the greenhouse is an almost perfect environment for plants. The light, water, fertilizers, and warm temperatures all work together to enable the plants to grow.

That's your goal at church. You want to develop an ideal environment where men can flourish in both growth and leadership. I feel fortunate to have spent thirty years in a feeding, nurturing setting. I have worked hard to create a similar environment for the men God entrusts to me. In this section I will share how you can develop a ministry where leaders are free to be all that God wants them to be—where they feel freedom to take risks, to grow, to step out and use the gifts God has given them. These are the environmental qualities you want to foster:

Give encouragement. Just as plants can't grow without a life-giving dose of water, people can't serve and lead without a life-giving source of encouragement. Encouragement can put a smile on the face of a child, lift the shoulders of a broken man, change the course of a young man's day, week, month, and even his life. Without encouragement we shrivel and die.

You can encourage through *notes.* A quick note at the right moment to a man on your team takes a guy a long way. When I receive a note from our senior pastor or one of our senior associates I'm ready to sign up for another year of service. A note says I'm a valued part of the team and that they are interested in what I am doing.

You can encourage through a *word.* Whenever you get a chance, thank the men for all they do, for the sacrifices they make, and for the impact they have on others' lives. A word spoken face-to-face will carry them a mile.

And you can encourage men through a *look.* I can still remember when I was in grade school playing for the divisional championship in baseball. I had just clobbered a game-winning home run, and as I rounded second base I looked to the stands for my parents. My father—a very quiet man—just looked at me and gave me a nod of approval. His look said, "I am proud that you are my son." It's a look I will carry with me the rest of my life. You will have ample opportunities to give a look to another man that says "thanks" or "that was great" or "I'm proud to be associated with you." When your men spend forty to sixty hours a week getting beat up at work and told they need to sell more, fix more, and do more, they find life-changing encouragement when you make a place where they feel encouraged.

Allow freedom to fail. I have mentioned that Stuart Briscoe, our former senior pastor, has a saying that is a watchword for our staff and the thousands who volunteer at Elmbrook. "If a job is worth doing," he says, "it's worth doing badly." Give your men freedom to fail. More than anything else you can do, it will allow them to take risks, to step out and discover their gifts—and to take personal ownership of the ministry. We have men in our churches that are running multi-million-dollar companies; they are by nature entrepreneurs and need space and freedom. If a man has to continually glance over his shoulder to see if someone is stomping up behind him to tell him what a terrible job he is doing, he will never reach his potential as a leader. His gifts will be wasted. When you give away responsibility you also give men the privilege of doing a job their way, with their unique style.

Recognize leaders. Everyone loves to be recognized for a job well done. Think of creative, meaningful ways to let men know they have done well and that you're glad they are on the team. One year I threw a catered appreciation dinner for leaders and their wives. Someone played the piano before and during the meal, and then I introduced each man and described the contribution he had made to the team during the last year. At our yearly Breakfast of Champions I hand out a Man of the Year award to the man who has gone beyond the call of duty in serving the men of Elmbrook. In our newsletter I will highlight different men and the impact their service has made to the ministry. Another year we had a simple evening of dessert and fellowship. Use these moments to reiterate your vision and talk about where you are headed in the future.

Take leadership retreats. Getaways for your leadership team are fantastic vehicles for accomplishing a number of important goals—one of which is to help them feel important, needed, and valued. Try to take your leadership team away once a year for a day or so to plan, pray, and play. You will develop a greater sense of team, and by including your team in planning this retreat, they will be more likely to open up and tell you what they feel the team needs most at the moment.

You can limit your retreat to your core leadership team or open it wide to all men in leadership positions. You can accomplish different goals with different types of retreats: A *training retreat* uses seminars and hands-on training to improve ministry skills. A *team-building retreat* aims to build relationships between all team members. You can spend your time sharing, worshiping, and playing together. A *planning retreat* is spent on evaluating where you have been, brainstorming where you want to go, and planning how to get there. Check back to chapter 8 on special events, and appendix B for hints on holding retreats.

Build a sense of team. Throughout this book I have purposely used the word *team* to describe the men who work with me in leadership. For me this is both natural and important. My leaders will blossom when they are all working toward the same goal and aren't interested in who gets the glory. The 1995 Packers are a great illustration. The previous year they lost one of their best players to a play-off injury. The next year—minus this supposedly key player—they were a much better team. Why? Chemistry. Any coach knows that chemistry or the lack of it can make or break a team. When you look for men to serve on your ministry, start with men who have servant hearts and are willing to do anything for the cause. Build on that by providing ample time in your meetings for talk and prayer. Keep reminding them of the common vision and keep their collective eyes focused on Jesus.

Grow love and acceptance. Last and most important for creating a winning environment for your leaders: Men take off when they realize they are accepted for who they are, not just what they can do. If encouragement is water, then love is the sun. Love takes phone calls any time of the day or night. Love gets excited about the things friends get excited about. Love listens to a man as he shares a wound he has carried for forty years. Love sees potential in others. Love believes that God can use a man and his gifts to make a difference in the kingdom. Love picks men up when they fall. Love feels as others feel. *Love.* Pour it out on your men.

Principle #4: Give Away the Ministry

In the movie *Miracle* (2004), the story of the 1980 U.S. Olympic hockey team, one of the most interesting scenes happens right after Herb Brooks' American squad beats the Russians in the semifinals of the medal round. Players on the ice hug each other, others cry out of ecstasy, flags wave everywhere, and the Lake Placid crowd chants, *"U.S.A.! U.S.A.!"* Then there's a shot of Brooks. An assistant coach tells Brooks to get out on the ice with the guys to celebrate one of the greatest upsets of all time. Herb looks at his assistant. "This is their time of glory," he says. "They earned it. Let's let them enjoy it." Brooks turns his back and walks off to the locker room.

Real leadership gets excited seeing *others* succeed. It pulls together a group of men, equips them, trains them, and then releases them to do ministry. Your ministry will only develop and grow as you develop leaders and allow them freedom. As long as you try to do everything yourself, the scope of your men's ministry will be small and its impact limited. I want to give you basic principles for giving away the ministry—how to delegate to the men you coach.

1. *Point people in the right direction.* Planning is an overlooked process—which is why I have talked so often about it in this book. Your first task as a leader or leadership team is to decide what you want to do. Vision is deciding where you are going with the ministry and discerning what has to happen for you to get there. As a leadership team, for example, we have decided to add one new ministry every year until we get everything going that we feel God has called us to do. There are times I would like to do more, and other times I feel our goal is too high. But try hard to look out into *your* future. You have to know where you want to take your men.

2. *Transfer ownership.* You may be sure where your group should head, but you can't get your men anywhere without help. You need to give your men the authority, freedom, and resources they need to perform as God has gifted them. Biblical delegation starts a man with small tasks, then moves him on to bigger assignments when he proves himself faithful. I start by putting men in charge of *things*, then move

them to *projects*, and finally to *people*. Since people are our most precious commodity, I want to make sure the guys we choose to lead them are men of character and ability.

You have to consciously work to give away ministry. Your first step to letting go is to make known what you need and expect. If I were going to get a man to head up a fall kickoff, I would sit down with him and go over the following:

What has to be done. I would cover the person's job description to ensure we are both thinking the same thing.

How it will be done. Greg Groh of Worldwide Leadership Council gave me a great suggestion in this area. He told me to have a man make a list of everything that has to be done for the project or job he has to do. Then we take the list and label each task 1, 2, or 3. A *1* means he doesn't have to check with me to do the task. Most jobs fall into that category. A *2* means he can go ahead and do it and tell me how it went. A *3* means he needs to talk with me first. This process is clear. It's simple. And it makes us partners.

When it will be done. I find it helpful to work with a man to develop a timeline for the area he is working on—not just a final date but intermediate checkpoints as well. For that fall kickoff we would set dates for getting help, scheduling a speaker, getting brochures out, and more.

Who will help. This part of the discussion hammers home the fact that a guy almost always needs help to get the job done. I suggest names of potential recruits. I let him know how I can be a resource to him. In the case of the fall kickoff, he would need men to take charge of publicity, program, food, registration, facilities, prayer, and budget.

3. *Release your leaders.* One summer I served with Greg Groh on a leadership school in the Middle East. We worked with pastors, evangelists, church planters, counselors—all of whom were working in difficult situations. As we taught on prayer, discipleship, evangelism, planning worship services, and other issues, we used a phrase that has stuck with me: *Catch and release.* Leadership means helping men to *catch* a vision for using their gifts and then *releasing* them to do it.

I will tell you up front that when you give a job away, your men won't do it like you would. They won't avoid the mistakes you would have seen a mile away. And they may never do their job as well as you could. But that's okay. Ministry isn't about perfection. It's about people—developing them into the men God wants them to be.

Releasing men is hard. It's also one of the most exciting things you will do as a leader. Each month when I get to speak at our monthly breakfast, all I have to do is show up and speak. A team of twelve men has planned the meeting. They will greet the men, emcee the event, cook the food, lead the music, and guide the table discussions. I feel like a proud parent. Those twelve guys understand what ministry is and they are doing it. What excitement!

4. *Stay in touch with your leaders.* You need to be available to meet with the men to talk through how they are doing.

One of the problems with delegation is the "dump and run" phenomenon. A leader gives away an aspect of the ministry and then never makes progress checks or offers follow-up help. As you give away your ministry, be available to support and encourage your hardworking men. What each man needs will be different. Some like a lot of room. They run with a job and forget all about you. Others need more time. You will learn how to best support your leaders as you get to know them. Be bold. Ask them to define what they must do to make their project successful. Make them tell you what you can do to help.

Principle #5: Organize the Ministry

The word *organization* evokes one of two reactions. For some, organization ranks right up there with root canals. For others, it's sheer delight—and the more graphs, charts, and systems the better. Wherever you may fall on the continuum one thing is certain: To grow your ministry you need to *plan* for growth and *structure* all you do in a way that facilitates growth, keeping in mind that the church is a living organism, not an organization. Here are some guidelines to help you assemble your ministry in such a way that the fire keeps burning and is not put out by the water of organization.

1. *Clearly define areas of responsibility.* I will say it again. Job descriptions ensure that your men know exactly what you need from them and

what doing a job well involves. A proper job description includes the responsibilities to be carried out, the time frame for finishing, whom to report to, and the resources available to do the job well. Job descriptions provide a man both freedom and direction and make him accountable for clearly stated duties.

2. *Clearly define areas of care.* If your men are going to invest time, money, and energy into ministry, they need leaders who care for them while they do ministry. The privilege of serving shouldn't be an invitation to dry up and blow away. One mistake that is easy for your leadership team to make is to give a man responsibility and authority but fail to give him the support he needs. Build into your structure men whose job it is to care for the personal needs of leaders. If you have ten small-group leaders in your ministry, have one man for every five leaders. Your encourager can call his men regularly, pray for them, help solve their problems, and dream up new ideas with them. They can also watch for leader burnout.

3. *Evaluate whether your structure accelerates or hinders ministry.* Organizations can get so complicated that people spend more time working through the bureaucracy than actually doing ministry. I know plenty of ministries where people spend more time in meetings than they do out with their people. Discuss this fine balance as a leadership team and be willing to revamp your ministry offerings, to revise who does what and who answers to whom. What works for you the first couple years of your ministry may not work in year four. Adding more leaders and coordinators will certainly mean you need to make changes. Failing to adjust will choke your ministry.

Don't expect men to attend an endless number of committee meetings. Streamline as much of your work as you can through phone conferences, e-mail, or fax machines.

4. *Develop a model that works for you.* There are as many ways to structure a ministry as there are ministries. What works for someone else's ministry may not work for yours. Have some of your organizational types talk through what might work best in your unique situation. Here are some models I have seen function well in churches I have worked with.

When the pastor is responsible for the men's ministry

In this setup the pastor's main responsibility is overseeing the key coordinators and leaders. He sets the vision and provides leadership to those men.

A meeting every six or eight weeks pulling together the pastor and coordinators of major areas of ministry gives an opportunity for everyone to share what they see going on in their areas, to pray for one another and their ministries, and to plan for the future.

As I mentioned earlier in the book, I recommend co-coordinators. It's a structure that furthers teamwork, spreads responsibility, and builds in accountability.

Each coordinator develops a team of men to do ministry in their area of responsibility. The coordinators of our small-group ministry work with a larger team of ten men. They meet weekly to nurture one another and to plan and carry out the ministry. A special-events coordinator, in contrast, may get his committee together only once a month, mostly to plan the upcoming event. How often and how long a team meets can be different for each area.

When the ministry is run by men working under a pastor

This situation assumes that the group's pastor is responsible not only for the men's ministry but a dozen other areas. In practice, the ministry is run by one or two men who pull in others to help them do the work.

If this working committee has four to six guys, each can take a specific area of the ministry and develop a team of guys to work in that area.

The committee needs to meet every four to six weeks to discuss the various areas as well as to plan and pray.

The pastor needs to decide which of the committee meetings to attend, and the committee needs to decide how to keep him up-to-date if he chooses not to attend.

When just one man is enthused about a men's ministry

In some churches it may be only one man who is really excited about seeing something happen among the men at his church.

He should first talk to the pastor for his input.

He will need to be careful not to attempt too much and set himself up for burnout. As he moves ahead and desires to develop a ministry he will need to coax others to help.

Most of this men's ministry will be informal, especially in the beginning—just meeting with men to encourage them and to spur them on in their walk with Jesus.

5. *Organize around weakness.* One final point: As you begin to determine the structure of your ministry, remember to evaluate your team's strengths and weaknesses. As you consider which men in your church to approach to help in your ministry, think about which ones best make up for your weaknesses. I am a visionary who loves to be out in front of the men leading the charge. I am weak in my grasp of details. I overlook smaller steps we need to take to get us to the destination. I also consider myself a weak shepherd. I need men on my team who are detail-oriented and others who can shepherd the men. Get to know yourself and the men on your committee. Ask yourselves what you need to round out your team.

NOTES

1. Robert Coleman, *The Master Plan of Evangelism* (Old Tappan, NJ: Revell, 1963), 21.

Special teams make or break a football team. A fumbled punt, a blocked field goal, or a kickoff returned eighty yards for a touchdown can all change the complexion of a game. But special teams are often the part of the game that coaches overlook, scrimping on time and effort. But here's a point too good to miss: When I coached ball and broke films down play by play, I found that almost a third of the action in any game involved special teams. Special teams done right can impact enormously the score at the end of the game.

Special teams have the same big effect on a ministry to men. Mission teams, service teams, evangelism teams, and other outreach specialties add excitement, diversity, and depth to your ministry. "As air is to fire," Stuart Briscoe says, "so missions is to the church." The same is true in a man's life as well. One of the best ways to see a man grow is to get him out of his comfort zone and serving others. Special teams may not be where you want to start, but you won't want to neglect them as time goes on.

Send Teams

We like to call our ministry trips "Send Teams." Having personally taken groups to the Philippines, Romania, and Russia, and planned many other Send Team trips, I have seen firsthand the benefit a one- to four-week trip has for an individual, a ministry, and the whole local church. I want to give you in this section some basic guidelines on carrying out short-term mission trips. We will cover the purpose for a trip, different types of trips you can take, planning a trip, trip recruiting and training, and the keys that make trips work.

Why Take a Trip?

Men work hard. They assume that the best way they can use time off from work is to hit the golf course or to head off to fish or hunt. Yet the incredible power of mission trips refreshes both the server and the served.

1. *Mission trips expose men to the realities of life in another culture.* A ten-minute walk in the squatter slums of Manila, Philippines, teaches men that everyone doesn't live like we do. Watching gypsies driving horse-drawn carriages through the Carpathian Mountains of Romania reminds us that not many enjoy the conveniences we do. Seeing food lines string out block after block in Moscow, men realize that not everyone eats the way we do. Comfortable men in nice suburban settings don't realize that two-thirds of the world lives in utter poverty, disease, and hopelessness. Taking people into these situations shocks them into reality. It forces them to deal with long-buried issues: *What is my responsibility? How can I help? How can I simplify my lifestyle? Where is God in all of this? Why has my country been blessed as it has?* National Geographic or a PBS special can give men the images, but a mission trip lets them pick up the smells, sounds, and emotions of life on the other side of the planet.

A mission trip also enables men to start to see the world as God does. They see the suffering and injustice present in our world. They begin to notice the billions of people on this earth who don't know Jesus. It's an eye-popping experience.

2. *Mission trips give men a chance to see what cross-cultural missions is all about.* We make sure our men understand that they are *not* missionaries—at least not in the sense of a cross-cultural worker who trains, prepares, and then goes long-term to another world.

These trips indeed give men a chance to do real ministry. They watch and work alongside missionaries, getting a peek at their lives. Whenever possible we like our teams to stay in or close to the homes of the missionaries we work with. They see that doing the laundry is more than a two-hour job, and that cooking often involves going to a morning market and spending a good part of the day preparing food. Trips help men grasp what it takes to work with people from another culture—people with different values and ways of doing things. It lets them see the extremely difficult situations missionaries work under and the sacrifice their families make for the cause of Christ.

3. *Mission trips let men assist in the work of Christian ministry.* Later we will discuss the types of trips you can take with your men. No matter what type you choose, though, you get the chance to encourage, support, and strengthen the work missionaries are doing. Lack of money or personnel or time almost always curtails some of what missionaries would like to do. Having a well-prepared team come from your church can get things done in a short time that may otherwise never happen. If a missionary family needs an addition on their home, church, or school, your church could raise the money to send the men to build it. If an outlying area lacks doctors, you could send a couple of doctors and nurses to give physical exams—likely to children who have never seen a doctor in their life. One of our prerequisites for sending a team of men is that it must in some way further the ministry of one of our Elmbrook-sponsored missionaries. We aren't interested in just sending teams to do projects. We want to connect with our missionaries and be a vital part of what they are trying to do.

4. *Mission trips stretch men spiritually.* One of my friends who went on our last Philippines trip said he would only be able to take part if God sent the two thousand dollars necessary for the trip. He watched in amazement as God provided exactly what he needed in a variety of ways. What a faith builder! John had never spoken a word in front of a congregation. When he arrived in Kabankalan—on the island of Negros—he was asked to preach on a Sunday morning at one of the forty-five outreach churches in the mountains. What made the challenge even greater was the fact that the invitation to preach came *after* he had arrived for the service that morning. He prayed fervently at the back of the sanctuary during the first half of the service—and then did a great job of sharing God's Word.

Everything that happens on a "Send Team" trip is the undoing of a "comfortable" faith. Financial concerns, culture shock, time changes, simple living situations, loneliness, busyness, hard work, sickness, detailed preparations—they all force a man to become more dependent on the Lord, more fired up for God.

The other ingredient in such a trip is the effect on your men of seeing the church in action in other parts of the world. In many ways the church in America is weak and sick compared to the church in other cultures, where it is generally much more vibrant and alive. Men go to Asia or Africa or South America to worship and pray and fellowship with men and women whose faith does not display the shallowness they often see in American Christianity. When I taught a leadership school in the Middle East this past year, it wasn't uncommon to hear men express their fear of being shot or imprisoned for their faith. Who would not be challenged by this? In Romania we attended worship services that lasted three hours. We caught a real glimpse of the people's love for God. In the Philippines we saw Christians gather at five o'clock morning after morning to pray for the people of the church and for the island outreach. Maybe that's why they have planted forty-five churches.

I think by now you get my point. I am convinced that these types of trips transform the hearts and lives of men and provide real service to the missionaries and nationals on the field.

Types of Trips

You can dream big when you think of the types of trips you can plan for the men of your church. You can wrap some of the following ideas together to accomplish two or three purposes on a given trip. On our last trek to the Philippines, we did both construction and medical work. These obviously aren't the only jobs to be accomplished, but they get you thinking of some possibilities:

1. *Construction trips.* Over the last couple of years we have sent men to Venezuela for construction work at a retreat center for pastors and missionaries; monthly work teams to Katrina-stricken areas; two teams of men to help Samaritan's Purse build a chapel at Angola Prison outside of New Orleans; five teams of men to Guatemala to help build a church; and numerous men to the Congo to build a school and chapel. None of these are the most glamorous trips in the world, but they're

very necessary and greatly appreciated by the missionaries. You could put an addition on a school, church, house, or hospital. You might cut down trees to carve out a landing strip in the Brazilian jungle. Whatever the project, it's a chance for men to help in the work of the kingdom.

Work teams range from one man going to help with a smaller project to a large number of men going to blitz the larger jobs. Several years ago a carpenter went to Papua New Guinea for a month to help build a furniture-making shop and to train nationals to build furniture. Last year a Presbyterian church in Chicago sent twenty-five men to Mexico for a week to help construct modular homes. One great aspect of construction projects is that not everyone has to be a tradesman to be involved. A willing heart to do whatever has to be done makes a man a candidate for a construction team. There's always dirt to shovel, concrete to mix, lumber to move, and walls to be painted.

Keep in mind:

Don't miss an obvious point: Do have a person on the trip thoroughly skilled in whatever the main purpose of the trip is—electrical work, plumbing, masonry, etc.

Find out early on exactly what is involved in the project and whether or not you will need to pay for the materials.

Try to get blueprints ahead of time so you can head off any problems.

Double-check on what tools are available and what you will need to bring along.

Get your non-construction guys in shape before you leave. There's nothing like mixing cement for ten hours a day in ninety-degree heat when all you normally do is sit at a desk.

Where are you going to be housed? Do you need to arrange for housing and food or are the hosts making the arrangements?

2. *Medical trips.* The need for medical help in developing countries is incredible. Dentists, pediatricians, nurses, surgeons, dental hygienists, physical therapists—all are needed in various parts of the world. We have had dentists and surgeons go to Ghana to work with Prison Fellowship in that country's prisons. Pediatricians have worked in the Philippines with kids who have never seen a doctor. Surgeons have done reconstructive

surgery in South American jungles, and nurses have provided care in a Haitian orphanage—all in the name of Jesus.

Most churches won't be able to field an entire team of medical personnel. You can nevertheless get your healthcare professionals aligned with one of many medical mission agencies. They continually organize efforts all over the world. They have vast experience that helps to ensure all the supplies are present and pre-screening has taken place.

Keep in mind:

Will the supplies you need be on site or should you bring all of your own?

Do your people need any special licensing to do medical work in your target country?

Do you need to complete any special forms to get medicine through customs?

Will the site be adequately staffed? What specialties are needed? Will there be an anesthesiologist, surgical nurse, etc.?

Who will pre-screen patients before you arrive? Your trips will be infinitely more productive if you can get right at your work.

You will need the best language interpreter you can get if you will be seeing patients.

3. Athletic trips. One of the simplest and most effective mediums for doing evangelism in other parts of the world is sports. Whether it's basketball, soccer, volleyball, or baseball, sports are a universal language. Again, a number of agencies specialize in sending sports teams all over the world. Last year we sent nine men to Guatemala on an eight-day, twelve-game ministry trip. They went from town to town playing the local all-stars and semi-pro teams. At half time they shared testimonies and a gospel message. In parts of the world like South America and Asia, it isn't uncommon to have two to five thousand people attend a game of this sort. If you have men in your group who are athletically inclined, this is a great way for them to spread the good news of the gospel. One of our Philippines teams saw so many people in a small barrio become Christians that the local church who sponsored us doubled in size. Another option is going to your local prisons and playing against the inmates. For years now we have been sending basketball, softball, and volleyball teams into prisons all over Wisconsin, and are having incredible ministry opportunities.

Keep in mind:

Who in the host country will set up all the games ahead of time?

Is the schedule realistic for your men?

Allow a day for the guys to get accustomed to the climate.

Will there be a sound system, or do you need to bring one? Don't underestimate the number of spectators. You want your half-time message to be heard.

What level of competition can you expect? Make sure you are evenly matched with the people in the host country.

What type of permissions do you need to get from the prison chaplains to get in and out?

4. *Business trips.* Some guys may want to take part in a mission trip, but they aren't athletically, medically, or mechanically inclined. I mentioned earlier that I took three businessmen to Romania to set up a clothing resale shop intended to underwrite a small church. It was one of the most exciting trips I have ever taken. I saw these astute businessmen use their God-given gifts to teach how to brainstorm, strategize, market, budget—everything necessary to start up a small business. Another one of our men, who is a farmer, recently spent three weeks in Africa helping the local people with irrigation and cattle-raising skills.

Keep in mind:

Are you going as Western world know-it-all imperialists—or servants of God and man?

What do you know about the country's economy and business practices? *Know* before you go.

What cultural differences can you expect that will impact how you do business?

Who do you know who can coach you in legal and procedural issues?

Will you have language interpreters available who know business terms?

5. *Prayer trips.* When I first talked to our men about a prayer trip, their first reaction was "What are we going to build?" "What are we

going to fix?" We have had teams from our church go to various cities around the world and spend two to three days walking the streets just praying for the city and asking what God would want to do in the future. The Christian workers in these cities believe that some of the spiritual strongholds will only be broken down through prayer. And until this is done, the gospel will not be received. This may not sound like a normal mission trip, but prayer is where the real battles are won for eternity. Prayer trips deepen the prayer lives of the men who go and of the people who send them.

Keep in mind:

You need to do a great deal of study ahead of time on the cities you will pray for—religious background, culture, societal issues, politics, and so on.

Team members must not be new Christians, but men who are real prayer warriors and who already have a ministry of intercession at home.

Team members should gather a prayer team to pray for them back home while they battle in prayer in these closed cities of the world.

Team members need to be versed in spiritual warfare.

Team leaders should have a working knowledge of the cities that will be visited.

6. In-country ministry trips. You don't have to leave this country to experience another culture or to help the cause of Christ. You could, for example, take a group of men to minister to the rural poor in the Appalachians, or the urban poor in any major city in this country. Plenty of Christian organizations need help restoring buildings. And many summer camps could use a group of men to help with building projects or general grounds maintenance. These domestic trips can be shorter in length—even a weekend—and usually considerably less expensive, making them a great way for many guys to get started.

Keep in mind:

What type of experience would be most beneficial to the men in your church?

What type of preparation does the organization provide, or what will your group need to do by way of preparation?

How to Plan a Mission Trip

In this section I will provide the basic steps to planning a short-term mission trip for your men. There are at least a couple of good books that go into much more depth than I can here. *Vacations With a Purpose*[1] has great material and checklists for putting a trip together. *Stepping Out: A Guide to Short-Term Missions*[2] is also a good guide for your planning and team training. One other book that is helpful is *Serving with Eyes Wide Open: Doing Short-Term Missions with Cultural Intelligence* by David Livermore.[3]

Getting Started

1. *Determine where you want to go and what type of trip you should take.* Go to these three resources to get info on potential projects, in this order:

Your pastor. Ask him if your church has any missionaries looking for help. If he is unaware of any current needs, you could ask him for a mailing list of missionaries supported by your church and then send them a letter to request information directly.

The second source is *your missions committee*, if your church has one. The committee coordinator should be able to detail some of the needs of the agencies and missionaries they work with.

The third source would be *your denominational mission headquarters.* Often they organize projects all over the world that you can tie in to. Trips sponsored by a denomination are a great place to start because they do the logistical work for you and you wouldn't need to field a whole team from your church to make it happen.

I am not against working with other organizations that send men on trips all over the world. My first choice, however, would be to link up with missionaries connected with your church. If your church has taken on obligations of prayer and funding for a particular project or missionary family, a mission trip to help them out is a natural for everyone involved.

Besides determining what type of trip to take, you will need to decide the cost, location, and length of it. An in-country trip is by far the easiest and least expensive. Going to Central or South America or Canada is relatively inexpensive and leaves you the option of going for just one week. Some things to keep in mind as you make these decisions:

How long can your guys be gone from work?

How much do you think they can reasonably raise for the trip?

What connections do you as a church have with missionaries and mission agencies?

How many men do you think would be interested the first time around?

2. *Develop a budget.* Once you have fixed your dates and location, your next step is to develop a trip budget. Budgeting will be done for you if you go with your denomination or a mission agency. These are some of the costs you can expect:

Travel
- Round-trip airfare
- In-country flights/transportation
- Daily transportation (from place of lodging to work site)
- Airport taxes

Food and Lodging
- Cost per day for lodging
- Cost per day for food
- Extra hotel and meal costs while entering and leaving country

Training Materials
- Team retreat
- Reading material
- Training manual

Miscellaneous Costs
- Passports/visas
- Shots

- Photography
- Printing and postage for team
- Money for building, medical, or athletic supplies

With a price determined you can start recruiting team members and put together a timeline.

3. *Plot a timeline for the trip.* This process may seem tedious, but you will suffer needless headaches if you don't plan ahead. If you start doing things far enough ahead, you won't be overloaded in the final few weeks before the trip. This is a bare-bones timeline—you will need to fill in the gaps based on your trip, church, and style:

Eight months before trip
- Establish a planning committee
- Determine when and where the trip will be
- Begin to develop a budget for the trip

Six months ahead
- Begin advertising the trip—prepare a brochure, put it in your church bulletin, hold an informational meeting
- Arrange for transportation
- Choose team leaders

Five months ahead
- Finalize your team
- Work with hosts on final arrangements

Four months ahead
- Begin training classes
- Apply for passports
- Plan fund-raising activities

Three months ahead
- Continue training classes

- Send out prayer and support letters
- Hold a potluck dinner for families

Two months ahead
- Go on a team retreat
- Do job-specific team training (bricklaying, basketball practice, etc.)
- Visa applications should be in (or earlier depending on country)

One month ahead
- Get immunizations
- Confirm flights and other travel arrangements
- Arrange for a send-off at a worship service
- Get traveler's checks for your team

This isn't an exhaustive list, but it gives you an idea of what you might need to include on your own timeline.

4. *Recruit team members.* It's one thing to draw up plans for a trip. It's another to convince others that it will be good for them to go. To be honest, it can be tough the first time. Once you have a history of trips and can show videos and share testimonies from former team members it gets easier—especially if the trip was a positive experience! While it's the job of everyone on the planning committee to help recruit team members, you may want to have one man oversee your efforts. Some recruiting tactics:

Brochures. Include the date, destination, what you will do, your purpose, cost, team leader, basic schedule, date of informational meeting, expectations, and application. You may want to include a map of the country where you will work to give people a better idea of where you are going.

Informational meetings. After the brochures and bulletin announcements have been out for a month or so, hold an informational meeting. This is your chance to describe the trip in greater detail, maybe to show a media presentation from previous trips, and to have a couple of men share testimonies regarding their experiences on a short-term project.

Make sure to leave plenty of time for questions and get a list of the men who attend so you can follow up on them.

Advertising blurbs. Use every means available to advertise the trip: the weekly church bulletin, church newsletter, and any other information system used at your church.

Former team members. These men are usually a great means of recruiting others for a trip. Once we schedule a trip, I usually contact all our former team members so they can start talking it up in their sphere of influence. They may also be potential team leaders.

Prayer. As the leader of our men's ministry, I am always listening and looking for men who need to take the next step in their Christian development. I keep those men in mind during my prayer time and ask God to help us know if this trip would be a good thing for them. Your planning committee should spend time praying that God would stir the hearts of the men who should go on this trip.

5. *Decide on the team.* This can be tricky. It helps if you are up front through the publicity process that team selection is not automatic. The men must apply and be accepted for the trip. I have found it helpful, as part of the application process, to have the men write a one-page letter explaining why they want to go on the trip. Set a deadline for applications and know ahead of time whether you plan to take everyone who applies or a just a few men. The sorting process also works best if your planning committee determines some objective means for choosing or excluding men—instead of leaving everything to subjective factors such as friendships and favorites.

Once you have received everyone's application, have your pastor look them over for any problems he might see. He may be aware of issues that would disqualify a man from going. Keep in mind the following issues when you make your selections:

- *Has the man been on a previous trip?* You might need experienced men on this one. Or you might want to open up opportunities to new men.

- *Does he get along with others applying for the trip?* Is there a good team fit?

- *Is he spiritually and emotionally mature enough to handle the trip?*

- *Is he looking to serve—or simply wanting a chance to travel?*

- *Do you have enough skilled men in the project area?* This needs to be a priority.

6. *Train the team.* With the team selected it's time to prepare them for the trip. From a perspective of growing the participants, I use the trip as dessert—and the preparation time as the real meat of the trip. Several years ago we were preparing a group of two dozen college students to go to the Philippines on a combination music/basketball/child evangelism/construction project. We had spent two months meeting weekly together. We had a wonderful weekend retreat. Two weeks before our departure date there was a coup attempt in Manila and all travel from the United States was stopped. Without hesitation, all of the team members said that even if they didn't go, their efforts were worthwhile because of the growth that had taken place in their lives. The good news is that the coup attempt failed and we were able to go anyway. What an experience for these young men to see tanks, armored vehicles, and soldiers everywhere they looked!

In order for your training to be effective, there are a couple things you will want to be sure to include.

1. *Training classes.* Six to eight weeks of classes work best. These shouldn't be solely sit-at-a-table-and-take-notes types. Include time for sharing and prayer, teaching, and discussions of how to handle the practical aspects of the trip. In your teaching time you will want to cover the following subjects:

Week One:	Devotions and prayer
Week Two:	Testimonies—how to put one together and how to give one
Week Three:	The biblical base of missions
Week Four:	The biblical base of missions (cont.)
Week Five:	Team building/relationships
Week Six:	Culture shock
Week Seven:	How to be a world-class Christian
Week Eight:	Packing

Give homework that matches the topic of the week. Some books that may be good for your team to read over the course of the training would be *In the Gap* by David Bryant,[4] *Unveiled at Last: God's Call to Be Involved in World Evangelism Throughout the Bible* by Bob Sjogren,[5] or *Run With the Vision* by Bob Sjogren and Bill and Amy Stearns.[6]

2. *Team retreat.* To get away to a retreat center for a day or two really helps the walls come down within the team. It also helps them get used to living together in close quarters. If you have a ropes course or adventure course nearby, it is a great way to accelerate the team-building process. You can also do some team-building exercises on your own at the retreat center—ask your youth pastor or sponsors for ideas. The retreat should also provide extended times of sharing, worship, and prayer together. By this time a question like "What was the most embarrassing moment in your life?" should go over well. Since you will be going as servants, I found doing a foot-washing service at the conclusion of the retreat to be memorable.

3. *Family potluck.* A month or so before you leave you might want to gather all the team members and their families for a meal. It gives the wives a chance to meet the other wives and to swap phone numbers so they can call each other for emotional support or practical help during the trip. It gives kids a chance to see photos or videos of where Dad is going and, better yet, to hear from others *why* he is going. If you have people in your church or community from the country where you will work, you might want them to come and share about their country and what the men will experience there.

4. *Background research.* It's important for your team members to learn as much about the country as possible before you leave. Have them go to the public library and check out books and videos on that country, read and watch, and then report back to the team. If there are language CDs available for your country, get those and learn some basic words.

Stress from the beginning that you are all going as learners and not as experts. When you learn about a country ahead of time, you are conveying to the people that they are important and that their country is important. It says, "I care about you, your background, and your struggles." By trying to learn the language and using it when you arrive—no matter how poorly—you say, "I am willing to humble myself and learn from you." This is the attitude you will want to foster among team members.

Ten Keys to a Successful Trip

You can know how to make a trip happen without knowing how to make it happen *well*. Here are some vital points to making it work:

1. *Flexibility.* "Roll with it" is the motto of any mission trip. Most of us like things to be structured—with some semblance of order and time. Life doesn't work that way in most countries around the world. Planes, buses, and trains don't leave on time, church services start late and run long, times and schedules constantly change. You'll never know when you might be asked to give a word of testimony or bring a message. Drill into your team members the need to be flexible.

2. *Prayer.* The real battles are fought in the heavenlies. As a result, it's imperative to have an army of people praying for the team while you are away. I encourage each team member to find five other men who will commit to pray for them every day they are gone. You could also set aside a room on the Sundays the team is away for family members and friends to gather to pray for the team. You could develop prayer cards with prayer requests and a picture of the team.

3. *Spiritual readiness.* If a team expects to see fruit on the field they must be spiritually strong going into the trip. It is easy as the trip draws closer for the men to worry about all the packing and physical things that need to get done and to forget about preparing their hearts. Jesus tells us in John 15 that there is a direct relationship between abiding in Him and bearing fruit. Anything you can do to keep the men close to Jesus will help.

4. *A servant heart.* I have said it already but I want to say it again: *Your men need to see themselves as servants to the missionaries and to Christians and non-Christian nationals, not as saviors from the West.* The nationals smell arrogant foreigners an ocean away. The greatest compliment you could ever receive is for people to say you were humble and served well. When you work with men it isn't hard to find out who has or doesn't have a servant heart. You want guys on your team who are willing to

do anything, not those who want their pillows fluffed and their egos stroked. We tell our teams all the time that they are to go as servants, learners, and listeners.

5. *Team building.* The more you can do, the better. Harsh environments bring selfishness to the surface. The chaos and rustic living conditions get old, the close quarters and lack of privacy irritating. People say and do things out of character. Relationships are strained. Men's ability to forgive, speak the truth in love, confront another person, and love unconditionally will all be tested. Build relationships before you go.

6. *Cultural sensitivity.* One quick way to ruin a trip is for a team member to use a word of slang or a phrase that is inappropriate for the country, or to act in a way that is disrespectful of the host country. In the Philippines, for example, you don't wave to a person indicating for them to come to you as you would in America. To wave in this fashion is how you call a prostitute in the Philippines. Read as much as you can and talk to veteran missionaries in order to develop sensitivity to the customs and culture of the country you serve.

7. *Debriefing.* When the trip is over, it is easy to check it off as another project completed and move on to the next thing. But your men's world has been shaken. They will need some time to readjust, come down to earth. Make the project a real growth experience by allowing plenty of debriefing time before coming home. Have each one share the highlight of his trip and how he was challenged in his Christian walk. Ask them to explain what steps they will take to become world Christians. Have them think about their response to questions Christian and non-Christian friends and family back home will ask, such as, "How was your trip?" and have them prepare a thirty-second answer. Take time to evaluate every aspect of the trip to discover what can be done better or differently next time. Debriefing not only brings closure to the trip but marks a new beginning for your men as they return home changed persons.

8. *Family involvement.* A man should only agree to go on a trip if his wife is in favor of it. As the planning process moves forward, make sure the men keep their wives informed. A phone chain for the wives while the men are gone can be helpful, as is distributing faxes or messages that come in from the team. A church in Chicago assigned men

from the church to shovel the driveway of each team member's home when necessary. What a great way to support the families!

9. *Churchwide support.* Some guys won't want to send out support letters asking for money. Some don't need to. But they should realize the letters aren't just about money. They are meant to share the vision of missions with others. If a man doesn't need to raise funds, have him send out a prayer letter instead of a support letter. Use your trip to fire up people beyond the team itself.

10. *Flexibility.* I know, I've said it before. But I needed a tenth point to make it an official top-ten list. And not only that—it needs to be repeated.

Short-term missions is a ministry that takes a lot of time to plan and carry out. But the impact it can have on your men's ministry is measureless. Let me close this section with the warning I put on all of our mission brochures.

WARNING:
Involvement in Men's Short-Term Missions
will cause world vision to spread
throughout your life and your ministry.

Focus on Evangelism

Surveys of evangelical Christians show that only about 25 percent have been trained in evangelism and only about 5 percent have shared their faith with another person. I don't know about you, but I sure wouldn't want to go to battle with only a quarter of the soldiers having been trained and only one in twenty with any experience. Yet that is exactly what is happening in our churches today. Evangelism is an often overlooked area of men's ministry. In chapter 6, I spoke about including evangelism as one of the components of a balanced ministry. In this section I want to mention a few things you can do to enhance this area of your ministry. Like a vacation with a purpose, once you get men sharing their faith with other men, their excitement grows as they spend time on the front lines.

They get caught up in what God is doing in the lives of other men and in their own lives as well. You *can* form evangelistic teams, but the real goal is to develop an environment that makes evangelism an everyday part of being a Christian—and a normal part of the men's ministry. Here are some things you can do to make it happen:

1. *Cultivate an evangelistic mindset.* From the first day you begin your ministry, remind the men of why it exists. This is much bigger than making men better husbands or fathers or more efficient workers. It's about doing kingdom business. It's about seeing men come into a relationship with Jesus and grow in it.

Make sure your men realize you aren't just going to have meetings and a program for them to come to and feel better about life. You do things so they can bring someone else in on their elbow, so they can be equipped to tell others about what Jesus has done in their life. A meeting doesn't go by that I don't remind the guys of why we gather. If they just want a nice little boys' club they can count me out. I realize that in some churches you face a circle-the-wagons mentality. It may take some time to break through that, but if you start from the beginning it's a little easier.

2. *Train your men.* Be creative. You don't have to announce a mandatory thirty-week course on evangelism. You can do a few things to make it more palatable. You could, for example, tell each of your small-group leaders that sometime in the next two years you want their groups to study a book on evangelism. Books such as *How a Man Stands Up for Christ* by Jim Gilbert,[7] *How to Give Away Your Faith* by Paul Little,[8] *Becoming a Contagious Christian* by Bill Hybels and Mark Mittelberg,[9] *Lifestyle Evangelism* by Joseph Aldrich,[10] and *Just Walk Across the Room* by Bill Hybels[11] are all great for small-group use. By doing evangelism training through a small group or Top-Gun group you aren't asking for another commitment from the guys. You're fitting the training into something they're already doing.

Make your training practical. Have your men write out their testimony and then give it to a couple of others in the group and allow them to critique it. I would do the same with a gospel presentation. It isn't enough just to read the material and know it. You want them to practice explaining what they believe in a safe environment. Within that safe environment they can make mistakes, try different styles, and receive constructive, loving feedback.

Emphasize that evangelism flows out of relationships. This goes back to what we said at the start. A good men's ministry begins with men developing relationships with other men. Out of these relationships naturally flow evangelistic opportunities. Most men think they have to become someone they aren't when they share their faith. If we can help men see that God will use exactly who they are and what they have been through to reach other men with similar backgrounds, we have accomplished a great deal. A second emphasis for your training is that evangelism is a process. So often we're so interested in closing the deal that we forget Jesus described coming into a relationship with Him as a process of sowing, watering, and harvesting. A final emphasis for a class like this is that the men must leave their comfort zone if they expect to be effective. You can't catch fish from your porch. You have to get in your boat and go to where the fish are. The fish don't come to you.

3. Form a "special forces" team. In time you will begin to notice the men who really do have the gift of evangelism. They love to meet with other men to tell them about Jesus. You may want to start a separate ministry for that group of men. We call our group Ambassadors. It is their job to contact any new male member of the church and to welcome him to the ministry. They have also been equipped to meet with other men one-on-one to take their spiritual temperature and to encourage them to move forward from wherever they are in their experience with Jesus. Interestingly enough, most of the guys on this team are salesmen. They love to be with people. They aren't afraid of rejection. I would love to see an entire army of men on the streets of Milwaukee meeting with other men just to encourage them and speak boldly to them. The team you put together could adopt much different strategies and methods from our group, but it should still aim at telling others about Jesus.

4. Use your special events as evangelistic opportunities. Without getting into too much detail, you can pick one or two special events in the course of your year to deliberately seek to reach the unreached. In appendix B, I describe sixteen great special events, some of which are evangelistic. Any well-planned breakfast, lunch, or barbecue, however, can be a great way to gather men together and bring them an inspirational message focusing on the gospel. Having too many of these causes them to lose their effect. But providing one or two a year can bring great results.

The heart of the issue in both mission trips and evangelism is whether or not your men's ministry is being proactive. To bring the fire home to your church means building men who are so on fire for Jesus that others are attracted to the fire—and those with the fire seek to share what they have.

Exercise 1—Special Teams Ministry

1. Share with the other leaders any cross-cultural experiences you have had and how they have impacted you as a Christian.

2. Considering the men in your church, what type of trip would be most appropriate?

3. What potential sources do you have for gathering information for future mission trips?

4. When in your yearly schedule would be a good time to have a trip?

5. What must you do to get started planning a trip?

6. What is your level of commitment to evangelism in your ministry? How is this evidenced?

7. How can you most effectively train men in evangelism within your existing program?

NOTES

1. Chris Eaton and Kim Hurst, *Vacations With a Purpose* (Colorado Springs: NavPress, 1991).

2. *Stepping Out: A Guide to Short-Term Missions* (Monrovia, CA: Short-Term Missions Advocates, 1987).

3. David Livermore, *Serving with Eyes Wide Open* (Grand Rapids, MI: Baker Books, 2006).

4. David Bryant, *In the Gap* (Ventura, CA: Regal, 1979).

5. Bob Sjogren, *Unveiled at Last* (Seattle: YWAM Publishing, 1992).

6. Bob Sjogren, Bill and Amy Stearns, *Run With the Vision* (Minneapolis, MN: Bethany House, 1995).

7. Jim Gilbert, *How a Man Stands Up for Christ* (Minneapolis, MN: Bethany House, 1996).

8. Paul Little, *How to Give Away Your Faith* (Downers Grove, IL: InterVarsity, 1988).

9. Bill Hybels and Mark Mittelberg, *Becoming a Contagious Christian* (Grand Rapids, MI: Zondervan, 1994).

10. Joseph Aldrich, *Lifestyle Evangelism* (Portland, OR: Multnomah, 1986).

11. Bill Hybels, *Just Walk Across the Room* (Grand Rapids, MI: Zondervan, 2006).

A few years ago I had the privilege of hearing Jim Collins speak at the Willow Creek Leadership Summit. He spoke on his book *Built to Last*, which became a bestseller for months on the Business Book list. He and Jerry Porras examined twenty long-lasting companies (each was started about a hundred years ago) and asked, "What are the qualities that made these companies last for the long haul?" "What makes a company a visionary company?" "What determines whether it will have long-term performance or be a one-night wonder?" Some of the companies they looked at were General Electric, Hewlett-Packard, Motorola, Boeing, Walt Disney, Nordstrom, IBM, and 3M. After a thorough investigation they were able to pinpoint a few qualities that allowed these companies to stand the test of time.[1]

I have thought a lot about this over the past few years, not only in terms of men's ministry leaders but also in terms of my own personal leadership. What is it that allows a man to sustain leadership and effectiveness over the long haul? How can I ensure that at the end of my life I am more in love with Jesus than I am today? How can I say, like Paul in 2 Timothy 4:7, "I have fought the good fight, I have finished the race, I have kept the faith"? How can I persevere to the end as mentioned in Hebrews 12:1? How can I ensure that I am not disqualified (1 Corinthians 9:27)?

Having spent the majority of this book discussing the nuts and bolts of starting a ministry to men, I want to turn my attention to you, the leader. If you are anything like me, you probably have stopped to ask the very same questions I did, and continue to ask them. I want to share with you four qualities of the leader who is built to last, who is prepared to lead over the long haul.

Life in Vital Union With Christ

One of the early lessons I learned in ministry is that our walk with Jesus is related to our work for Him. Perhaps the greatest danger you will face as a leader is that oftentimes the way we are doing the work of the Lord is hindering the work of God in our lives. The leadership lesson is this: What you are in private will determine what you do in public. This principle can be seen in every sphere of society.

Jascha Heifetz, one of the greatest violinists of the twentieth century, started playing violin when he was three. He practiced four hours each day until the day he died at eighty-seven. That is over 100,000 hours of practice for an occasional one-hour performance.

Leonardo da Vinci, the great Italian painter, wanted nothing less than perfection with his paintings of the human body. For one picture, he drew a hand more than a thousand times until he felt it was right.

Mike Singletary was six feet tall, two hundred pounds, and considered very small by NFL standards for a middle linebacker. Yet he was elected to ten NFL Pro Bowls, and then voted into the NFL Hall of Fame as one of the best to ever play the game of football. These achievements did not come by accident but were due to his hard work and legendary training regimens.

Lance Armstrong, seven-time Tour de France winner, trained like no other racer. In *It's Not About the Bike*, Armstrong describes his preparations for the 1999 Tour de France: "I went back to training. I rode, and I rode, and I rode. I rode like I had never ridden, punishing my body up and down every hill I could find. . . . I remember one day in particular, May 3, a raw European spring day, biting cold. I steered my bike into the Alps, with Johan following in a car. By now it was sleeting and 32 degrees. I didn't care. We stood at the roadside and looked at the view and the weather, and Johan suggested that we skip it. I said, 'No. Let's do it.' I rode for seven straight hours, alone. To win the Tour I had to be willing to ride when no one else would ride."[2]

We love great music, great art, and great athletes, but they all come with a price. We forget the discipline it takes on a daily basis to perform at this level, and it is no different in the Christian arena, especially for leaders. Paul says in 1 Timothy 4:7, we are to train ourselves for godliness. So often we marvel at what Jesus did during His public life, but lose sight of what He did in private to prepare himself for those moments. I like to tell leaders around the world that if we are going to become like Jesus on the field, then we must become like Him off the field. What Jesus did in private prepared Him for what He did in public. I'm not sure if anyone could say it better than Dallas Willard in his wonderful book *The Divine Conspiracy*: "My central claim is that we can become like Christ by doing one thing—by following Him in the overall style of life He chose for himself. We can become like Christ by practicing the types of activities He engaged in, by arranging our whole lives around the activities He himself practiced in order to remain constantly at home in the fellowship of the Father."[3]

With the principle being what it is, allow me to share a few disciplines we need to arrange our lives around in order to be in a place where we can be taught, touched, and transformed by Jesus.

Silence

In silence we close off our souls from "sounds," whether those sounds are noise, music, or words. We need to keep in mind that God speaks in the silence, not in the noise or busyness of our lives. Chuck Swindoll says it well in his book *Intimacy With the Almighty*: "Silence is indispensable if we hope to add depth to our spiritual life. It guards the fire within our souls; silence makes us pilgrims. It sharpens the keen edge of our souls, sensitizing us to those ever so slight nudgings from our heavenly Father. Noise and words and frenzied schedules dull our senses, closing our ears to His still, small voice and making us numb to His touch."[4]

I can still remember the day I tried to incorporate silence into my daily time with the Lord. I folded my hands, closed my eyes, bowed my head, and was quiet before the Lord. After about one minute I couldn't take it any longer and had to start talking and telling God what He needed to do! Since those first few seconds, I have learned to sit before God and allow His Spirit to speak with mine. Start slow and grow your ability to be silent before God. Over time you will find yourself being able to be silent for a longer period of time.

Solitude

In solitude we purposefully abstain from interaction with others, denying ourselves companionship and all that comes from conscious interaction. Solitude has been called by many the furnace of transformation. *Solitude* is a nasty word in our society today. If you tell people you are going to have a time of solitude, they would probably say you don't have enough to do. In his book *The Way of the Heart,* Henri Nouwen says, "In solitude, I get rid of my scaffolding: no friends to talk with, no telephone calls to make, no meetings to attend, no music to entertain, no books to distract, just me—naked, vulnerable, weak, sinful, deprived, broken—nothing. It is this nothingness that I have to face in my solitude."[5] When you build times of solitude into your daily, weekly, and yearly schedules, you will have your vision clarified, purposes set, and resolve solidified.

Study

To study is to engage with the written Word. The problem with so many of us is that we spend so much time *under* the Word listening to others that we are not *in* the Word. A second problem is that we may spend a lot of time preparing to speak or to lead a small group, but that time in the Word is generally for the sake of others rather than for the renewing and replenishing of our own heart. May I encourage you to build into your daily schedule a time when you can slowly read through a small portion of Scripture and then spend time reflecting on it and making application to your life. For many years I have found it helpful to read through five Psalms and one Proverb each day. This gets me through all 150 Psalms and all thirty-one Proverbs each month. I will normally choose one main verse or point each day and then spend time praying about it. We need to train our minds and hearts to read the Bible for the sake of transformation, not information. Most of us today are educated way beyond our obedience.

Prayer

Prayer is the talking part of our relationship with Jesus. Prayer involves fellowship with God, aligning our will with His will. It is listening to the nudging of the Holy Spirit. It is praising God for who He is and all He has done for us and it is expressing our dependence on God. Years ago I read Bill Hybels' book *Too Busy Not to Pray,* and he provided a simple acronym as a guide for praying—ACTS. A is for adoration, C is for Confession, T for Thanksgiving, and S for Supplication. Since then, I have used it as a guide for my daily prayer times and have found it to be very helpful. To get your prayer time off to a good start, I recommend finding a time best suited for you, a place void of distractions, and then allow the Scriptures to guide you as you pray.

Journaling

A final spiritual discipline that I have found to be very helpful is journaling. It is the practice of writing down your inward groans, fears, sins, experiences, feelings, and aspirations for the purpose of seeing God at work in your life. I don't journal every day, but at least weekly, and it is during this time that I record what God has been saying to me through the Scriptures, through my various experiences during the week, and through things I have been thinking about or wrestling with. It is a wonderful way to keep track of God's work in your life and to see the progress you are making.

One application for this is to plan a personal half- or all-day retreat. Go away to a camp or park, or any place where you will not be disturbed and are able to read the Word, pray, and journal for an extended period of time. These have been some of my best times for reflection and think time. Most leaders are behind in their think time, and a retreat such as this gives you the necessary time to do just that.

Some time ago I heard the story of Tom Landry, the great Dallas Cowboys football coach, as he walked among the players early in the fall. A host of media followed behind. They stopped in the middle of the practice field and one of the reporters asked, "Coach, how many of these players have the potential to be all-pro?" His answer: "All of them; we would not draft a player into the Dallas organization unless he had the potential to be all-pro." The reporter's comeback: "Well then, coach, how many of them will become all-pro?" Coach Landry's response: "Very few . . . very few are willing to pay the price to be all-pro."

The same is true in the Christian life. How many of us have the potential to finish strong and to be the leader that God desires? All of us. We all have the same Holy Spirit living in us, access to the Word of God, and are free to worship and fellowship with other believers. But not all of us are willing to pay the price of building into our lives the disciplines necessary to be transformed by Jesus. Before you go any further, I encourage you to take a look at the disciplines you are currently incorporating into your life, and evaluate what needs to be changed.

Personal Exposure to Significant People

Throughout the course of the book I have spoken a great deal about the need to encourage the men of your church to become involved in a small group. It is no different for you as a leader. As a leader you need the support, encouragement, and accountability to lead properly. All of the studies conducted on leaders show one common contributing factor in those who have fallen—it is a neglect of community. I have come to realize more and more that the Christian life was meant to be lived in community, and that ministry flows from relationships and community. A few years ago I heard Rick Warren of Saddleback Community Church give a talk on leadership, and in the talk he said that every leader needs four types of relationships in their lives. Allow me to share these with you.

Models That Inspire

In John 13:15 Jesus said, "I have set you an example that you should do as I have done for you." Paul says basically the same thing in Philippians 3:17: "Follow my example." When I was in middle school, I took a woodworking class. In order to complete the project, I had to follow the pattern that the teacher provided. As long as I cut my piece of wood exactly along the lines of the pattern, I would be in good shape. Patterns are meant to be a guide, to show us the way. We each need others who have gone before us to show us the way. For me, it has been my father. He served faithfully in the church I grew up in and modeled for me humility and a willingness to do whatever it took to get the job done. I have sought to model my life after him and a few other men as well.

Mentors for Advice

The book of Proverbs is full of wonderful wisdom on the importance of seeking the counsel of others. Proverbs 19:20 says, "Get all the advice and instruction you can, so you will be wise the rest of your life" (NLT). In Proverbs 15:22 it says, "Plans fail for lack of counsel, but with many advisors they succeed." Mentors help us with our roles, goals, and souls. They provide perspective in life. I have a number of mentors in my life that I will go to with various questions and issues. I have mentors in the area of finances, leadership, spiritual formation, parenting, and ministry. These men are available by phone or to get together so I can ask questions or run things by them. They all want to see me win in life, and their encouragement breathes fresh wind into my sails.

Partners Who Accept Me

The third type of relationship I need is partners who accept me for who I am. These are people going in the same direction as I am. They are co-workers here at church and men who are on my leadership team. Those in the church have a desire to see you achieve your life mission. The only way the church will be successful is if everyone does their part and fulfills their role. We need to surround ourselves with like-minded men who are pulling their own weight.

Friends Who Support Me

Finally, we all need friends that we can hang out with, laugh with, cry with, be ourselves with. They are there for us emotionally when we're hurting, intellectually when we're looking for wisdom, and spiritually when we're weak. Colleen and I are close to a few couples, and we love to go out to dinner with them. I don't have to fix them, counsel them, or referee a fight. We just love each other and love being with each other. We all need friends like that.

Several years ago I took up biking to strengthen my back as well as to stay in shape. My friends, who have been biking for years, took me out west of Milwaukee on an early Saturday morning ride. The sun was just coming up, and the dew was still wet on the fields. There was hardly a car on the road—a perfect time to bike. The three of us had gone a few miles when I heard what sounded like a tornado coming. It was a loud sound of wind getting closer and closer. As it got louder, my friends told me to get off the road and hang on! Out of nowhere came a pack of forty to fifty bicyclists, all clumped together, just flying past us down the road. What was so amazing was to watch the guys in the middle. It seemed like they were barely pedaling. When I asked my friends, the experts, about it, they told me there was nothing like it. They said you can be in the middle of the pack and just be swept along by the pull of the other bikers.

That is exactly why we need other men in our lives. The role of leadership is tough and draining, but when surrounded by men who love you and want the absolute best for you, they will pull you along toward Christ and His purposes for your life. Do you have men like that in your life? If not, you need to find some before it is too late.

Embraced by a Sense of Mission

Leaders who last are men who exhibit a growing awareness of their sense of destiny. They are able to say, "For this I was born." I can still remember when I was younger going with my father to see the movie *Patton* and loving it. Not that war is fun, but to see a man so focused on winning and so committed to his troops was inspiring. I still remember the scene where General Patton is walking through a field where a battle had taken place the day before. There are burned-out tanks and trucks, bodies everywhere, smoke rising from the ground, and as he looks out over this field he says, "Oh, how I love this." Of course it was not that he loved death, but he loved what he was doing and knew what God had made him for.

The Bible is full of men with this sense of mission and purpose:

Nehemiah—I will rebuild the walls.
Moses—I will lead the people to the Promised Land.
Paul—I will take the gospel message to the world.
Abraham—was a blessing to many nations.
Barnabas—I will establish the church in Corinth and encourage others.
Caleb—at age eighty, said, "Give me this mountain."

These men understood the power of a focused life. If we are going to last for the long haul we need to focus our efforts in the direction God has called us to and made us for. What I have discovered in working with hundreds of leaders is that those who have a sense of mission and purpose in their lives benefit in the following ways:

First, *it gives them a sense of direction.* It serves as a compass for their lives and allows them to make decisions. Ask yourself if an activity aids your purpose or distracts you from what you should be doing. Leaders understand that you will define your life more by what you say no to than what you say yes to.

A second benefit is *it will increase your motivation.* When you have a sense of mission, it will get you out of bed in the morning. It will give you hope and allow you to hang in there when things get tough.

A third benefit is *it will allow you to concentrate on what you do best.* The power of light depends almost entirely on focus. Light that is diffused doesn't have much of an impact. Through a magnifying glass, light can set something on fire. Through a laser it can cut through metal. Most of us in leadership are trying to accomplish way too much.

A final benefit to having a sense of mission and purpose is *it will prepare you for God's final evaluation of your life.* When you die He will ask you two questions: The first is *what did you do with my Son, the Lord Jesus?* The second is *what did you do with the gifts, talents, and treasures I invested in you?*

Allow me to give you a few practical suggestions for working this out in your life.

First, take the time to seek the Lord and develop a personal mission statement. It should answer the question "For this I was born." Second, take a note card and write down three things you do well, and on the other side three of your weaknesses. Most people spend a great deal of time doing things they are not good at rather than spending time on things they are gifted for. Ask others to do what you don't do well to allow yourself time to do what you do best.

Next, develop a rigorous, worthwhile schedule. If you do not determine your schedule, someone else will. As I mentioned above, you will be defined by what you say no to more than what you say yes to. In the end you will discover what I did years ago: The greater the focus, the greater the impact for God.

One of my favorite scenes in the movie *Braveheart* is found at the end when Wallace is in chains awaiting his execution. On the strength of his determination and passion he had led all of Scotland to revolt against their English oppressors. In this scene a young woman urges the imprisoned Wallace to do whatever he can to give in to the enemy so that his life might be spared. His response communicates one of the deepest truths of human existence: "Every man dies," he says, "not every man really lives." And he was right. There is no greater joy than to know who made you and what He made you to do. To be embraced by a sense of mission will allow you to truly live.

Get Rid of the Distractions

To be leaders who last for the long haul, we will need to eliminate from our lives those things that distract us from our stated mission in life. I like to call this "planned abandonment." If our stated goal is to follow Jesus, to become more like Jesus, to contribute to the cause of Jesus, then we had better get rid of anything that entangles us or hinders us from that goal. The writer of Hebrews says it pretty clearly in Hebrews 12:1–3: "Therefore, since we are surrounded by such a great cloud of witnesses, let us throw off everything that hinders and the sin that so easily entangles, and let us run with perseverance the race marked out for us. Let us fix our eyes on Jesus, the author and perfecter of our faith, who for the joy set before him endured the cross, scorning its shame, and sat down at the right hand of the throne of God. Consider him who endured such opposition from sinful men, so that you will not grow weary and lose heart."

Unfortunately as men we have a tendency to play around on the fringes and see how close to sin and trouble we can get. Some of us are living some high-risk lifestyles and are in danger of being disqualified from finishing strong.

Let me mention some of those risky lifestyles that hinder and entangle us as men:

1. *A love of money.* Now, money is not bad; it is the love of money that is the problem. Some are obsessed with making money, investing money, and protecting money. Others struggle with being upright in their financial dealings. Whatever it may be, money can be a huge entanglement for many men.

2. *A neglected family.* A second problem area for many is spending so much time with work, ministry, hobby, or friends that your wife and children are neglected. One of my greatest fears is being successful in ministry but losing my family. It seems like not a week goes by that I don't hear of another ministry leader who has to bail out because they have allowed their family and marriage to fail.

3. *Emotional adultery.* A third risk area is becoming involved in an emotional affair. I will always remember Steve Farrar speaking at Elmbrook a few years ago when he said, "The emotional affair always precedes the physical." In order to survive you will need to establish some pretty solid boundaries with the women at work, socially, and in the ministry.

4. *Impure thought life.* This is absolutely epidemic in our society. With access to the Internet we can go to our secret place and fill our minds with destructive material. We need to keep in mind that our eyes are connected to our heart and what we allow our eyes to see and our minds to think about will eventually find a resting place in our hearts. Again, we will need to be ruthless with what we look at.

5. *Spiritual apathy.* David Watson, a great English preacher, once said,

"What is hard to detect and yet over the long run may be the most dangerous of all Satan's temptations, is to be sub-Christian—a style of worldly materialism, social distinction, middle class morality, western influence, covered with a thin veneer of spirituality." Satan wants people to believe that 80 percent commitment is okay; he wants to vaccinate us with a mild case of Christianity to protect us from getting the real thing. As a leader of men it is extremely important for you not to settle for just going through the motions but to keep your faith alive and vibrant.

The story is told of a certain man who wanted to sell his house for $2,000. Another man wanted to buy it very badly, but he was a poor man and didn't have the full price. After much bargaining, the owner agreed to sell the house to the man for $1,000. But the reduced price came with a stipulation. The owner would sell the house, but he would keep ownership of a large nail that protruded over the front door. Several years later, the original owner decided he wanted to buy the house back. Understandably, the new owner was unwilling to sell. As a result, the original owner went out, found the carcass of a dead dog in the street, and hung it from the nail he still owned. Soon the house became unlivable, and the family was forced to sell to the owner of the nail.

I heard this story from a Haitian pastor, who concluded it by saying, "If we leave the devil with even one small peg in our life, he will return to hang his rotting garbage on it."

Gentlemen, what is the one peg in your life that you need to give up to the Lord? The one peg that puts you in harm's way.

In closing, allow me to share the story of John Acquire, from Tanzania. He ran the marathon in the Olympic Games held in Mexico City in 1968. He started strong like all the other runners, but then stepped in a pothole at the fourteen-mile mark. Instead of dropping out, he limped, crawled, and walked the final twelve miles. He was still on the course hours after everyone else had finished and gone home. Later in the evening while the track events were going on in the stadium, John entered the arena to finish his final lap. He slowly made his way around the track and fell across the finish line in pain and exhaustion. The reporters asked him why he didn't stop. His answer: "My country did not send me 7,000 miles to start, but to finish."

Friends, it is the same with us. Jesus did not save us just to get us into heaven, but to do His work here on earth. There is no greater joy than to see a man come into a new relationship with Jesus, to see his life transformed, to see him getting in the game and serving, and then taking his talents and treasures and investing them in eternal matters. These are the things that await those who follow hard after Jesus for the long haul.

Personal Leadership Inventory

1. Which spiritual disciplines do you regularly practice during the course of the week (silence, fasting, solitude, prayer, Bible reading, journaling, confession, worship, service, other)?

2. What does your plan for staying spiritually vibrant look like?

3. What steps do you need to take to grow in this area?

4. Which of the following do you have in your life; list by name:

    models—

    mentors—

    partners—

    friends—

5. Answer this question: "For what was I born?"

6. If you are unsure how to answer #5, what steps must you take to discover God's purpose for your life?

7. As you read through the list of potential distractions, to which are you most susceptible? What does planned abandonment look like for you?

8. Is there anything you must do to arrange your life in such a way so as to finish strong?

NOTES

1. Jim Collins, *Built to Last* (New York: HarperCollins, 2001).

2. Lance Armstrong, *It's Not About the Bike: My Journey Back to Life* (New York: Berkley, 2001), 221–22.

3. Dallas Willard, *The Spirit of the Disciplines* (New York: HarperCollins, 1988), preface, ix.

4. Chuck Swindoll, *Intimacy With the Almighty* (Dallas: Word, 1996), 38.

5. Henri Nouwen, *The Way of the Heart* (New York: HarperCollins, 1991), 27.

In the opening chapter of this book I talked about the fields that are ripe for harvest—about the fact that everywhere we look we see men who are friendless, emotionally isolated, success-driven, and spiritually hungry. These are men ready to respond to the gospel and ripe to get involved in a men's ministry based in the local church.

This truth was brought home powerfully to me on Saturday morning, February 3, 1996. As a bit of background, let me tell you that throughout that year we had seen steady growth in our monthly Saturday morning meetings. We started with 110 men attending in the fall, and by January had 155. Needless to say, the guys running the breakfast were excited. In our committee meeting that January, we boldly projected we should plan for 175 men in February. That's a lot of eggs—but not much trouble having those on hand. Where to put that many men was another issue.

The week before the February meeting, the temperature in Milwaukee never got above 0°F. Wind chills ranged from –50° to –75°. Schools closed because of the danger the extreme cold would pose to kids walking to school or waiting for a school bus.

I woke up at 5:30 AM on Saturday and listened to the cancellations on the radio, expecting my daughter's park-and-rec basketball game to be called off. While listening to an endless list of non-events, I leaned over to Colleen and asked if she thought they would cancel our men's breakfast. "Hey," she said out of her sleep, "if it was to be canceled, *you* would have had to call it in." So I got up and went to church.

Saturday was officially the coldest day of the year: –28° with a –75° wind chill. The cooking committee was fixing food when I walked into the kitchen at 7:00. Because of the cold, they had decided to cook only enough for a hundred men. With the meeting scheduled to start at 7:30, there were only half a dozen men there at 7:15. I mumbled to myself that I would be leading a small-group discussion instead of speaking to the usual large audience. I went up to my office to pray and go over my notes. When I came down at 7:45, more than 220 men were crammed into the fellowship hall—eating, sharing, laughing, and enjoying one another's company.

We had a great time of worship that morning. I spoke about the stumbling blocks men face today and then gave time for discussion and prayer at the tables. It was an incredible morning. When I looked out over this great gathering of men of all ages and backgrounds, I was reminded once again: *The fields are ripe for harvest.* Men are hungry. They are looking for truth. For relationships with other men. For a life-changing experience. They are looking to have even the tiniest flicker of faith fanned into a raging fire. There is no doubt that the hottest place in Milwaukee that cold, cold February day was the fellowship hall of Elmbrook Church, where a fire lit many years ago was still burning brightly.

As I survey the landscape of our society—its trends, values, and outlook—I am more convinced than ever that the time is right for every church in this country to have a ministry to men. It isn't enough for men to go to a weekend retreat or a men's conference or a missions trip—all good things in their own right. What men need now, more than ever, is a place where they can plug in with other men—week in and week out. Where they can be encouraged, comforted, challenged, held accountable, and taught together. A place where they can be sharpened—in their marriage, their integrity, their prayer life, their use of God-given gifts. Where the fire can be lit or re-lit: the fire of their faith in Jesus, the fire of their marriage, the fire of their friendships.

Men, it is time to bring the fire home to the church.

Top-Gun Ministry APPENDIX A

In the winter of 1991–92, I was asked by our senior pastor to lead the men's ministry at Elmbrook Church. After surveying many men and talking to a number of leaders ministering to men around the country, I assembled some somber findings. It was obvious that the church in America was shallow, superficial, and spectator-based—especially with respect to the men. I saw the need to develop leadership among our own men, and I set out to write a curriculum that would help men to go deep—deep in their relationship to the Lord, deep in their relationship to their spouse, and deep in their relationships to other men. I wanted to build a program that was an inch wide and a mile deep.

I fully realized I had to get away from the numbers game that is so easy to play. As Robert Coleman says in his wonderful book *The Master Plan of Evangelism*, Jesus didn't work to reach the masses by himself. He worked to build men to reach the masses. When the fields are ready for harvest, men need to be equipped with a vision and know-how to reap the harvest. The result was the development of a program called Top-Gun Basic Training. It has the following characteristics:

1. *A small-group format. Basic Training* forms groups of ten to twelve men who meet weekly for two hours, for a period of thirty-four weeks.

2. *A relational component.* During the first hour of a *Basic Training* small-group meeting, the men divide up into groups of three or four for sharing, prayer, and accountability. It is during this time that the walls come down and men can be vulnerable with one another.

3. *A character-training component.* We aren't just interested in men acquiring more skills, but rather attaining to godliness.

4. *A service emphasis.* Not only is the group required to do two service projects over the course of the year, but each man makes a commitment to be active serving within the local church by the time the course is completed. During the third module of the curriculum, Servant Leadership, men do spiritual gift assessments that help them discover where they should plug into service in their church.

5. *A leadership component.* The nine-month equipping process is designed to encourage and equip men to provide leadership, based on sound biblical principles, in each area of their life—home, work, community, church, and the world.

We started Top-Gun Basic Training in the fall of 1992 with two groups. I took one of the groups and one of my deacons took another group. I wrote as we went, and at the end of the year I was really unsure what type of effect it had on the men who participated. When we did our evaluations with all of the participants, I asked if any of them would be interested in leading a group next year. Sixteen men said they would. That was all the answer we needed. Knowing we wouldn't get enough men for sixteen groups, we had the men co-lead, which we felt was something the Lord orchestrated. Since that time we have seen incredible growth both at our church and in hundreds of churches across the country. In the fall of 1995, more than 150 men signed up to go through what is a rigorous course. Since that time we have had nearly 700 men from our church go through the material, with over 400 churches around the country having used it as well. For the rest of this section, allow me to share some of the basic aspects of our Top-Gun Ministry (TG).

Purpose of Top Gun

1. *To share life* (1 Thessalonians 2:8–9). The small-group format allows men the chance to be encouraged, challenged, comforted, prayed for, and held accountable. It becomes more than just a sharing of information. It is sharing life with one another. It is a chance for men to develop solid friendships with other men. It is a chance for them to share wounds, dreams, failures, and successes that they have perhaps never shared with anyone else. One of the desired outcomes of the course is that men

would see the need to participate in a small-group setting the rest of their lives.

2. *To grow in Christ* (Colossians 2:5–7). It is possible to spend time with other men and never get around to really seeking after godliness. The stated purpose of TG is to help men grow closer to Jesus, to increase their love for Him, and to reflect Him to the world in which they live. There is a heavy emphasis on the spiritual disciplines and on living a consistent lifestyle. A second desired outcome of the course is that men would develop the habit of a daily devotional time with the Lord.

3. *To be equipped to influence others* (Ephesians 4:11–12). The course is designed to help men discover, develop, and deploy their spiritual gifts. Every man who calls himself a Christian has a spiritual gift. We want to help him find out what it is and then use it to its fullest. So a third desired outcome is that men who have finished the course would serve somewhere in the local church.

How Top-Gun Basic Training Benefits Churches

1. *It develops leadership.* When I started the men's ministry, I had about eight leaders. Four years later, I had more than eighty men working in the men's ministry, and many more have gone on to serve in other ministries of our church. Today, we have well over a hundred men serving in some capacity in the ministry to men. When I am consulting with other churches and doing all-day seminars on how to start and run an effective men's ministry, one of the things I suggest is that they use Top Gun to develop their leadership. There is nothing wrong with taking a year to develop a nucleus of guys who will be the future leaders of your ministry. The same holds true for a church. Top Gun is a great tool for a pastor to use to develop the leadership within his congregation.

2. *It moves men out of the pews and onto the field.* For many years the only place you would see men serving was ushering or mowing the church lawn. The TG course helps men appreciate the true nature of servanthood and then to realize that they have a gift they can use in a local congregation.

3. *It starts men growing in Christ.* One of the complaints I hear on a regular basis is that men are tired of just getting together with other men over breakfast and sharing what is new in the world of sports. They say that before they got involved in TG they wanted to grow in Christ but didn't know how. Unfortunately, most men think they are more mature than they really are. The other group has the Peter Pan syndrome—they just don't want to grow up. As a result, men need something to help them cover the basics of Christianity and get grounded in the disciplines of prayer, Bible study, Scripture memorization, solitude, service, and fellowship.

4. *It provides the next step for men after a men's conference.* One of the comments I hear in my travels is "The Men's Conference was great, but when I got home there was nothing." TG has been described as "Promise Keepers every week of the year." It is easy for a man to come home from a mountaintop experience like Ignite, Iron Sharpens Iron, or Men at the Cross, and settle in to his old lifestyle. A program like TG is easily transferable to your church setting and brings the fire home that was lit at the conference.

5. *It starts new small groups.* When a group finishes the nine-month curriculum, we challenge them to stay together and continue on as a small group. We have launched many small groups this way. Because for nine months the men have been together, had a retreat together, and served together, it is only natural that they become a small group. They can meet for an hour or so a week and go through one of the many study books available to men today. So in a way, TG is an effective launching pad for your small-group ministry.

How We Accomplish Our Goals

We bring together a number of resources to help the men realize the goals of the Top-Gun program.

Basic Training Manual. Each man receives a manual containing six modules. The modules have anywhere from four to nine lessons in them. The modules they study are:

Intimacy With Christ
Evangelism
How to Study the Bible
Building Your Family on Biblical Principles
Servant Leadership
Building Your Work on Biblical Principles

Every lesson has the stated goals for that lesson, an assignment, a Bible study, discussion questions for the small-group sharing time, and discussion questions for a large-group discussion.

CDs. Each man receives a CD binder with nine CDs that are used over the course of the year. The CDs, which include presentations by a number of Christian leaders from around the country, supplement the program's reading.

Books. Each module is coupled to a particular book that the men read and discuss over the course of the specific module. During the first module, Intimacy With Christ, the men read John Ortberg's *The Life You Have Always Wanted.*

How Your Men's Ministry Can Start Top Gun

In an ideal world, it would be great for anyone who is going to lead a Top-Gun Basic Training group to go through a TG group first, but I realize this is impossible. We have put all the training on DVDs, which you can get from our ministry, and then train your leaders right at your church. In the near future the training will be on the Top-Gun Web site as well. When we train our own leaders, we have them listen to all the DVDs on their own and then get together for discussion and go over any questions they may have. If you have questions about the TG ministry and how you can use it, go to our Web site, *www.topgunministries.org,* or contact us here:

Steve Sonderman
Elmbrook Church
777 S. Barker Rd.
Brookfield, WI 53045
(262) 786-7051
ssonderman@elmbrook.org

To order contact:
Church Smart Resources
800-253-4276
www.churchsmart.com

In summary, of everything we have done in our men's ministry, Top Gun has had the greatest impact in the lives of our men. It generates an excitement that is contagious, and its life-changing power brings glory to God. The greatest testimony to TG comes from the wives of the men who are in it. A week doesn't go by that I don't receive a letter or phone call from a wife telling me what a change TG is making in their life and marriage. For me, that is all the encouragement I need.

In this appendix I would like to provide you and your leadership team with several ideas for special events for your ministry. All the events here have been tested with our men or those of another church. (Don't worry—I'm not just making these up as I go!) For each event I give a basic description, a reason to do it, and some guidelines to ensure its success.

Note: We have learned that men often won't come the first time you do something. They want to hear how it went and find out whether it's worth bringing a friend to. It's important, then, to do what you do with excellence so you can build confidence among your men that you will provide a quality event.

The events are not in any specific order.

1. Golf Outing

What: The men of your church and their friends spend an afternoon playing golf at a local course. You may want to consider having a lunch beforehand or a dinner after golf. We have had a speaker each time, as well as testimonies from the men on how God has used the men's ministry in their own growth. If you have the speaker at lunch, it gives the men a chance to talk with their guests about what was said while they are playing. We have also included wives for dinner afterward and found both men and their wives appreciated the event.

Why: A golf outing can be just for the men of your church—for a time of fellowship—or it can be an outreach event. You can encourage men to bring friends from work or the neighborhood to expose them to other Christians and a Christian message.

Guidelines:

1. Plan far in advance with the golf course. Not many can handle a lunch or dinner.
2. Settle on a purpose and make sure your men know why you are doing the event.
3. If you do a lunch, make sure the food providers know you are on a tight schedule.
4. Have the guidelines for whatever game you are playing on the carts ahead of time (if you play "best ball," for example, have the guidelines typed up and run off ahead of time).

2. Father/Child Canoe Trip

What: Your trip can be as short as a day or as long as a week, depending on what you want to do. It can be a simple float on a local river to a white-water rafting trip. We have tried a variety of formats and it seems to work best as a long weekend—leaving early Friday, putting in that afternoon, and then pulling out Sunday morning and traveling back on Sunday afternoon.

Why: Combining camping and canoeing is an excellent way for a dad and child to foster their relationship. It is a chance for them to hang out in a more rustic setting away from distractions and to really talk and work together.

Guidelines:

1. Use an outfitter that provides camping and canoeing equipment. Many Christian camps can provide a reasonably priced trip for you. If you go to one of the more popular canoeing areas in the country, there are also local outfitters who can help you.
2. Have a what-to-bring list available for the dads. A good outfitter provides these.
3. Have everyone put their sleeping bags and clothes in plastic bags. (I speak from experience on this one!) A duffel bag by itself will not—let me repeat, *will not*—keep your gear dry if it goes in the water.
4. Be realistic about what you and your group can cover each day. We have learned that kids under ten can handle only three or four

hours on the water a day. Extra time at the camp is a great way for bonding to take place.

5. Build into each day a devotional time for the dads and children to break away and talk about certain things. For example: In one session, you could have them share what they appreciate most about each other. It is helpful to guide the discussions.

3. Father/Child Bike Trip

What: Like the canoe trip, there are many ways to do this—from a one-day excursion beginning and ending at the church to a week-long trip for hard-core cyclists. It can include camping or more comfortable arrangements, such as a church camp or a hotel.

Why: This is a great relationship builder between a father and one of his children.

Guidelines:

1. This is probably an event for children who are at least junior high age. Our own junior high ministry runs a fairly demanding trip kids can do during the summer after their seventh-grade year.

2. Again, use an outfitter that can provide you with safe, dependable equipment. Check with local bike shops and Christian camps.

3. You will have a better time if you can shuttle equipment in a couple of vans—"sag wagons"—rather than carrying all of it on your bikes.

4. Encourage the participants to work out before the trip so the first day doesn't kill them.

5. Have tire repair kits.

4. Men's Retreat

What: A retreat is an ideal opportunity for the men of your church or even a small group of men to get away for a night or two of fellowship, instruction, and play. You can do many different types of retreats—a teaching retreat, a play retreat, a personal growth retreat, or a planning retreat. Decide up front what you want to do. I speak at retreats at least once a month and have found them incredibly helpful to men's ministries everywhere.

Why: Retreats provide a man a chance to get away from the distractions and pressures of life—to relax and be refreshed. They can also provide an opportunity for concentrated teaching on a specific area relevant to men.

Guidelines:

1. Decide on your purpose and clearly carry it through in your planning and publicity.
2. Use a facility where the accommodations are appropriate for men of all ages. I have been to rustic retreats where it was difficult to sleep. Needless to say, that doesn't go over well with most men. A nicer camp or even a hotel is a better place for a retreat—unless you deliberately choose a "rough-it" weekend and advertise it as such.
3. Plan your retreat a year in advance. You need ample time to schedule a location and line up a speaker.
4. Potential schedule:

Friday Evening

5:00　Registration
7:00　Large Group (introduction to weekend, worship, teaching, testimonies, crowd breaker)
8:15　Small Groups (a chance to get to know one another and to talk about what the speaker discussed)
9:00　Free Time

Saturday

7:00　Devotions (supply one for those who aren't sure what to do)
8:00　Breakfast
9:00　Large Group (worship, testimony, speaker)
10:15　Small Groups
11:00　Free Time
12:00　Lunch
1:00　Free Time
5:30　Dinner

7:00 Final Session (worship, testimony, speaker)
8:30 Go Home

5. Leave plenty of time for the guys to unwind and spend time with the Lord and with one another. There is nothing worse than going on a retreat and coming home more tired than when you left.

6. Make sure you have small-group time planned after the speaker is finished so the men get a small-group experience. When the retreat is wrapping up, give the men a chance to join a small group. Remember: Always build a bridge to the next part of the process.

5. Barbecue

What: This event is an evening of food, fellowship, and fun. You might want to use it as a kickoff for your fall program. It could include a pig or chicken roast, music, and a short program. Do it at church, a park, or in a big backyard.

Why: Barbecues are low-key events that give men on the fringe an opportunity to see what your ministry is doing as well as to spend some time with other men from the church.

Guidelines:

1. If you use this as your ministry kickoff, be careful in your planning that you don't interfere with anything else on the church calendar.

2. Build into your schedule a chance for testimonies and an explanation of what the ministry is all about. You may want to pass out a calendar for the year, or show a media presentation of last year's activities.

3. If you do something elaborate like a pig roast, consider hiring a caterer.

6. Kickoff Event

What: This event can look entirely different from church to church, but its purpose is to get your men's program off to a flying start in the fall. It could be a concert, an evening program with a keynote speaker, a cook-out, etc. Be sure to include testimonies from men who have benefited from whatever ministry you have done up to that point, and have your leadership team share the vision of the ministry and what is happening in the coming year. This can also be a main event to sign up men for a small group.

Why: To kick off the men's program. To introduce the men of your church to what is going on in the coming year and how they can be involved.

Guidelines:

1. Plan your kickoff far enough away from the start of school so you aren't competing with school and church events.
2. Have a flyer/brochure available that outlines upcoming activities for your ministry.
3. Have it be a low-key activity with plenty of time for guys to hang out and talk with one another.

7. Outreach Breakfast or Lunch

What: This is an event designed specifically for evangelism. A great format is an event between an hour and an hour and a half in length. It includes a meal, a testimony by someone in the community—an athlete, businessperson, entertainer—and a clear gospel presentation. Your goal is to develop a safe environment for this to take place. Each year we do a Breakfast of Champions at a local hotel on a Saturday morning. The men of our church pool together to buy tickets for a table—spots for six to eight guys—and bring their friends.

Why: An outreach meal is a chance for men to bring unchurched people to hear a clear presentation of the gospel. Often men have shared their own testimony with a friend, but they need another person to share it as well.

Guidelines:

1. Potential Schedule

   8:00–8:10 Arrive and find your table
   8:10–8:15 Emcee welcomes men and prays

8:15–8:45 Breakfast is served
8:45–8:50 Special music
8:50–8:55 Introduction of speaker
8:55–9:25 Message/testimony
9:25–9:30 Closing remarks

2. Encourage your men to come only if they are bringing another man.
3. Have the small groups in your ministry buy up tables.
4. Do a study on evangelism before this event, giving your men an opportunity to use what they have learned.
5. Don't have singing or anything else that needlessly makes visitors feel uncomfortable.
6. Choose a restaurant or hotel you know will do a first-class job. Make sure the servers are instructed not to pick up plates during the message.
7. Make up an invitation the men can use to invite other men.
8. Have some materials that you can give to the guests when they leave.

8. Sporting Event

What: With this event you gather a group of men and go to a sporting event together—a basketball, football, baseball, hockey, or soccer game. By going out to dinner or having a tailgate party, you add time to talk and develop relationships with the other men in the church.

Why: Sporting events are easy events for building relationships with other men.

Guidelines:
1. Check on group ticket rates. Some stadiums have alcohol-free family sections that can make the evening more enjoyable.
2. Some clubs allow you to reserve a place in the parking area for a tailgate party.
3. Decide ahead of time if the men can bring their families, or if you want a men-only event. Both are great options, but head off the confusion that *will* arise if you don't decide beforehand.

9. Fishing Outing

What: This one-day to one-week event is another great way for the men of your church to build relationships. It is also a chance to give men normally not involved a taste of the ministry. Some groups have planned one-day fishing excursions and others have opted for longer trips. We have a group of men that heads north every spring for a long weekend of bass and walleye fishing. They have had the time of their lives. If you plan on going for more than a day or two, you may want to consider using an outfitter/guide, or going through a Christian camp that does fishing trips on a regular basis.

Why: To have fun together, to enjoy a hobby together, and to build relationships with other men.

Guidelines:
1. Provide a what-to-bring list if you go overnight or longer.
2. Make reservations far enough in advance if you choose to go to wilderness areas where you need permits. (In the Boundary Waters Canoe Area of Minnesota, for example, you need permits ahead of time.)
3. Provide assistance to the novices on what type of fishing gear they need and what you will be fishing for. Consider enlisting one of your experienced men as an "expert" to help guys shop and prepare, or provide a comprehensive, specific list of supplies needed.
4. Have someone responsible for sharing devotions on a daily basis.
5. If you use your own camping and cooking equipment, make sure you check it thoroughly before you leave home to be sure it is functional.

10. Financial Weekend

What: A two-day seminar on money management for men or couples. You can prepare your own material, bring in a speaker, or use CDs from nationally known experts. Ron Blue's weekend presentation for our men and their wives was extremely helpful. He covered such topics as the biblical base of money, developing a family budget, and saving for retirement.

Why: A financial weekend serves a number of purposes. It provides solid instruction on Christian stewardship. It helps men and women deal with an area of their marriage that is usually a major source of disagreement. And it's another way to reach people who may not normally come to a men's event.

Guidelines:

1. Use materials that take a balanced, biblical approach.
2. Provide enough time for couples to talk with each other about their specific financial situation.
3. Have a workbook to take notes and a folder to hold any extra materials that are available.
4. Check out what audiovisual equipment will be needed and make sure everything is in working order.

11. Steve Farrar Conference

What: Steve Farrar is a great example of a nationally known men's writer (*Point Man, Finishing Strong*) who also speaks to churches and city-wide weekend conferences. His conference "Men Leading the Charge" provides men with practical biblical principles for becoming a godly man, father, and husband. You will want to mobilize a number of churches from your area to have Steve or another major speaker come in.

Why: This event is great for bringing in new men as well as providing instruction for the men of your church and community.

Guidelines:

1. Most major speakers schedule at least a year in advance.
2. These types of events are an excellent way to start small groups. After Steve spoke to our men's ministry, we started eight groups that all went through his book *Point Man*. A number of the groups were still going three years later.
3. Start talking to men's ministry leaders from other churches about sponsoring a joint event.

12. Regional Men's Rally

What: This event is a chance for all the men's ministries from a city or region to come together to worship, fellowship, pray, and receive instruction from God's Word. For the past sixteen years we have had gatherings of men in the Milwaukee area at Elmbrook called "No Regrets." We started with 1,800 men, and this year we expect about 6,000 men for a Saturday men's conference. The nice thing about a men's rally is that it can flow from the efforts of local churches and can break down racial and denominational walls. With the Ignite Conferences during the summer, a citywide conference in the winter is a good alternative.

Why: A regional men's rally challenges men to grow in their relationship with Jesus and be involved in bringing others to Christ as well. It can really boost the men's ministries in a city.

Guidelines:

1. Develop a committee that represents a number of churches. You will need men to cover the following areas: prayer, registration, publicity, facilities, volunteers (greeters, ushers, ticket sales), program, technical support (audio, video, lighting), financial, and food.

2. Start working on your speakers and musicians at least a year ahead of time. The farther ahead you can work out these arrangements, the better.

3. Work closely with all the men's ministry leaders in the city to get the word out and to rally support for it.

4. Have a prayer rally a couple of months ahead of time in preparation for the event.

5. Have a good balance of music, teaching, prayer, and testimonies in the program. We have found that the seminars draw the men year after year.

6. For more information on what a church men's conference can look like, go to *www.noregretsconference.org.*

7. If your church is interested in being a venue for No Regrets, contact Elmbrook Men's Ministry at (262) 786-7051.

13. Iron Sharpens Iron Conference

What: Each year ISI offers conferences around the country that begin on a Friday evening and run through Saturday evening. The conference includes great speakers, music, and testimonies.

Why: ISI Conferences can act as one of your men's ministries' special events. It is important not to use ISI as your whole men's ministry, but rather *one* of the things your ministry can use as a resource for instruction and fellowship.

Guidelines:

1. Plan ahead. These conferences usually sell out quickly, so you will want to order tickets for your church as soon as they go on sale.
2. Try to carpool together and stay at the same hotel so you can have the extra time for fellowship.
3. Ask your pastor ahead of time if you would be able to share on a Sunday morning what happened at the conference.
4. Have a follow-up meeting a month or so later where the men can share what God is doing in their hearts and you can share some potential next steps for them. One might be how they can get into a small group.

14. Sweetheart Banquet

What: An evening that the men's ministry hosts at a local restaurant or hotel banquet hall for the couples of your church. The program could include a nice dinner—complete with dinner music, of course—followed by a short program that might include a message for couples. Some groups get special prices for the hotel so a couple can stay the night if they wish.

Why: To help guys plan something for their wives so they aren't surprised when February 14 comes around. Seriously, this can be a very special time for couples to get away and have a nice dinner and evening together with other Christian couples.

Guidelines:

1. Do it right if you are going to do it. Have it at a place that has a pleasant atmosphere and good food.

2. Work with the hotel to ensure everyone is served promptly and that servers aren't picking up dishes during the program.
3. Have your guys put it on their schedule far in advance.

15. Super Bowl Party

What: A party where men can invite other men to join them to watch the Super Bowl. For a smaller group this can take place at someone's home; for a larger group it could happen in the fellowship hall or gym of your church. Many groups hold gatherings centered on major sporting events, and some churches invite professional athletes to do an evangelistic talk at half time. Another way to go is to order the special half-time DVD that Sports Spectrum puts out each year. It includes testimonies from NFL players and a clear presentation of the gospel.

Why: Fellowship and outreach.

Guidelines:
1. Borrow or rent a large-screen TV. Make sure it works!
2. Divide up responsibilities for the food.
3. Order your half-time DVD in advance so it arrives in time for your men to preview it and decide how it will fit into your event.

16. Adventure Sports

What: Extreme sports can be a way to bring in younger men, as well as more energetic men that will not darken your door for just one more men's breakfast. It's one more opportunity for men to build relationships with unchurched neighbors, older kids, or twenty-something guys that are not interested in other activities. Some activities could be mountain biking, backpacking, off-roading, archery or shooting, paintballing, climbing, white-water rafting, running events—the wilder the better for some of these guys. For those who are less experienced or adept but willing to give it a try, it's a great time to laugh at one another and just have fun. (Check out one of the most aggressive extreme sports ministries in the nation: *http://baysideadventuresports.com*.)

Why: Relationship building with the goal of one-on-one evangelization and discipling.

Guidelines:

1. Use well-established and professional services for all of your outfitting needs.

2. Consult with legal counsel before setting up events, and have all participants sign a waiver that has been pre-approved by your counsel.

3. Publicize the event or outings well on the Web and on Community Events listings in your local paper.

4. Tell your guys to personally invite their unsaved friends.

RESOURCES FOR MINISTRY

APPENDIX C

Small Groups

Training materials for leaders

The Big Book on Small Groups by Jeffrey Arnold (Downers Grove: Inter-Varsity, 1992).

Brothers! Calling Men Into Vital Relationships by Geoff Gorsuch (Colorado Springs: NavPress, 1994).

Building a Church of Small Groups by Bill Donahue and Russ Robinson (Grand Rapids: Zondervan, 2001).

Growing People Through Small Groups by David Stark and Betty Veldman Wieland (Minneapolis, MN: Bethany House, 2004).

The Seven Deadly Sins of Small-Group Ministry by Bill Donahue and Russ Robinson (Grand Rapids: Zondervan, 2002).

Simple Small Groups by Bill Search (Grand Rapids: Baker Books, 2008).

Walking the Small-Group Tightrope by Bill Donahue and Russ Robinson (Grand Rapids, MI: Zondervan, 2003).

Materials to use in a small group

CHRISTIAN GROWTH

The Body: Being Light in Darkness by Charles Colson (Dallas: Word, 1992).

Design for Discipleship series—six books on the basics of Christianity (Colorado Springs: NavPress).

The Disciplines of a Godly Man by Kent Hughes (Chicago: Crossway Books, 1991).

Dream by Kenny Luck (Colorado Springs: Waterbrook Press, 2007).

How a Man Prays for His Family by John Yates (Minneapolis, MN: Bethany House, 1996).

Knowing God by J. I. Packer (Downers Grove: InterVarsity, 1993).

The Life You Have Always Wanted by John Ortberg (Grand Rapids, MI: Zondervan, 1997).

LifeChange series—study guides on Bible books (Colorado Springs: NavPress).

Risk by Kenny Luck (Colorado Springs: Waterbrook Press, 2006).

Spiritual Disciplines for the Christian Life by Donald Whitney (Colorado Springs: NavPress, 1991).

Too Busy Not to Pray by Bill Hybels (Downers Grove, IL: InterVarsity, 1988).

HUSBAND/FATHERING ISSUES

Better Dads, Stronger Sons by Rick Johnson (Grand Rapids, MI: Revell, 2006).

Dad, If You Only Knew by Josh and Jim Weidmann (Sisters, OR: Multnomah, 2005).

Fathering Like the Father by Kenneth Gangel and Jeffrey Gangel (Grand Rapids, MI: Baker Books, 2003).

The Five Love Needs of Men and Women by Gary and Barb Rosberg (Colorado Springs: Tyndale, 2000).

The Heart of a Father by Ken Canfield (Chicago: Northfield Publishing, 2006).

If Only He Knew by Gary Smalley and Steve Scott (Grand Rapids, MI: Zondervan, 1982).

Point Man by Steve Farrar (Portland, OR: Multnomah, 1990).

The Seven Secrets of Effective Fathers by Ken Canfield (Wheaton, IL: Tyndale, 1992).

Strong Fathers, Strong Daughters by Meg Meeker (Washington, DC: Regnery, 2006).

MEN'S ISSUES

Finishing Strong by Steve Farrar (Portland, OR: Multnomah, 1996).

Four Pillars of a Man's Heart by Stu Weber (Sisters, OR: Questar Publishers, 1997).

God Built by Steve Farrar (Colorado Springs: David C. Cook, 2008).

Healing the Masculine Soul by Gordon Dalbey (Dallas: Word, 1991).

Man in the Mirror: Solving the Twenty-Four Problems Men Face by Patrick Morley (Nashville: Thomas Nelson, 1992).

Tender Warrior by Stu Weber (Portland, OR: Questar, 1993).

The Transformation of a Man's Heart by Stephen Smith (Downers Grove, IL:: InterVarsity, 2006).

WORK

About My Father's Business by Regi Campell (Sisters, OR: Multnomah, 2005).

The Church in the Workplace by Peter Wagner (Ventura, CA: Regal, 2006).

The Fourth Frontier by Stephen Graves and Thomas Addington (Nashville: Word, 2000).

How to Balance Competing Time Demands by Doug Sherman and William Hendricks (Colorado Springs: NavPress, 1989).

Keeping Your Ethical Edge Sharp by Doug Sherman and William Hendricks (Colorado Springs: NavPress, 1990).

The Nine-to-Five Window by Os Hillman (Ventura, CA: Regal, 2005).

Your Work Matters to God by Doug Sherman and William Hendricks (Colorado Springs: NavPress, 1987).

Leadership

Courageous Leadership by Bill Hybels (Grand Rapids, MI: Zondervan, 2002).

Developing the Leader Within You by John Maxwell (Nashville: Thomas Nelson, 1993).

In the Name of Jesus by Henri Nouwen (New York: Crossroads, 1993).

Leadership Essentials by Greg Ogden (Downers Grove, IL: InterVarsity, 2007).

The Next Generation Leader by Andy Stanley (Sisters, OR: Multnomah, 2003).

Ordering Your Private World by Gordon MacDonald (Nashville: Thomas Nelson, 1985).

Spiritual Leadership by Henry Blackaby (Nashville: Broadman, 2001).

Spiritual Leadership by J. Oswald Sanders (Chicago: Moody Press, revised 1994).

Transforming Leadership by Leighton Ford (Downers Grove, IL: Inter-Varsity, 1993).

Discipleship

Discipleship Essentials by Greg Ogden (Downers Grove, IL: InterVarsity, 1998).

Eternal Impact by Phil Downer (Eugene, OR: Harvest House, 1997).

The Master Plan of Evangelism by Robert Coleman (Old Tappan, NJ: Revell, 1963).

One Conversation at a Time by Michael Henderson (Kansas City, MO: Beacon Hill Press, 2007).

Transforming Discipleship by Greg Odgen (Downers Grove, IL: Inter-Varsity, 2003).

Missions

How to Be a World-Class Christian by Paul Borthwick (Wheaton, IL: Scripture Press, 1993).

In the Gap by David Bryant (Ventura, CA: Regal, 1989).

The New Global Mission by Samuel Escobar (Downers Grove, IL: Inter-Varsity, 2003).

Perspectives by Ralph Winter and Steven Hawthorne (Pasadena: William Carey Library, 1999).

Run With the Vision by Bob Sjogren, Bill and Amy Stearns (Minneapolis: Bethany House, 1995).

Unveiled at Last by Bob Sjogren (Seattle: YWAM, 1992).

Vacations With a Purpose: A Planning Handbook for Your Short-Term Missions Team by Chris Eaton and Kim Hurst (Colorado Springs: NavPress, 1991).

Evangelism

Becoming a Contagious Christian by Bill Hybels and Mark Mittelberg (Grand Rapids, MI: Zondervan, 1994).

The Coffee House Gospel by Matthew Paul Turner (Lake Mary, FL: Relevant Books, 2004).

Going Public With Your Faith by William Peel and Walt Larimore (Grand Rapids, IL: Zondervan, 2003).

How to Give Away Your Faith by Paul Little (Downers Grove, IL: Inter-Varsity, 1988).

Just Walk Across the Room by Bill Hybels (Grand Rapids, MI: Zondervan, 2006).

Out of the Saltshaker and Into the World by Becky Pippert (Downers Grove, IL: InterVarsity, 1979).

Men's Organizations

Battle Zone Ministries—*www.battlezone.echurchnetwork.net*

Champions of Honor—*www.championsofhonor.com*

Character That Counts—*www.characterthatcounts.org*

Christian Businessmen's Connection—*www.cbmc.com*

Dad the Family Shepherd—*www.dtfs.org*

Discipleship Network of America (Phil Downer)—*www.dnaministries.org*

Every Man Ministries—*www.everymanministries.com*

Great Dads—*www.greatdads.org*

Heritage Builders—*www.heritagebuilders.com*

Iron Sharpens Iron Conferences—*www.ironsharpensiron.net*

Man in the Mirror—*www.maninthemirror.org*

Men at the Cross—*www.menatthecross.org*

Men's Fraternity—*www.mensfraternity.com*

National Center for Fathering—*www.fathers.com*

National Coalition of Men's Ministries—*www.ncmm.com*

On Target Ministries—*www.ontargetinstitute.org*

The Potter's Inn (Stephen Smith, The Transformation of a Man's Heart)—*www.pottersinn.com*

Pure Life Ministries—*www.purelifeministries.org*

Steve Farrar Ministries—*www.stevefarrar.com*

Top Gun Ministries—*www.topgunministries.org*

Young Business Leaders—*www.ybl.org*

ACKNOWLEDGMENTS

Thank you to the men of Elmbrook Church, who have allowed me to try out these principles on them over the last seventeen years.

Thank you to the sixteen coordinators of the men's ministry, who really run the show. It has been a great ride thus far, and I can't wait to see where God takes us next. I love each of you deeply and count it a great privilege to work alongside you.

Thank you to Stuart Briscoe, my former senior pastor, boss, and, most important, friend. Your preaching led me to the Lord thirty-five years ago. You called me to serve at Elmbrook some twenty-five years ago, and have given me the encouragement and freedom to do ministry since that time. You have lived and taught the principles found in this book.

Thank you to Dave H., a friend and mentor. Your godly counsel and wisdom allows me to do what I am doing.

Thank you to Diane, my administrative assistant, who encourages me along the way, protects my schedule, and helped organize the ministry for me. Without her nothing would get done.

To Dave and Kathy, Phil and Mary, and John and Kris—our Couples Prayer Group. Over the past twenty years your faithful and fervent prayers have carried me through this project.

To Dave Wennstrom—thank you for allowing me to run ideas by you and for being such a cheerleader during the process.

Thank you to the Top-Gun ministry team. You inspire me with your dedication and passion for ministry, your love of life and for one another. You are a living illustration of what ministry to men is all about; you truly get it.

Thanks to my brothers Phil and Dan and Brian for your weekly calls to check in and see how things were going and asking if there was anything you could do to help.

To Mike Noel and Rob Adams, my brothers, fellow workers, and fellow soldiers.

A huge thanks to Jeff Braun, my editor at Bethany House Publishers. Thank you for believing in me and giving me the opportunity to do this project. Your patience, guidance, and encouragement will always be remembered and appreciated.

To my parents, Lowell and Doris Sonderman—thank you for being Jesus to me when I was young and telling me about Him as I grew up. You are my biggest cheerleaders.

To my wife, Colleen, and our four wonderful children, Kristin, Angela, Tim, and Jon—thank you all for putting up with me when I went to my study to work on "the book." Each of you has been so excited about this project, and I am proud to be your husband and father.

Books by
Steve Sonderman
FROM BETHANY HOUSE PUBLISHERS

How to Build a Life-Changing Men's Ministry

Mobilizing Men for One-on-One Ministry